"I am happy to endorse Derek Cooper's *Christiani*
to his *Christianity and World Religions*, which students who took my introductory course on world religions appreciated greatly. The ambitious volume is a rigorous, critical, yet compassionate engagement with a variety of the world's new religious movements on their terms. His book, which includes many intriguing insights and color images relevant to understanding the settings of these religious movements, is the product of true love and intellectual curiosity."
—**Jose Abraham**, Associate Professor of Islamic Studies, Fuller Theological Seminary

"My friend Dr. Derek Cooper has done it again. His compassionate spirit and courageous fervor to engage the individuals that many Christians would meet with disgust, debate, or dismissal is amazing. Unfortunately, most Christians lack the knowledge to defend their faith. This limits their ability to engage with anyone who possesses a different theological system. Dr. Cooper gives a sensitive explanation of well-known 'new religious movements' to help equip faithful followers of Christ with the tools necessary to understand, engage, and evangelize as the Spirit leads—because our Lord's desire is that none would perish."
—**Larry L. Anderson Jr.**, Coauthor, *Ask Me Why I'm Not in Church* and *The Pastors' Diaries*

"Derek Cooper has provided the body of Christ with a useful and creative work in *Christianity and New Religious Movements*. Building on his *Christianity and World Religions*, in which he surveyed the major global religions, this offering introduces a selection of 'new religious movements.' The movements chosen are well known, and believers today are likely to encounter adherents in day-to-day life. The work is well researched. Cooper engages the ideas and faith experiences of those he encounters in these movements from a unique standpoint that can be described as a 'confessional yet compassionate Christian disposition.' The book aims to understand these movements (their history, beliefs, worship), to compare them with Christian teaching, and to 'offer a way for committed Christians to engage them.'"
—**Ken Cuffey**, President and Professor, Urbana Theological Seminary

"Dr. Derek Cooper's latest book is brilliant, compassionate, and innovative. His exploration of new religious movements around the world is expertly written. One always expects great competence when reading a new book by Cooper. What stands out in this book is the empathy he displays toward people of other faiths, as well as people of no faith. I found his chapter on the 'Nones' to be studded with insight and written with humility and compassion. This book will challenge Christians everywhere to treat people of other religious perspectives with the loving dignity that they deserve."
—**Dyron B. Daughrity**, Professor of Religion, Pepperdine University

"What a remarkable follow-up for Dr. Derek Cooper to his *Christianity and World Religions*. Cooper packs excellent scholarship into an extremely enjoyable and readable format, which, together with the first volume, provides a thorough and helpful road map with which to navigate the current religious landscape. His tone is generous and peaceable as he capably guides readers through each chapter's contents.

Each chapter has discussion questions and resources for further study, which will not only help readers process what has been written, but also encourage them to dig deeper. The callouts and figures are perfect little tidbits that offer additional information in a digestible format. And finally, the Name and Topical Glossary ensures that everyone can follow along with Cooper's rich resource.

This will no doubt prove to be a wonderful publication, for both students and churchgoers alike. Dr. Cooper has done the church a great service with this volume, and I commend it to anyone interested in learning more about today's new religious movements and how they themselves might fit into this complicated but fascinating landscape."
—**Dan Lowery**, President and Associate Professor of New Testament, Pillar Seminary for Contextual Leadership

"Unlike major world religions—which might be broadly understood, whether rightly or wrongly—new religious movements are both mysterious *and* misunderstood. The rise of such movements makes Derek Cooper's book all the more necessary. He is able to parse them in understandable and accurate ways. I know of no other all-in-one helpful guidebook like this, and Cooper makes for a readable and reliable interpreter. This book is highly useful not only for classrooms but also for personal study."
—**Allen Yeh**, Professor of Intercultural Studies & Missiology, Cook School of Intercultural Studies, Biola University

"As our neighborhoods become increasingly diverse in the West, we can cry out in fear, *The barbarians are coming!* or we can say with settled confidence, *What opportunities God is bringing our way for thoughtful Christian witness.* Derek Cooper teaches us how to do the latter, showing that this is part of what it means to love our neighbors well. Like C. S. Lewis, Cooper is a 'translator'—that rare person with a genius for taking complex ideas and explaining them in ways that can be easily understood by ordinary followers of Jesus. He has done that again in this must-read sequel to *Christianity and World Religions*."
—**F. Lionel Young III**, Senior Research Associate, Cambridge Centre for Christianity Worldwide

Christianity & New Religious Movements

Christianity & New Religious Movements

AN INTRODUCTION TO THE WORLD'S NEWEST FAITHS

DEREK COOPER

P&R PUBLISHING
P.O. BOX 817 • PHILLIPSBURG • NEW JERSEY 08865-0817

ISBN: 978-1-59638-591-9 (pbk)
ISBN: 978-1-59638-592-6 (ePub)

Cover design by Jelena Mirkovic
Cross image, Mormon temple, Jehovah's Witness Bible, and Sikh man: ISTOCK.COM

Printed in the United States of America

Library of Congress Cataloging-in-Publication Data

Names: Cooper, Derek, 1978-, author.
Title: Christianity and new religious movements : an introduction to the
   world's newest faiths / Derek Cooper.
Description: Phillipsburg, New Jersey : P&R Publishing, [2023] | Includes
   bibliographical references and index. | Summary: "In this user-friendly
   textbook, Cooper explores the world's most dominant new religious
   movements-such as Jainism, Nation of Islam, Mormonism, and
   Scientology-from a confessional yet compassionate Christian
   perspective"-- Provided by publisher.
Identifiers: LCCN 2023006298 | ISBN 9781629955919 (paperback) | ISBN
   9781629955926 (epub)
Subjects: LCSH: Cults--Case studies. | Christianity.
Classification: LCC BP603 .C666 2023 | DDC 261.2--dc23/eng/20230628
LC record available at https://lccn.loc.gov/2023006298

To my dear friend and colleague Justin Gohl,
seeker of truth, keeper of wisdom, defender of faith.

Contents

Foreword

W HEN I WAS growing up in an evangelical Protestant family, religious pluralism might have meant living next door to Roman Catholics or Mormons. But I can't take the dog for a walk today without expecting—or at least hoping—that I'll run into one of my Muslim neighbors for another enjoyable conversation.

It is always welcoming when non-Christians demonstrate some familiarity with Christianity. And the same is true when we exhibit even rudimentary knowledge of the beliefs and practices that our neighbors hold dear. In both cases, separating fact from fiction is a significant advance beyond suspicion and distance. Even in the context of persecution, the apostles reminded believers, "But in your hearts honor Christ the Lord as holy, always being prepared to make a defense to anyone who asks you for a reason for the hope that is in you; yet do it with gentleness and respect, having a good conscience, so that, when you are slandered, those who revile your good behavior in Christ may be put to shame" (1 Peter 3:15–16). This is a crucial but often difficult balance: to be ready to offer a defense of the faith *and* to do it "with gentleness and respect." On the first day of class, I tell my students that their papers must first of all represent a view sympathetically, in terms that the advocate would acknowledge as his or her position, before earning the right to offer a challenge. The ninth commandment requires that we defend not only the truth but the honor and good name of our neighbor. With exactly that combination, Derek Cooper's previous book *Christianity and World Religions* provides a terrific map for understanding the beliefs and practices of an increasingly diverse society.

Cooper employs the same skill in *Christianity and New Religious Movements*. If it requires humility and knowledge to summarize world religions, explaining new religious movements presents additional challenges. In the first place, many of these new movements claim not to be religions at all but something closer to a spiritual philosophy that

ix

eschews formal institutions, dogmas, and rites. And yet in increasing numbers people today identify as "spiritual but not religious."[1]

Whether or not they describe themselves with this phrase, most people in the United States are open to views that both modern science and traditional religions—particularly Christianity—consider "superstitious."[2] A 2018 Pew Research study found that 62 percent of U.S. adults affirm at least one New Age tenet (spiritual energy in material objects, reincarnation, astrology, and so on). The number rises to 77 percent among the "spiritual but not religious."[3] The number of U.S. adults who believe in astrology is larger than the membership of all the mainline Protestant denominations combined. Overall, 58 percent of American 18- to 24-year-olds believe that astrology is scientific.[4] Reincarnation is affirmed by 33 percent of U.S. adults, more so by younger generations (40 percent of those age 18–29 vs. 23 percent of those 65 or older). Twenty-nine percent say that they have experienced a "direct revelation from God or other higher power."[5]

Wicca is "technically the fastest-growing religion" in America, and interest in witchcraft among the educated is rising.[6] Among political conservatives, the influence of mind-science theosophy is evident in

1. According to a 2017 Pew Research study, more than a quarter of Americans (27 percent) identify themselves as "spiritual but not religious," up from 19 percent in 2012. According to a western European survey, over a mere five years, the percentage of "spiritual but not religious" jumped 8 percent (19–27 percent) from 2012 to 2017 (https://www.pewforum.org/2018/05/29/attitudes-toward-spirituality-and-religion/, accessed May 1, 2020). A June 2005 study found that 70 percent of Europeans considered astronomy scientific and that 41 percent considered astrology to be so. See https://ec.europa.eu/commfrontoffice/publicopinion/archives/ebs/ebs_224_report_en.pdf, accessed June 20, 2020. Significantly, 53 percent claim to be "neither spiritual nor religious." Yet I offer evidence below for the conclusion that even among these, spirituality (or at least interest in the "supernatural," particularly the occult) is quite high.

2. Among U.S. evangelicals, 47 percent hold one or more New Age tenets, compared with 78 percent of "nones" (those who identify as having "no religion in particular"). See https://www.pewresearch.org/fact-tank/2018/10/01/new-age-beliefs-common-among-both-religious-and-nonreligious-americans/, accessed June 22, 2020.

3. Thirty-three percent of evangelicals believe in psychics, and 36 percent of Roman Catholics believe in reincarnation. https://www.pewresearch.org/fact-tank/2018/10/01/new-age-beliefs-common-among-both-religious-and-nonreligious-americans/, accessed June 22, 2020.

4. https://www.nsf.gov/statistics/seind14/index.cfm/chapter-7/c7h.htm, accessed May 1, 2020.

5. Moreover, the statement "Things happen that can't be explained by science or natural causes" is affirmed by 83 percent (34 percent of atheists; 65 percent of agnostics). Seven in ten respondents agreed that the living can experience the presence of the dead, and half say that they have been personally helped by them (even two-thirds of nones). Although Protestants traditionally deny the assistance of souls in heaven, 38 percent of evangelicals believe that one may receive help from the deceased, and 35 percent believe that they can communicate with the dead. https://www.pewresearch.org/religion/2021/11/23/views-on-the-afterlife/, accessed August 1, 2022.

6. Bianca Busker, "Why Witchcraft Is on the Rise," *Atlantic*, March 2020. See especially Tara Isabella Burton, "The Rise of Progressive Occultism," *American Interest* 15, no. 1 (June 7, 2019). See Burton's considerable documentation and explanation of the rise in *Strange Rites: New Religions for a Godless World* (New York: Public Affairs, 2020).

the popularity of positive-thinking and prosperity-gospel movements.[7] Fascination with shamanism has returned with considerable force in Western culture, from academic studies to movies and video games. Christian apologetics is often focused on atheism, but only 4 percent of American adults identify as atheists. We are clearly living not in a disenchanted age, but in an increasingly post-Christian one.

In this context, it is crucial not only that Christians know what they believe and why they believe it, but that they gain some familiarity with the views of people they encounter at work, in the neighborhood, and, increasingly, in their own families.

Christianity and New Religious Movements is concise and accessible, but don't let that fool you. Beneath each chapter is a wealth of research. I will be using and recommending both of Cooper's books. After reading this one, I'm sure you will feel the same way.

Michael S. Horton
J. Gresham Machen Professor of Systematic Theology and Apologetics
Westminster Seminary California

---

7. On the evolution of the prosperity gospel (and much else in American religious culture) from New Thought, see the superb study by John S. Haller Jr., *The History of New Thought: From Mind Cure to Positive Thinking and the Prosperity Gospel* (West Chester, PA: Swedenborg Foundation, 2012). The prosperity gospel (also called "Word of Faith") has been enormously successful abroad, especially in Africa and South America. Though the object of a barrage of evangelical critiques in the past thirty years, many recent advocates (including, at the time of my writing, close advisers of President Trump) are now considered by the media—and political allies—as mainstream evangelicals. The list of evangelical critiques of the movement is too lengthy to include here. For one example, see D. R. McConnell, *A Different Gospel: A Historical and Biblical Analysis of the Modern Faith Movement* (Peabody, MA: Hendrickson, 1994).

A Word from William Edgar

A S A YOUNGER man, I was introduced to books and documentaries on the world's greatest religions. Usually featured were Buddhism, Hinduism, Confucianism, Islam, Judaism, and Christianity. Fairly typical examples are J. N. D. Anderson's *The World's Religions* (Grand Rapids: InterVarsity Press, 1955) and the more recent *The World's Religions* by Huston Smith (New York: HarperOne, 1991). But I remember early on wondering why there were no books on the world's *not-so-great* religions. I admit that this was a bit peevish, but today I recognize that my question had considerable pertinence. Religion is a huge category, encompassing far more than the rigid grouping of the older books.

There is an increasing understanding of the breadth of religious awareness. Johan Herman Bavinck (1895–1964) (Herman Bavinck's nephew) has effectively guided us through the matter of universal religious consciousness. Among other things, he was a missionary to Indonesia, taught biblical studies at Kampen, and became chair at the Free University of Amsterdam. A recently published English translation of his essays is a well-kept secret, full of insights.[1] His primary interest is in the psychology of religious consciousness.

Bavinck's views in no way slouch into traditional natural theology. Rather, he makes the assumption that God's revelation gets through and can be measured, taking fully into account the perversion of revelation that human beings construct. Bavinck has extensively studied Hinduism, Islam, and various other religions encountered by him on the field. He concludes that the awareness of God, being the *principium essendi*, can be measured in various cultures. This view can be verified in such biblical texts as Acts 17:27ff. and Romans 1:18ff.

Presupposing such an understanding, all kinds of religions, *great* and *not-so-great*, can be studied and compared to orthodox Christianity. One

---

1. *The J .H. Bavinck Reader*, ed. John Bolt, James D. Bratt, and Paul J. Visser (Grand Rapids: Eerdmans, 2013).

example among many of such enquiries is the series *A Journey through New York City Religions* by Tony Carnes. Topics include Central Park as a repository of many religions, the perils of secularism in Brooklyn's Bushwick Park, persecution of Jehovah's Witnesses, Korean-American religion in Flushing, Queens, Pastor J. Johansson, and the theology of the Coney Island roller coaster.[2]

Modern sociologies are increasingly aware of "minor" religions. They often struggle to categorize them. An example (among many) of this kind of research is *Sociology of Religion: A Reader*, 3rd ed. (New York: Routledge, 2018), edited by the team of William A. Mirola, Michael O. Emerson, and Susanne C. Monahan. These essays tend to organize religious organizations according to their size and influence.

The volume you hold in your hands is a bold venture into the multifaceted phenomenon of *new* religious movements. Many of the subjects scrutinized are not new in the sense of novel or recently emerged (though some are). Unlike the pioneering work of Phillip Charles Lucas and Thomas Robbins or Danièle Hervieu-Léger, who wrestle with the challenges of new religious movements in the face of Western modernity, Derek Cooper has a broader reach. Lucas and Robbins study church-state relations, nonconventional religions, and the opposition to the cults.[3] Hervieu-Léger has studied the underlying reasons for the resurgence of the cults in our world. She avers that the explosion of traditional religions today creates a vacuum, to be filled by more personal views, supposedly free of dogma, open to "à la carte" constructions.[4]

Cooper's concerns are different. He looks deeply into smaller offshoots of Hinduism, Islam, and so on. He also studies the tenacity of unaffiliated religions, and even the "nones." He surveys the "new atheists," Richard Dawkins, Christopher Hitchens, and company. Cooper's analyses are deep, historically responsible, and full of facts and details usually unknown to the average person.

Understandably, there is something disjointed or messy about these studies. From spiritual communities to agnostics to religious zealots, Cooper includes a large diversity of religions without sacrificing details. The book is an apologetics treasure trove. It should equip believers not only to observe more carefully but to engage adherents and bring them the gospel, with both accuracy and compassion.

---

2. See https://www.linkedin.com/in/tony-carnes-b26b3a34.

3. *New Religious Movements in the Twenty-First Century: Legal, Political and Social Challenges in Global Perspective*, ed. Phillip Charles Lucas and Thomas Robbins (New York: Routledge, 2004).

4. Danièle Hervieu-Léger, *La religion en miettes ou la question des sects* (Paris: Calmann-Lévi, 2001).

This work allows Cooper to put into question popular views of "the cults." Most importantly, he ends each section with a "point of contact" whereby we may not only compare the religions to the Christian faith but find entrance points for conversation. This is a marvelous book. It needs to be read by many people.

William Edgar
Professor of Apologetics
Westminster Theological Seminary, Philadelphia

Acknowledgments

I WOULD LIKE TO THANK so many delightful people who helped in the writing, research, and editing of this book. First, I am deeply indebted to the countless men and women from various new religious movements who graciously welcomed me into their places of worship, patiently answered my revolving door of questions, and eagerly shared their personal stories of faith with me. Second, I give my heartfelt gratitude to all our travelers at Thomas Institute who courageously visited foreign places of worship with me all over the world. You have deeply inspired me. Third, Cliff Gehret has been a trusted collaborator in a vast number of writing projects. I always appreciate you and your feedback. Fourth, my friends and colleagues from Dodekagram, Shanna Cummings and Jenny Abraham, are always a tremendous source of encouragement. Fifth, I want to thank the wonderful people at P&R Publishing. I have been happy to publish several books with such a professional, courteous, and purposeful publisher. I am especially grateful to John Hughes, who demonstrated kindness, support, and patience as I delayed in completing this book. You certainly made it a much better product. Finally, I have dedicated this book to my friend, colleague, and colaborer Justin Gohl. Thank you for being you.

Introduction

> Humanity is not limited to the small set of better-known "world religions" that dominate the planet today. People across history have recurrently generated new religious ideas, movements, experiences, and practices.
>
> *Christian Smith[1]*

War in Waco

The relatively unknown city of Waco, Texas, captured national headlines on February 28, 1993, when ATF agents raided a compound that housed a new religious movement called the Branch Davidians. Agents had no idea of the amount of resistance that they were soon to encounter. The compound's charismatic yet controversial leader, David Koresh (1959–93), was almost instantly wounded. And tragically, several ATF agents and Branch Davidians were killed within minutes. For the next fifty days, the world watched with bated breath on national television as the FBI replaced the ATF and proceeded to blockade the compound, attempting to negotiate the release of the faithful members inside, especially its leader.[2] In fact, despite his gunshot wounds and his lack of medical treatment, David Koresh led regular talks with the FBI, sometimes elatedly so. Framing the standoff in apocalyptic terms that were inaugurating the end of days prophesied in the Bible and interpreting himself to be the second coming of Christ, Koresh earned the epithet "wacko from Waco."[3]

---

1. Christian Smith, *Religion: What It Is, How It Works, and Why It Matters* (Princeton, NJ: Princeton University Press, 2017), 235.

2. Although the Bureau of Alcohol, Tobacco, and Firearms (ATF or BATF) initially led the siege at Mount Carmel against the Branch Davidians, the Federal Bureau of Investigation (FBI) quickly took over and remained in control for the duration of the operation, ultimately receiving approval from the U.S. Attorney General for the use of tear gas on April 19.

3. Eugene Gallagher, "The Branch Davidians," in *Controversial New Religions*, ed. James R. Lewis and Jesper Petersen, 2nd ed. (Oxford: Oxford University Press, 2014), 67–68.

Things, however, eventually came to a standstill. The FBI was embarrassing itself in front of millions of onlookers, being bullied by a wounded anarchist eking out an existence in a house filled with mothers and children. The agency had to act soon. And so on the fateful day of April 19, the FBI fired tear gas into the compound as a final attempt to force the Branch Davidians to surrender and vacate the premises. As the hours passed that day, fire erupted inside the compound and swiftly expanded. Although a few escaped, almost all the faithful members remained trapped inside and died—including Koresh and his right-hand man, Steve Schneider (1949–93), who apparently shot and killed Koresh at very close range upon Koresh's orders before then killing himself. No children escaped. In total, seventy-six members of the community perished.

I grew up in East Texas, not far from Waco. My most distinct memories from 1993 are from the hours I spent watching the Waco siege unfold from February 28 to April 19. The images of ATF agents courageously entering and then shamelessly exiting a second-story window on the first day of the siege—and the consuming flames and thick black smoke ascending from the compound to the heavens on the last day—are forever cemented in my mind. David Koresh, born Vernon Howell, had set up his Branch Davidians base in nearby Palestine, Texas, only a few miles from my house, before building the infamous compound (called Mount Carmel) outside Waco. And unbeknownst to most people, Koresh—in contrast to the international fanfare that his movement had provoked for weeks on end—was quietly and discreetly buried in a cemetery in my hometown, mere minutes from where I lived.

As a kid watching the Waco siege, I was profoundly saddened, yet strangely fascinated, wondering why anyone would follow a leader such as David Koresh to the death, especially given the stories—notoriously, "The Sinful Messiah" series as reported by the *Waco Tribune-Herald*[4]— alleging Koresh's long-standing exploitation, religious manipulation, sexual coercion, and delusions of grandeur. Decades later, as a historian of religion, I still marvel at these questions and ponder why Koresh's followers were willing to sacrifice everything for him and the cause he championed. But today, in contrast to when I was a kid, I have a much deeper understanding of the brokenness of the human condition, I am acutely familiar with the hope and healing that religion pledges, and I can empathize with those who see nothing but confusion surrounding all the different religious traditions that exist.

---

4. "The Sinful Messiah" was a seven-part investigative series appearing in the *Waco Tribune-Herald* about David Koresh. The first part of the series appeared on February 27, 1993, the day before the Waco siege began.

Fig. I.1. The relatively unknown city of Waco, Texas, captured national headlines in 1993 because of a government standoff involving a new religious movement called the Branch Davidians.

Cults, Sects, and New Religious Movements

The emergence of the Branch Davidians in the early 1990s from obscurity to international notoriety raises many questions, to be sure, including when the Branch Davidians emerged, where David Koresh entered the picture, why their members reacted the way they did during the siege, and how they understood themselves in relation to the world. Regarding the latter, although the Branch Davidians believed themselves theologically to be the true body of Christ in contrast to their Seventh-day Adventist Church cousins who had lost their way, most people just characterized them as a cult or a sect led by a madman whose real motives proved much more fleshly than spiritual: centering on having sex with as many women as possible, exploiting others as an abuse of power, and building an arsenal of weapons.

This is possibly very accurate, but it is also short-sighted. As historian of religion Eugene Gallagher explains, "The application of the very simplified 'cult' stereotype to the Branch Davidians did more to obscure who they really were, what they cared about, and how and why they lived their lives the way they did."[5] He has a point. For the most part, the average person is unable to articulate exactly what a cult is,

---

5. Gallagher, "Branch Davidians," 74.

other than to assume that it is sinister in nature and that you would never want anyone from your family to be in one. Cults, after all, are commonly interpreted to be breeding grounds of mind control, social isolation, financial manipulation, and even sexual exploitation. According to scholar of religion Philip Jenkins, the media commonly perceives cults to embody "blind fanaticism, megalomaniacal leaders, and the following of incomprehensible dogma."[6]

In fact, few people today can precisely distinguish a cult from a sect or differentiate an established world religion from a new religious movement. More often than not, these terms are used interchangeably, or simply inaccurately, which only reinforces misunderstanding. This is compounded by the fact that no cult accepts such a label or would ever entertain the notion that it might be one. Instead, the moniker *new religious movement* has become the agreed-upon term that better describes "all of those leftover groups" that fall neatly under neither the category of "world religions" nor the culturally outdated categories of *cults* and *sects*.[7] To be sure, the term *new religious movement* boldly attempts to encompass a rather broad—and arguably disjointed—hodgepodge of spiritual communities ranging from those who believe in aliens to those who are atheists to those who consider themselves the only true body of Christ. I concede that it is far from perfect. But then again, what scholarly term is?

Classifying New Religious Movements

Historically, scholarly research in new religious movements has been dwarfed by the study of world religions, even though the former increases with no indication of stopping. As sociologist of religion Christian Smith argues, "humans will continue to generate new religions" as mankind marches on.[8] In fact, it is precisely because religions continue to be formed, continue to be spread, and continue to be neglected by scholars that more needs to be written about them. In this way, this present book is meant to serve as a companion to my prior book *Christianity and World Religions: An Introduction to the World's Major Faiths*,[9] which discussed global religions having widespread cultural and societal

What Is a New Religious Movement? The terms *cult* and *sect* are no longer used by scholars of religion. Several terms have emerged as replacements, including *new religion, alternative religion, fringe religion, new religious tradition,* and *nontraditional religion.* These all have merit. Yet the term that has become most widespread is *new religious movement* (often abbreviated as NRM).

6. Philip Jenkins, *Mystics and Messiahs: Cults and New Religions in American History* (Oxford: Oxford University Press, 2001), 5.

7. J. Gordon Melton, "An Introduction to New Religions," in *The Oxford Handbook of New Religious Movements,* ed. James R. Lewis, vol. 1 (Oxford: Oxford University Press, 2008), 20.

8. Smith, *Religion,* 235.

9. Derek Cooper, *Christianity and World Religions: An Introduction to the World's Major Faiths* (Phillipsburg, NJ: P&R Publishing, 2012).

acceptance and recognition. Just as *Christianity and World Religions* provided a user-friendly and experience-based engagement of the world's most dominant faiths from a confessional yet compassionate Christian disposition, so, too, *Christianity and New Religious Movements: An Introduction to the World's Newest Faiths* aims to lay bare the essence of the most dominant new religious movements in the world as well as offer a way for committed Christians to engage them.

In *Christianity and World Religions*, I organized the world's most widespread religions into Indian world religions (Hinduism and Buddhism), Chinese world religions (Confucianism and Daoism), and Middle Eastern world religions (Judaism and Islam). In this book, I organize each faith into Hindu new religious movements (Jainism and Sikhism), Muslim new religious movements (Baha'i and Nation of Islam), Christian new religious movements (Mormonism and Jehovah's Witnesses), Pagan new religious movements (Wicca and Scientology), and uncommitted new religious movements (nones and atheism). These religions are not exhaustive, and they are not universally recognized. Nor are they perfectly precise. After all, every major religion has produced hundreds of offshoots, and many new religious movements have sprouted from hybrid trees. Sikhism, for instance, developed out of both Hinduism and Islam, though I discuss the religion primarily in the context of the former.

In total, there are thousands of new religious movements. They exist in virtually every country, and they are constantly being created, being adapted, and being readapted. Some countries, such as the United States, are up to their eyeballs in them. Some are illegal, some are clandestine, and some are outlandish. In fact, some new religious movements are pernicious organizations that threaten human flourishing, while others are culturally accepted and claim to promote a healthy and happy lifestyle. Still others make national headlines because of their extreme practices, bizarre rituals, or illicit activities. Most new religious movements represent groups that you have never heard of and are populated by people whom you might least suspect. Rather than sift through thousands of smaller movements, however, we will focus our attention on the most historic, most prominent, and most recognizable, including ones with members that we have a higher chance of meeting. This is intentional.

The goal of this book is to learn about new religious movements in order to actually engage both them and the people who are part of them from a confessional and compassionate Christian perspective. I am not interested in dissecting them like an impartial scientist or degrading them like an overbearing bully. On the contrary, I believe it more helpful to isolate faith movements that most intersect with our cultural contexts, theological beliefs, and daily lives—for a specific and practical purpose. After all, when the apostle Paul entered Athens in Acts 17 and began engaging the seekers there, he did not cite Scandinavian gods or offer a discourse about Aztec religion. Instead, he appealed to beliefs and practices most germane to the Athenians, with the result that some connected with his message and embraced Christianity.

PART 1

Hindu New Religious Movements

In this section, we discuss the two most influential religious traditions emerging out of Hinduism (other than Buddhism, of course, which also arose from Hinduism): Jainism and Sikhism. Although spread apart historically by centuries, these two religions owe their geographic origin to Greater India. This region of the world has produced one of the most fertile religious soils on the planet, and it offers a great place to begin our study of new religious movements. If you would like a refresher on Hinduism and Buddhism, be sure to read the chapters dedicated to them in my prequel, *Christianity and World Religions*.[1]

1. Derek Cooper, *Christianity and World Religions: An Introduction to the World's Major Faiths* (Phillipsburg, NJ: P&R Publishing, 2012).

chapter 1

Jainism: The Story of Nonviolence

The main thrust of . . . Jainism is nonviolence (ahimsa). One should not injure another [whether in] mind, speech, or body.

Saman Srutaprajna[1]

Right path, right knowledge, and right conduct together constitute the path to moksha.

Tattvartha Sutra[2]

The goal of Jainism . . . is the removal of the karmic matter that obscures the true nature of [a soul] and causes it to be bound to the cycle of rebirth.

Jeffrey Long[3]

Part 1: The Beginning

There was no beginning. There is no middle. And there will be no end. Nor is there any god who intervenes in the meantime. What exists is a timeless universe among universes whose beings circulate through the cosmos one life at a time like a slowly moving yet eternally revolving door. When it comes to our realm, there is an axis at the center called Mount Meru sitting atop a flat disc. From the center radiates a concentric series of rings of islands separated by the waters. What we

1. Saman Srutaprajna, *The Path of Purification* (Gujarat, India: Peace of Mind Training Center, 2005), 151.
2. Tattvartha Sutra 1.1. This is the first verse of the most authoritative religious text in Jainism.
3. Jeffrey D. Long, *Jainism: An Introduction* (London: I. B. Tauris, 2009), 96. The original word is *jiva*, which, as I will discuss below, is variously translated in Jainism as "life," "soul," or "spirit."

3

call the *world* mirrors the shape of a human being who is standing with each hand touching the waist and each leg outstretched and firm like an athlete about to do squats. This realm consists of three worlds, each of which has sublevels or subislands. And it also consists of a series of realities that contain beings who live in various stages of existence based on their karma from former lives.

Above the waist is the higher world—what some might call *heaven*—which houses beings who have accrued exceptionally good karma. Here there is no suffering. And the gods dwelling here are mindful and mobile. At the very top of this realm are those who have reached the highest peaks of enlightenment and so contain no karma. Here they remain in a conscious, complete, and contented state of understanding. Meanwhile, the lower that one descends through the realms, that is, below the waist, the worse the plight of the beings residing here. This lower place is what some might call *hell*. This dreadful place contains beings whose grievous actions in their former lives weighed them down with bad karma that will take eons to burn off. For them, every day is a living hell. Their existence includes extreme temperatures, horrid smells, conscious suffering, and constant conflict. There are seven layers of this hellish abode. The beings here are tortured by hellish deities who have also committed horrid deeds. But despite the horror they experience, the beings in hell will eventually be reborn in a better place where they can ideally make better choices. And the same is true of the gods—they also will eventually be reborn. The place they might be reborn next is what some might call *earth*. Located near the anatomy of the waist, it is the place that you and I currently call home. This is where animals, plants, and humans live, only the latter of which are capable of enlightenment.

Nonetheless, other than the enlightened beings remaining at the very top of the universe, all the rest of the living beings will eventually complete their time in whichever realm they inhabit and thereby take on another form as a human, god, hell-being, plant, or animal. Exactly what their existence will look like in their next life—as well as the exact place they will live—is completely dependent on one impersonal, indifferent, inescapable, and infinite factor: karma. In a word, karma is the glue that binds all the universes together. And unless you have exhausted all your bad karma and attained complete understanding, you cannot overcome it. It will win in the end—and in the beginning, and in the middle, and in the end again.[4]

Road Map to Jain Creation Story. Every religion conceives of creation differently. Jainism visualizes the three temporary realms of existence as a person whose head and torso represent the highest realm (a temporary Heaven), whose waist represents the middle realm (a temporary Earth), and whose legs represent the lowest realm (a temporary Hell).

---

4. This description of the Jain cosmos is taken from Tattvartha Sutra, especially the third chapter.

Fig. 1.1.
Representation of the universe in Jain cosmology in the form of a *lokapurusha* or "cosmic man."

Part 2: Historical Origin

Jainism is the lesser-known sibling of the Indian religious family of Hinduism and Buddhism. This means that its historical roots run deep into the religiously fertile soil of Greater India. The long religious history of this region makes Jainism difficult to describe in full detail, including capturing its exact beginning. Like Hinduism, for instance, which is called *sanatana dharma*, or the "eternal religion," Jains maintain that Jainism has always existed. And although Mahavira is often regarded as the "founder" of Jainism, we should apply that term only if we understand it to really mean "forebear," since Jains believe that Mahavira was one among many who discovered the same path to enlightenment. In fact, Mahavira was the twenty-fourth spiritual master in a millennia-long series of guides. This is similar to many other religious traditions. For instance, neither Siddhartha Gautama in Buddhism, nor Abraham in Judaism, nor Muhammad in Islam is believed by practitioners to have actually founded his respective religion. Instead, the religions of these men predated them by millennia. Thus, these spiritual leaders simply reconnected people to eternally existing truths that never should have been forgotten.

The Fordmakers—The Jinas

The religious tradition of Jainism is connected to twenty-four mysterious figures called *fordmakers*, *ford finders*, or *builders of the ford* (*tirthankaras*) who lived before the advent of historical record and who formed a chain of unbroken knowledge. These fordmakers were so called because they were the ones who had learned "the way across the river of rebirth to the further shore of liberation [to] build a *tirtha*, or 'ford,' that others [could] use to make their way across as well."[5] This is a common concept in Indian religious traditions. It symbolizes the shallow water through which one can safely cross to the other side of a river. And it parallels the Buddhist figure of the Bodhisattva—with the most famous example being the Dalai Lama ("Ocean Teacher")—who agrees to be reborn again and again in order to liberate others rather than achieve nirvana and therefore liberate only himself.

Fig. 1.2. Statues of Jinas in Jaisalmer, India.

Another name for the fordmaker was *jina*—"victor" or "conqueror"— and over time, the one who followed a jina's teaching was called a *Jain*

5. Long, *Jainism*, 3.

(or *Jaina*).[6] Naturally, the victory referred to here was not a physical victory won at war but a spiritual victory won in the ego. This involved strenuous commitment. The twenty-four fordmakers are believed to have existed since the beginning of time and, in fact, will continue to live on age after age in human forms not yet known. When visiting a Jain temple, you will often see them prominently displayed in statues and iconography. Of these, the last fordmaker in our current life cycle or epoch was a man named Mahavira. His accomplishments—as well as those of the twenty-three preceding him—were exceptionally rare, and there will not be another fordmaker or jina on this earth for tens of thousands of years.[7]

Mahavira (6th Century B.C.)

Mahavira serves as a foundational figure within Jain history. Precise dates vary, but it is generally believed that Mahavira was a contemporary of Siddhartha Gautama—better known as *Buddha*. In this way, Mahavira lived roughly twenty-five hundred years ago in the same region of northeastern India (sometimes called Greater Magadha). In my chapter on Buddhism in *Christianity and World Religions*, I described the Four Signs of Buddha, in which the young prince successively saw old age, disease, death, and an ascetic on his way to becoming who he was destined to become.[8] Jainism shares a similar history. But rather than being the Four Signs of Buddha, it is the Five Auspicious Events of Mahavira. They comprise Mahavira's (1) conception, (2) birth, (3) renunciation, (4) enlightenment, and (5) demise. These were important developments in Mahavira's life that illustrate how he achieved enlightenment.

Similarities between Mahavira and Buddha

In truth, this is not the only similarity between Mahavira and Buddha. There are many additional commonalities between the two, seven of which I will mention.[9] First, like *Buddha*, *Mahavira* is a title, not a name.

Five Auspicious Events of Mahavira. Jains celebrate five "auspicious" moments from Mahavira's life: conception (*garbha*), birth (*janma*), renunciation (*vairagya*), enlightenment (*kevalajnana*), and demise (*nirvana*). Each offers a model of emulation in which believers reflect on their own spiritual development.

6. Though the terms mean slightly different things, I will use *fordmaker, tirthankara,* and *jina* interchangeably to refer to any of the twenty-four spiritual masters who traditionally serve as the object of adoration and study in Jainism.

7. But here it is important to distinguish between what may happen on earth and what may happen in some other currently existing universe. For it is very possible that another fordmaker is alive and teaching the way of liberation in another universe.

8. Derek Cooper, *Christianity and World Religions: An Introduction to the World's Major Faiths* (Phillipsburg, NJ: P&R Publishing, 2012), 29–30.

9. This history comes from the Kalpa Sutra, the Jain scriptures focused on the life and miracles of Mahavira.

It means "Great Hero" or "Great Man," indicating his spiritual authority; his childhood name, however, was Vardhamana. Second, Mahavira and Buddha were both Indians who were reacting against the dominant religious system of Hinduism. They were connected to a similar movement called Shramana, but their way of teaching developed into distinct religions that we refer to today as Jainism and Buddhism. Third, both were from the same warrior caste in India called the Kshatriya caste. This was one of the most revered castes in Indian society, second only to priestly Brahmins, and it ushered the two young boys into a life of luxury and status unknown to virtually all their contemporaries. Like Buddha, Mahavira married a princess and fathered a child, though adherents of the more traditional of Jain denominations (the Digambaras) believe that he was a lifelong bachelor who eschewed such worldly pleasures.[10]

Fig. 1.3. Statue of Mahavira in Jain temple in Rajasthan, India.

10. Padmanabh S. Jaini, *The Jaina Path of Purification* (Berkeley: University of California Press, 1979), 11.

Fourth, Mahavira and Buddha were the same age—the age of thirty—when they renounced their worldly possessions and left their families in search of enlightenment. (Ironically, both Jesus and Guru Nanak, the founder of Sikhism, whom I will discuss in the next chapter, were also thirty when inaugurating their ministries.) According to tradition, Mahavira renounced all his possessions at this time and demonstrated it by removing his clothes,[11] pulling out his hair (one hair at a time), and assuming the life of a wanderer rather than remaining with his family in luxury (again, almost exactly paralleling the renunciation of Buddha). Fifth, during this time, both Mahavira and Buddha experimented with various spiritual practices such as yoga, meditation, and fasting. And it was the latter, in particular, that characterized Mahavira, since he would regularly go days at a time without food or water (even more austerely than Buddha). Sixth, after years of experimentation and almost to the point of physical death from lack of eating, they both attained enlightenment while meditating under a tree. Seventh, there are countless legends about the birth, signs, and death of Mahavira and Buddha. For instance, both were prophesied to become either great warriors or great saints—the latter of which happened. Subsequently, both attracted disciples who recorded their teachings and enlarged their communities. And in fact, the religions that formed in the wake of their lives eventually divided over the issue whether these two were spiritual saints to be venerated or gods to be worshiped.

Twelve Similarities between Mahavira and Buddha

1. Both lived countless lives and accrued untold good karma before being born.
2. Both were historical contemporaries, living roughly twenty-five hundred years ago.
3. Both spent their whole lives in northeastern India and likely spoke the same local language.
4. Both were born in the Kshatriya caste, the revered warrior caste in Indian society.
5. Both were princes and raised in luxury.
6. Both married princesses, and each fathered one child.

The Movement That Inspired Mahavira, Buddha, and Others. Mahavira and Buddha were figures within a much larger and more ancient movement called *Shramana*. This movement was active thousands of years ago in India. Their teachings and lifestyles were very similar, but for reasons that are not completely clear, entire religions only developed around a few of them.

11. The intentional removal of clothes is a point of contention within the two denominations in Jainism. In short, the Digambaras (or more traditional Jains) believe that Mahavira renounced all clothing at this time, while the Svetambaras (those of the more recent tradition) maintain that Mahavira wore a white loincloth that eventually fell off and that since Mahavira was so unattached to material things by this time, he did not notice that he was naked. For more about this, see Jaini, *Path of Purification*, 12–14.

7. Both renounced their lives and family at the age of thirty.
8. Both wandered and experimented with austere spiritual practices for many years before "starting" their own religions.
9. Both achieved enlightenment while meditating under a tree.
10. Both gathered disciples and formed a new religious community.
11. Both were attested by signs and miracles from infancy to death.
12. Both were given important titles and are worshiped or venerated by millions.

Why Does Jainism Embrace Swastikas? The swastika is an ancient Indian symbol used for centuries before Nazism. In Jainism, the four lines of the swastika symbolize the four classes who have not attained moksha: humans, gods, hell-beings, and animals and plants. The three dots stand for the three jewels of Jainism (right path, right knowledge, and right conduct).

As the last of the fordmakers in our cycle, Mahavira exerts tremendous influence over Jainism—not completely unlike the influence of Muhammad in Islam (though, to be sure, Muhammad is never worshiped). For instance, Jains regard Mahavira's life as a model for how to live their own; thus, each stage of his story, particularly after renunciation, is intensely studied and debated. This includes his teachings, practices, and lifestyle. Naturally, Mahavira would have accrued eons of good karma to be in the place he was to attain what he did, but he is the guide to follow (and, in the case of some Jains, worship). And having attained enlightenment or supreme knowledge (*kevala jnana*), Mahavira officially became the twenty-fourth fordmaker or jina. This means that when he died on earth at the age of seventy-two, he attained nirvana, thereby exiting the cycle of birth and rebirth, victorious over karma and reincarnation—the bonds that enslave all other living beings. But Mahavira will not be the last fordmaker; others will eventually follow.

Mahavira established four *fords* or *tirthas*, which are very important to Jainism and continue to play a role today. This includes monks (*sadhus*), nuns (*sadhvis*), laymen (*shravikas*), and laywomen (*sravakas*). And together they constitute the core of the Jain community or *sangha*. Surprisingly for many, this fourfold model is symbolized by the swastika—and when I lead groups overseas to South and Southeast Asia, travelers are shocked to see the swastika appearing prominently in countless ways, especially during Jain religious rites. It is crucial to recognize, however, that the swastika has its origin in the Indian religious tradition, not Nazism. There is no similarity in belief between the two.

Mahavira's division of the Jain community into four roles persists to this day and also remains the source of confusion among outsiders. In short, most Jains fall under the latter two roles: laymen and laywomen. Only a small percentage of Jains are able—or, more accurately, sufficiently buoyed by eons of good karma—to be in a place where they can renounce everything and focus exclusively on liberation from the cycle of death and rebirth that characterizes life. Only the *sadhus* and *sadhvis* practice this. Although they are highly revered in India, and reliant on the resources of the *shravikas* and *sravakas*, they constitute only a tiny percentage of the Jain community. This is similar to other religions such as Hinduism and Buddhism, in which most practitioners are ordinary people trying to live their lives to the best of their ability, while only a precious few become ascetics. To state it differently, the overwhelming majority of Jains today are laypeople who materially support the small number of Jain monks and nuns with food, water, and other resources. And in turn, they receive moral guidance and good karma. In this way, it is an essential reciprocal relationship. Each needs the other. But each has different religious aims. And the majority do not pretend to be able to renounce everything as the monks and nuns do.

Fig. 1.4. The swastika is an ancient Indian symbol preexisting Nazism by hundreds of years. In Asia, the symbol has nothing to do with German Nazism.

Jainism Today

Today, the Jain religion contains about six million adherents. Most still live in their homeland of India, where they are overshadowed by the overwhelming Hindu majority. But this small number is slightly offset given that Jain practitioners have traditionally specialized in business and received higher education, and so achieved a higher financial status in comparison to their Hindu counterparts.[12] They are also highly literate

12. Lawrence A. Babb, *Understanding Jainism* (Edinburgh: Dunedin Academic Press, 2015), xiii.

in comparison to their Hindu or Muslim peers, particularly male Jains. The historical Jain relationship to education and business is, of course, related to the caste system—which, though not officially endorsed by the government, still exercises considerable influence over Indian society. On the one hand, it is interesting that a religion so intent on nonattachment would come to be associated with the merchant class, which is highly educated and often the recipient of top jobs. On the other, this class allows lay Jains—again, the vast majority within the religion— to abide by the key concepts of ahimsa ("nonharm" or "nonviolence") and vegetarianism, as well as other core teachings, which I will discuss below. Interestingly, it also allows the laypersons to be able to finance the lifestyle of ascetics.

The Caste System. Coming from the Portuguese word *casta,* "color," the caste system was a racial framing of the Sanskrit term *varna,* which refers less to skin color and more to the stratification of society into classes, dating back to the Rig Veda. Though unsanctioned, caste is a hereditary system that remains an everyday feature of Indian society.

In the diaspora, that is, outside India, virtually all Jains are of Indian descent, and they have not yet created submovements appealing to Westerners to the degree that other Indian religious traditions have done in the West through yoga, meditation, and mindfulness. Scholar of Jainism Paul Dundas has categorized Jains today into one of three orientations or mindsets: (1) orthodox, (2) heterodox, and (3) neoorthodox. These are not universally accepted terms, and they have their limitations. Yet they do provide a helpful framework from which to understand what may be regarded as contradictions or tensions within the Jain community. The orthodox encompass traditional Jains, mostly in India, who accept the authority of Mahavira and follow the accustomed rituals and teachings. They are more exclusivist in practice. The heterodox are those who have adopted a more theistic worldview in which jinas (sometimes also called *gods* or *deities*) can and do intervene in human affairs. An example could be Dada Bhagwan (1908–88), who founded the Akram Vignan movement, which offers "instant salvation" to its Jain followers through the mediation of Simandhara—a jina living in another universe.[13] Finally, the neoorthodox include more progressive Jains who accept modern science and Western ways of thinking and living.[14] An example could be Chitra Bhanu (1922–2019), who established a more modernized form of Jainism in the United States. In truth, the same phenomenon can be said of all other Indian-based religions as well as practically all other world religions. There is always a tension between the traditional (or conservative) and the progressive (or liberal), with a good percentage of practitioners falling somewhere in between. But in the West, it is much more common to find Jains who would fall into the heterodox or

13. Peter Flügel, "Present Lord: Simandhara Svami and the Akram Vignan Movement," in *The Intimate Other: Love Divine in the Indic Religions*, ed. Anna King and John Brockington (New Delhi: Orient Longman, 2005), 196–97.

14. Paul Dundas, *The Jains* (London: Routledge, 2002), 272.

neoorthodox category—without at all, of course, implying that they are not good Jains or not in good standing.

Part 3: Religious Writings

As with most other holy scriptures in religions around the world, the sacred writings in Jainism were transmitted orally by their seminal leader's disciples before being recorded in written form decades or centuries later. But here an important issue arises. Were the oral sayings of jinas such as Mahavira written down accurately? Of the two major denominations within Jainism, which I will discuss in depth below, only one of them (Svetambara) accepts most of the written record. The other (Digambara) believes that much has been inaccurately recorded in written form, and so its canon is much smaller.

The holy scriptures within Jainism are called *agamas* ("that which has come down"). And they were written in what is called a Prakrit language—a language that Mahavira either spoke in everyday affairs or used only for specialized purposes, but that, significantly, was decidedly not the sacred and high-caste-based language of Sanskrit (with its echoes of and deference to the Brahmins and Vedas in Hinduism). As in Christianity, the number of scriptures varies according to denomination. According to the Svetambaras, members of the less traditional denomination within Jainism, the Jain holy writings are almost three thousand years old. The oldest portions—fourteen texts called *Purvas* or "Old Texts"—date to the twenty-third jina, but they are no longer in existence. Instead, what survives are dozens of texts customarily divided into six portions that cover a range of genres and topics: rules for monks, philosophical teachings, doctrinal beliefs, descriptions of different beings within the Jain worldview, and so on. The exact number is usually given as forty-five or thirty-two—but again, only the Svetambaras accept these scriptures. Of these, the oldest are eleven *angas*, or "limbs," which are more than two thousand years old and serve as foundational texts that describe the life and legacy of Mahavira.

Besides these holy scriptures within the Svetambara denomination, a postcanonical text has become authoritative for both major denominations within Jainism. It is titled Tattvartha Sutra ("On the Nature of Reality"), dating to the 300s or 400s.[15] And unlike the original holy scriptures in Jainism, it was written in the sacred language of Sanskrit. Composed of ten chapters, it is philosophical in nature and offers an excellent summary of Jain teaching. It begins with a now-famous phrase:

---

15. Babb, *Understanding Jainism*, 29.

"Right path, right knowledge, and right conduct together constitute the path to moksha." And it ends with instructions on how to achieve enlightenment: "Omniscience or perfect knowledge [*kevala jnana*] is attained through destruction of delusion and destruction of knowledge-covering, perception-covering, and obstructive actions [*karmas*]." Once this occurs—that, is, upon one's following all the teachings contained in the book—liberation from the endless cycle of birth and rebirth is achievable: "Owing to the absence of the cause of bondage [*bandha*] and with the functioning of dissociation of actions [*karmas*], the annihilation of all actions [*karmas*] is liberation [*moksha*]."[16]

Fig. 1.5.
Palm of hand symbolizing *ahimsa* in Jainism.

Five Core Ethical Teachings of Jainism

1. Nonviolence (*ahimsa*)
2. Nonlying (*satya*)
3. Nonstealing (*asteya*)
4. Noncarnality (*brahmacarya*)
5. Nonattachment (*aparigraha*)[17]

16. Tattvartha Sutra 1.1, 10.1, and 10.2, respectively.
17. Tattvartha Sutra 7.

One other important notion taught in Jain scriptures is a strong dualism that characterizes the religion. According to Jainism, there are two types of a being or entity: one is *soul* (*jiva*) and the other is *matter* (*ajiva*).[18] In a pure state, a soul possesses three qualities that are unhindered by matter: consciousness (*caitanya*), bliss (*sukha*), and energy (*virya*).[19] Although these exist when a soul is joined with matter, the matter darkens our consciousness, deflates our bliss, and diminishes our energy. The opposite of soul is matter (*ajiva*). Existence is essentially understood as follows. Matter—in the form of karma, and so often called *karmic matter*—attaches to or binds to a soul. Or, to state it differently, the soul is sticky, and matter effortlessly sticks to it. In this way, the goal of a human being is to return to that state of being a pure soul without having any stickiness. This means that there is no longer any karmic matter sticking to the soul and binding it to the unrelenting cycle of samsara. When this happens, through the steps outlined in Jain scriptures, a person loses stickiness and experiences moksha.

Part 4: Beliefs

Jainism naturally shares many common beliefs with its more famous religious family members of Hinduism and Buddhism. To begin with, like the assumed reality of gravity among the scientific community, Jains have always taken for granted the universal moral principle of cause and effect known throughout the world as *karma*. Based on the Sanskrit term for "action," karma reigns as a sort of cosmic and impersonal judge and king that dispenses justice across the universe based directly on the actions of the living. In this way, every time we think or act, we are generating karma that will return to us in either a positive or a negative way. In Jainism, karma takes on a physical force—highlighting how our physical actions (in addition to our mental intentions) can do either good or bad—but many subtypes of karma are mentioned in Jain scriptures. Or, to change metaphors, karma operates like an unrelenting, unrivaled, and unfeeling tennis player who always returns the ball with the same intensity, nuance, and force as it receives it. You cannot outsmart or outplay it. What you give, you get. For what goes around comes around. But here, it is important to underscore that it is not some personal God who dispenses karma. Jains do not believe in a God that corresponds in any way to the God of the Bible.

Key Differences between Jainism and Hinduism. Despite many similarities between Jainism and Hinduism, there are also differences. Historically, two of these distinctives revolve around the Vedas and the caste system. While Jainism does not regard the Vedas as authoritative and it questions the caste system, Hinduism has traditionally ascribed a sacred status to the Vedas and accepted the caste system.

18. There are, of course, different ways to translate these words. For instance, *jiva* could be translated as "life" or "soul"; and *ajiva* as "nonlife" or "nonsoul."

19. Jaini, *Path of Purification*, 104–5.

Belief in karma coincides with another foundational assumption within Indian religions: reincarnation. As the Jain scriptures teach, "The mark of a substance is existence."[20] In other words, nothing really dies—it just takes on a new form. Unlike monotheistic religions such as Judaism, Christianity, and Islam that envision human life as linear, temporal, and unrepeatable, Hinduism, Buddhism, and Jainism believe that life is cyclical, eternal, and recurring—a concept called *samsara*. And in fact, it is karma, in proportion to a person's own decisions, that determines how many lives a living being will have as well as the quality of each life lived.

The Goal of Jainism

The way to eliminate karma is to follow the so-called three jewels of Jainism: right path, right knowledge, and right conduct. This is based on Tattvartha Sutra 1.1, the opening of the most authoritative religious text among Jains. The three jewels are practiced in a sequential order. First is "right path," which is belief in the jinas who have gone before and who taught the true path to enlightenment. Second, "right knowledge" refers to the actual understanding of what the jinas taught. And third, "right conduct" includes behaving in a way that is consistent with and reflective of these core teachings. In short, as scholar of Jainism John Cort summarizes it, "The Jain who wants to travel the path to liberation must have faith in the Jain worldview, must have knowledge of the details of that worldview, and must act properly in accordance with that worldview."[21] And what exactly is this worldview? It is a worldview codified in Jain scriptures, and it has nine components. These nine truths encompass the existence of a soul, matter, attachment of the two, the soul's bondage to karmic matter, the opportunity to accrue either good or bad karma, and the ability to diminish karma, which is practiced through detaching one's soul from it in the hope of one day—perhaps after eons and eons of former lives—experiencing complete liberation from it.

Nine Truths in the Jain Worldview

1. Soul (*jiva*)
2. Matter (*ajiva*)
3. Karmic matter contacting the soul (*asrava*)

---

20. Tattvartha Sutra 5.29.
21. John E. Cort, *Jains in the World: Religious Values and Ideology in India* (New York: Oxford University Press, 2001), 18.

4. Bondage of the soul by karma (*bandha*)
5. Good karma (*punya*)
6. Bad karma (*papa*)
7. Blockage of karma (*samvara*)
8. Detachment of the soul from karma (*nirjara*)
9. Complete liberation from karma (*moksha* or *nirvana*)[22]

Briefly stated, those who successively and successfully pass through these stages may reach the last and final one—what is called *moksha* in Hinduism, *nirvana* in Buddhism, and *salvation* in Christianity. Unlike Christianity, however, but very much like Hinduism and Buddhism, Jainism assumes that freedom from the principle of cause and effect is reached only by those who have undergone countless lives, have accrued immeasurably good karma, and are now ready to be at one with the universe. In Jainism, the one who is able to achieve this is often called *Nigantha*, "one who breaks bonds," referring to the bond of karma that historically enslaves all living beings. But the overwhelming majority of people are not ready for this, so their goal in life is essentially doing good deeds in keeping with their station in life and so ideally accruing enough karma to return to earth one step higher in their next life.

Fig. 1.6.
Mahatma Gandhi was a champion of *ahimsa*.

22. Uttaradhyayana Sutra 28.14.

In addition to these shared religious concepts with Hinduism and Buddhism, Jainism also, of course, has its own distinct beliefs and practices. The first is called *ahimsa*, which is often translated as "nonharm" or "nonviolence." It is the cardinal theological distinctive of Jainism, offering the dominant narrative from which to frame the entire religion. And it is most famous for being the doctrine that Mahatma Gandhi (1869–1948) most deeply incorporated into his campaign against the British Empire in the first half of the twentieth century. Rather than being passive, ahimsa is active. After all, Jains believe that violence attracts negative karma, which, in turn, keeps us in bondage to a cycle of birth and death. By contrast, the cultivation of ahimsa repels bad karma and nurtures good karma. This is the goal of Jainism, and it is what distinguishes it from every other religion.

Historically, Jains illustrate ahimsa through the care they take in walking and even breathing, both gently brushing aside any living organisms they might otherwise tread on and wearing a face mask to refrain from accidentally inhaling a microscopic bug. But the majority of those who practice Jainism today—what are traditionally called *laypeople*—are fully committed to ahimsa without ever using a whisk to brush away insects before walking or wearing a mask to avoid inhaling a microscopic organism. And in fact, not even all monks or nuns are required to go to these extremes. Only certain sects do, and so it is less common than one assumes. But what unites all the disparate practices is the unified cultivation of ahimsa.

Another important doctrine within Jainism is fasting to death. The technical term for this is *sallekhana* (or *santhara*). As you might imagine, it is controversial. According to tradition, virtually every jina fasted to death as a perfect embodiment of ahimsa. Following in their footsteps, several Jain ascetics—and some laypeople—have adopted their practice. Jains are quick to point out, however, that this practice is not equivalent to suicide. In other words, it is not performed as a desperate measure or as a way to terminate the pain of depression, loneliness, or sickness. Instead, it is performed—by a very rare number of individuals—out of compassion for all living things and simultaneously in complete detachment from worldly things. Proceeding in stages, it is a willful choice that is premeditated. And in fact, it is not altogether different from martyrdom—as practiced in Christianity, and that was very common in the early centuries of the church.

Finally, I also want to mention one more important doctrine in Jainism that plays an important role. It is called *anekantavada*, and it means something like "non-one-sided" or "multifaceted reality." The concept sounds postmodern, but it is actually premodern. In a nutshell, the doctrine of *anekantavada* maintains that there are countless valid perspectives on any given matter, since truth is ascertained in context and in part. For instance, in a multireligious context such as India, it was necessary to explain why and how Jainism was distinct from Hinduism, Buddhism, and other religious and philosophical traditions. Thus, only a jina is really able to view the whole picture and know the whole truth. But when applied in normal life, the doctrine means that truth cannot be reduced into one single concept; instead, it can be approached from many angles.

Two Historic Denominations in Jainism

Jainism is historically divided into two denominations that are just as divisive and critical of each other as denominations within Christianity (and of course, each denomination has lots of subdivisions). Both comprise mostly laypeople, but monks and nuns are found in both and play a prominent role. And although I will focus on the role that monks and nuns have played, it is important to recognize that most Jains are laypeople. The names for adherents to these denominations are the "sky-clothed" (Digambaras) and the "white-clothed" (Svetambaras), and as you will see, their names get to the core of the historical dispute between them: namely, clothing. What, you might be thinking, is the relationship between clothing and liberation? In Jainism, the two have a long and contentious history. As religious scholar Padmanabh Jaini explains, "the history of Jainism is rather remarkable for the almost total lack of doctrinal accommodation between [these two denominations] . . . regarding the issue of nudity."[23]

The *Digambaras*, meaning "sky-clothed," are Jains—specifically, only the male monks within this denomination—who go naked as Mahavira did. Rather than donning clothes, Digambara monks are clad in the sky and so wear nothing. In fact, they own no possessions and eat only what they can hold in their hands. They do not receive medical care, brush their teeth, or participate in society. Their decision to wear no clothes derives from their belief that clothes signify attachment, shame, and violence against life (in the plant fibers used), none of which can lead to liberation—moksha. Even the laypersons within the Digambara denomination—who do wear clothes—believe this, thereby sealing their fate that they cannot attain moksha in this lifetime like their (male) monk brothers. In fact, for Digambaras, "nudity remains

23. Jaini, *Path of Purification*, 5.

the necessary condition for moksha."[24] Although it seems strange and even bizarre that only a tiny fraction of the denomination can achieve liberation—and perhaps it is—it must be stressed that the Jain worldview is cyclical in contrast to the Christian worldview, which is linear. This means that, to put it bluntly, Christians get only one lifetime to get things right, while Jains have ceaseless lifetimes to do so. In this way, most Jains are content to forgo attempting to achieve moksha in this life and, instead, simply hope to be born into a better situation in their next life—perhaps then considering moksha a viable or even preferable option.

Fig. 1.7.
Jain pilgrimage site in Mehsana, India, where both Digambaras and Svetambaras visit.

What about Digambara (female) nuns? Are they able to achieve moksha in this lifetime? Female nun Digambaras do exist, but they wear clothes and, as a result, are believed to be "incapable of practicing nonattachment to the degree of which a man is capable."[25] Consequently, female Digambaras—as well as laymen Digambaras—must be reborn as male Digambaras to achieve moksha. And so they strive to lead an exemplary life in the hope of returning to earth as males capable of attaining the highest spiritual goal. Moreover, Digambaras revere Mahavira, believing him to be more than a human.

The other traditional denomination within Jainism is less strict. Its adherents are called *Svetambaras*, meaning "white-clothed," since they

24. Jaini, 20.
25. Long, *Jainism*, 17.

wear white clothing rather than go naked like the Digambara monks. Monks and nuns within the Svetambara denomination travel with a begging bowl in which they collect food to return to their religious communities to eat. And they may also wear a face mask and carry a whisk to refrain from harming any insects or small creatures. Svetambaras include males and females, both of which are able to achieve moksha in this lifetime—a concept that is, of course, rejected by Digambaras. Svetambaras even recognize two groups of male monks within the denomination: one that lives alone and naked in the forest and one that lives clothed and in a religious community. Most Jains today are part of this denomination, and they mostly reside in Northern and Western India.

Part 5: Worship Practices

Where Do Most Jains Live? Today, Jains can be found anywhere in the world. But historically in India, the Svetambaras are clustered in Gujarat and Rajasthan, with the Digambaras in Karnataka and Maharashtra.

Jain worship practices are not as austere as some of their distinct beliefs may suggest. And their worship of gods appears quite similar to that of most other modern religions. In fact, Jain services and temples present joyful experiences that reflect a zeal for living and a worshipful devotion to their revered ones. I will classify Jain worship practices into three categories: personal piety, corporate worship, and mendicant life.

First, there is personal piety, which is usually practiced in the home. For instance, Jain families have a small shrine at home that contains images of their preferred figures that have renounced the world—such as one of the five groups mentioned in the figure below—often simply called *gods* or *deities*. The specific ones vary, and not surprisingly, Mahavira is quite common. As in Hinduism, these images may be ceremonially fed, bathed, adorned, and even put to sleep. The family shrine centralizes family devotion each day, typically in the morning, with this traditional prayer:

I bow before the worthy ones.
I bow before the perfected ones.
I bow before the leaders of the Jain order.
I bow before the teachers of the Jain order.
I bow before all Jain monks in the world.[26]

All five of these figures are former or current mendicants who lived countless lifetimes to be in a place to renounce everything and detach themselves from the things of the world.

---

26. This foundational Jain prayer is usually called the *Mahamantra*, and various translations are offered. Such mantras are common in Indian religions.

Five Supreme Beings in the Mahamantra

English (Prakrit)	Referent
Worthy ones (*arhats*)	Those who achieved nirvana (jinas)
Perfected ones (*siddhas*)	Those who attained moksha
Leaders (*acaryas*)	Those who oversee monastic communities
Teachers (*upadhyayas*)	Those who teach in monastic communities
Monks (*sadhus*)	Those who are in monastic communities

Second, corporate devotion takes place in Jain temples, at pilgrim sites, and on specific holy days during festivals. When visiting these temples, you should remove your shoes, dress modestly, and act respectfully. In Jain temples, people gaze at, bow before, and pray to the images of the jinas or deities depicted. And most Jains illustrate this through adoring and praising representations of them in the form of *murtis*, or "images." Murtis, as in Hinduism, offer a material embodiment of a being worthy of respect and honor, and they are depicted in human forms either seated or standing. Temples usually have a primary murti of a jina in addition to side shrines of others. And unlike Christianity, no priests or ordained clergy are needed to intercede between the worshiper and the image.

Fig. 1.8. Jain temple in Ranakpur, India.

Jains pray to these murtis for the same things that people around the world pray for regardless of religious affiliation: health, favor, prosperity, protection, wisdom, and so on. In this way, a Jain service may appear to outsiders as worship of an image of an actual god—just like devotional Hinduism. And for all practical concerns, this is accurate. Other Jains, however, may be less inclined toward praising an image of a jina and instead show their devotion to a living guru who offers advice, teaching, and blessings to devotees. What's more, pilgrimages are also important in Jain spirituality. It is common for Jains to visit sacred sites where jinas achieved enlightenment. And there are also several famous shrines that pilgrims visit—one of which is the sixty-foot statue of Bahubali, the first person to attain moksha in our epoch. What is more, probably the most popular festival for Jains is *Paryushana* ("coming together"), which is an eight-day ritual that re-creates the life of a monastic.

A third type of worship takes place among the mendicant (monk and nun) communities. Although they receive the bulk of scholarly attention, Jains who take the five vows to become monks or nuns—whether in the Svetambara or Digambara denomination—are very much in the minority.[27] Their devotional practices differ in many ways from those of lay Jains. For instance, as mendicants, Jain monks and nuns do not cook their food but rely exclusively on laypeople,[28] have no possessions, wear distinct clothing (or, in the case of Digambara male monks, wear nothing), practice meditation, refrain from any sexual activity, offer blessings and teachings (especially during the rainy season in India), perform daily rituals, and follow more austere spiritual practices.

One common spiritual practice in Jainism, regardless of station in life, is meditation. This is commonly done daily in a practice known as *Samayika*, which is designed to last twice the number of fordmakers, thus forty-eight minutes. The ultimate purpose of meditation is, as in Buddhism, to remember and cultivate our true self—in which we are neither bound to nor shaken by the vicissitudes of life. In this way, meditation allows one to foster and nurture a disposition toward detachment no matter what circumstances are encountered. This is related to a concept called *equanimity*. Literally meaning "even soul" or "even mind," it refers to the disposition of being so aware of life's transience that it does not get shaken or stirred.

Outside India, and particularly in the United States, it is common for Jain communities to share space with Hindu ones. This is a strange concept

Who Are the Jain Gods? Although Jainism does not claim a personal and creator God as in Christianity, there are references to "gods" and "deities" in Jain literature. These gods temporarily live in another realm, and so will eventually be recirculated through the cosmos like every other being.

27. Their numbers are only in the thousands. And they are really found only in India. For more, see Babb, *Understanding Jainism*, 65.

28. It goes without saying that Jains are vegetarians. The central tenet of ahimsa proscribes the eating of an animal.

from a monotheistic perspective—after all, it would be quite shocking to attend a mosque, for instance, that also housed a church. But this is not strange from an Indian religious mindset, particularly in the United States, and you should not be surprised if you attend a Jain worship service only to find that most of the people there are Hindus who are worshiping their own gods and simply share holy space with Jains. This is not to imply that Jainism and Hinduism are identical or follow the same rituals. Nor is it to imply that this arrangement exists or is accepted in India. It is merely to indicate that—particularly in a foreign context—there are many more similarities than differences between the two religions, and that the pooling of resources from such a small community is needed to afford a worship space at all. In India, however, the differences are more pronounced, meaning that you will not as often encounter such an arrangement.

Part 6: Point of Contact

Probably the most distinct teaching of Jainism is ahimsa. As I discussed, the term is variously translated as "nonviolence," "nonharm," or "noninjury." In my conversations over the years with Jains, both in India and in the United States, this is the topic that I most often return to. After all, when you first learn the concept, it is attractive and sounds surprisingly modern. Essentially that message is: "Do no harm." *Yes*, we think, *that is a mindset that I can incorporate into my daily life!* In fact, it is a mindset that one of the world's most famous leaders, Mahatma Gandhi, adopted in his colossal struggle to nonviolently liberate India from British rule in the first half of the twentieth century. But as you dive deeper into ahimsa, moving away from the theoretical and entering into the mundane realities of the practical, it is shocking to learn that the most notable figures in the Jain religion—all twenty-four jinas—were revered because they took the teaching of ahimsa to the extreme by willingly starving themselves of food and water so as not to harm any living creature, including microscopic organisms that we cannot even see in plain sight. This occurred in a practice called *sallekhana*.

As a Christian, I am fascinated by how an otherwise completely foreign concept in another religion relates to Christianity. For instance, I believe that Jainism's practice of sallekhana aligns closely with Christianity's practice of martyrdom. At the heart of the Christian faith, after all, is Jesus' death on the cross, which ensured salvation for those who believe in his sacrifice. We live because he died. In addition, Jesus encouraged his followers to take up their crosses and be willing to put their lives on the line for their faith. In this way, I resonate with Jains who willingly risk their lives for their beliefs. This is, in fact, how most of the Christian disciples died, and there has hardly been a generation since in which missionaries, clerics, and even laypeople have not died for Christ.

But here is the primary difference between Jain sallekhana and Christian martyrdom. Those practicing sallekhana actively participate in their death, while those undergoing martyrdom passively participate in their death. One is done in foresight, the other in faith. One is done for oneself, the other for Another. One is done to forever renounce the body, the other to eventually resurrect the body. But let me get more to the point: Is it not the case that ahimsa is actually violated by sallekhana, since the persons doing it are intentionally harming themselves? Are they not simply substituting the life of insects and microscopic organisms for a human life?

Jesus presents what I believe to be a more authentic version of ahimsa. For example, Jesus did not hand himself over to the authorities; he was arrested. Jesus did not climb the cross; he was put on it. And Christ did not plunge a spear into his heart; he was stabbed. In this way, I would contend that Jesus demonstrated ahimsa more effectively than Mahavira. That is to say, Jesus remained faithful to ahimsa from beginning to end. He preached that when being taken advantage of, a person is to turn the other cheek. And when he himself was unlawfully arrested and put on trial, he taught to not use the sword. In short, I think we can round out our understanding of ahimsa within Jainism by realizing that Jesus illustrated his glory by transcending nature rather than opposing it. For instance, like Jains, Jesus believed in fasting. But he practiced it occasionally and temporarily to symbolize that we do not live by bread alone. And when he had made his point, he resumed eating. Similarly, when Jesus healed the sick, exorcised the demons, and calmed the waters—however momentarily, selectively, and remotely—it was done symbolically to illustrate that it was God's ultimate design for humankind to be whole, for spirits to be clean, and for nature to be domesticated. Although there is great value in temporarily opposing nature by fasting from food and water, it is our ultimate design to eat from the tree of life in a restored nature that lovingly provides for its creatures.

Discussion Questions

1. How would you explain what Jainism is in a conversation with a friend?
2. What characteristics or features of Jainism do you think believers and seekers find attractive?

3. What commonalities and differences are there between Jainism and Christianity?

4. What is the difference between Jainism, Hinduism, and Buddhism? Which do you believe has been most influential in the West? Why?

5. Why does clothing (or lack thereof) play such an important role in Jainism? As you think of worldwide Christianity (including all its denominations), how is clothing used to differentiate or set apart certain individuals? Why is this?

For Further Reading

Babb, Lawrence A. *Understanding Jainism*. Edinburgh: Dunedin Academic Press, 2015.

Cort, John E. *Jains in the World: Religious Values and Ideology in India*. New York: Oxford University Press, 2001.

———, ed. *Open Boundaries: Jain Communities and Cultures in Indian History*. Albany: State University of New York Press, 1998.

Dundas, Paul. *The Jains*. London: Routledge, 2002.

Jaini, Padmanabh S. *Gender and Salvation: Jaina Debates on the Spiritual Liberation of Women*. Berkeley: University of California Press, 1992.

———. *The Jaina Path of Purification*. Berkeley: University of California Press, 1979.

Long, Jeffrey D. *Jainism: An Introduction*. London: I. B. Tauris, 2009.

chapter 2

Sikhism: The Story of Union

Sikhism has a rich and distinctive history, during which it has forged a unique identity while interacting with the other major religions of India—Hinduism and Islam—as well as impacting in a major way on the culture of the colonial power that was eighteenth- and nineteenth-century Britain.

Jagbir Jhutti-Johal[1]

The Sikhs believe there is only one supreme being, or God. . . . To them, the God of their religion is the same God as that of all other religions. For example, the Sikh God is the same one that Muslims and Christians worship.

Michael Regan[2]

Sikhs are . . . those who have undertaken a path of self-perfection under the guidance of a spiritual master called Guru.

Arvind-pal Singh Mandair[3]

Part 1: The Beginning

In the beginning was the one God whose name was truth. This God was the creator who formed all that exists—planets and galaxies, water and wind, animals and humans, sticks and stones. God created

1. Jagbir Jhutti-Johal, *Sikhism Today* (London: Continuum, 2011), viii.
2. Michael Regan, *Understanding Sikhism* (Minneapolis: Abdo Consulting Group, 2019), 18.
3. Arvind-pal Singh Mandair, *Sikhism: A Guide for the Perplexed* (London: Bloomsbury Academic, 2013), 3.

all these things without fear and without hate but, on the contrary, with complete love. Neither male nor female, this God is timeless in form, beyond birth, the same from age to age, self-existing, and never-ending. Nobody, other than God, knows exactly when God created everything. And nobody knows how great God is. We know only that there are endless worlds existing both above and below the one we inhabit. And that God is infinite in goodness.

Humankind is naturally bent toward itself and will die and be reborn countless times. But in the grace of God, salvation is available for those who listen to the divine music beating in their hearts and sing the praises of their maker. In fact, the repetition of the maker's name is the holiest and most sacred of rites. Although the wisest sages and the most devout of believers from all religions have attempted to describe God, none have succeeded, and their attempts are as inadequate as drops in an ocean. And to the gods who are worshiped in each religion, the true God is their creator. God forever sees them, but they never see God.

Like a king whose throne extends across the oceans, God alone possesses authority. Like a judge whose courtroom traverses the land, God alone passes judgment. And like a deity whose temple spans the galaxies, God alone deserves praise.

> What God wills, God ordains.
> No one can give an order to God.
> For God . . . is the King of Kings.
> As God wills, so we must live.[4]

Road Map to Sikh Creation Story. Sikhism does not spend much time pondering where we come from. In fact, in Sikhism, God never takes on a body or materializes. And because Sikhism affirms reincarnation, it is not possible for humanity to collectively conceive of an initial stage of existence. The focus is our current existence, not our previous origins.

Part 2: Historical Origin

Greater India is the mother of countless religious traditions. In addition to giving birth to the older religions of Hinduism and Buddhism, which I discussed in my prequel, *Christianity and World Religions*,[5] and Jainism, which I explained in the previous chapter, Sikhism is the youngest child of Asia's very fertile religious mother. Unlike her older siblings, however, Sikhism emerged at the dawn of the modern world—when Martin Luther (1483–1546) was nailing his criticisms of Roman Catholicism on a public church door, when Hernán Cortés (1485–1547) was laying siege to the fabled kingdom of Tenochtitlán, and when Nicolaus

4. This is based on the Japji, the opening section of the Guru Granth Sahib, Sikhism's holy scripture. The Japji contains thirty-eight sections originally written by Guru Nanak, the first Guru. The quotation at the end comes from the last stanza in chapter 27.

5. Derek Cooper, *Christianity and World Religions: An Introduction to the World's Major Faiths* (Phillipsburg, NJ: P&R Publishing, 2012), 1–49.

Copernicus (1473–1543) was publishing the revolutionary theory that the earth revolved around the sun.

In short, the world was changing—and not just in the West. Everywhere, it seems, religious traditions were being seriously questioned, newly disseminated, or doubly fortified. The Ottoman Turks, for instance, were propagating Sunni Islam in the Middle East; the Spanish and Portuguese were extending Roman Catholicism across Asia, sub-Saharan Africa, and Latin America; and the Ming Dynasty was seeking to maintain the assumed harmony of the so-called Three Teachings of Buddhism, Confucianism, and Daoism in China. As for India, its religious profile varied greatly depending on geography, ethnicity, heritage, language, and tradition. Hinduism, of course, was the majority religion, but many other minority religions, such as Buddhism, Christianity, Jainism, and Islam, flourished and were actively practiced. And then, over a series of events, a new religious child was born that sought to bring peace to sibling rivalry.

The Punjab and Its Connection to Hinduism and Islam

The modern country of India can be compared to the continent of Europe inasmuch as each Indian state is so different from the others that each one is better understood as the equivalent of a different nation rather than as part of a monolithic Indian country. Not only do different Indian states historically speak unrelated languages and follow distinct customs, but their ethnic backgrounds and religious traditions are quite dissimilar. This truth helps us understand that Sikhism is intimately connected to a region in North India and Eastern Pakistan called Punjab, which is composed mainly of Punjabis who speak a language that is also called Punjabi.

This also underscores the complicated and controversial history of this region since 1947, when the British overlords of Greater India arbitrarily partitioned the British province of Punjab into two countries—the modern nation of Pakistan and India. Subsequently, the people groups found themselves in the precarious position of living in a country different from both their near and distant relatives. When Pakistan and India were partitioned, most of what we today call Sikhs moved to North India while Muslims relocated to Eastern Pakistan. This was because Pakistan became a Muslim nation that grew antagonistic to native-born Indian religions such as Hinduism and Sikhism while India reacted negatively to Islam. This is, of course, a simplistic explanation of a complex history in which millions of inhabitants were displaced—and some very violently and horribly so.

Pronunciation of the Punjabi Language. Though *Sikh* is commonly pronounced as "seek," the Punjabi language voices the *i* as a short vowel, meaning that the more accurate pronunciation is closer to "sick"; hence, it is more properly pronounced as "sick-ism" rather than "seek-ism." The term *Sikh* means "learner" or "disciple," in which case Sikhs are disciples of the Guru.

In fact, the history of Punjab is as ancient as the Indus Valley civilization itself, dating back thousands of years. Because of its central location as the gateway to Greater India and because of its fertile soil, this region found itself regularly subjected to a revolving door of foreign overlords ranging from Aryans to Greeks to Mongols to Persians to Afghanis. Though dominated religiously by Hinduism, Punjab was first introduced to Islam by Arab conquerors in the eighth century. Over time, the rulers who gained control over the region sowed religious discord into the soil, yielding division and isolation among the sparring religions of Hinduism and Islam. This conflict ensued for centuries, sometimes with Hinduism's having the upper hand and sometimes with Islam's having it. But what united the people was a common language and a mutual love for the land they inhabited.

A Fusion of Two Religious Traditions: (Bhakti) Hinduism and (Sufi) Islam

From this context, we can begin to understand how Sikhism emerged as a religious tradition that had been brewing for centuries within the religious basin of the two historical, sizable, and rival religions of Hinduism and Islam. As historian Khushwant Singh explains, "Sikhism was born out of a wedlock between Hinduism and Islam after they had known each other for a period of nearly nine hundred years."[6] As I discuss in detail in *Christianity and World Religions*, Hinduism and Islam are two religions that could not be more different. In short, Hinduism believes in many gods, endless life reincarnations, and widespread veneration of images, while Islam affirms the existence of only one God, one life on earth, and an absolute rejection of religious imagery. Not surprisingly, therefore, it is only natural that these religions would chafe under each other's existence. And it is equally natural that a movement would eventually emerge attempting to bridge the gap between the two. This came from the fringes of both religions. In short, both devotional (*bhakti*) Hindus and mystical (Sufi) Muslims urged tolerance, but the time was ripe for a new religious tradition to emerge.

Just as the Protestant Reformation gestated for centuries within Western Europe before it was finally born in the person of Martin Luther, so, too, Sikhism had many predecessors before it coalesced under the leadership of Guru Nanak (1469–1539). One of the earliest of these was a Hindu philosopher named Adi Shankara (c. 700–750). He was a prolific

---

6. Khushwant Singh, *A History of the Sikhs*, vol. 1, *1469–1839* (Princeton, NJ: Princeton University Press, 1963), 17.

author who taught that there is only one true God, and that idol worship was illegitimate. Three centuries later, in the eleventh and twelfth centuries, another Hindu guru emerged who was named Ramanuja (c. 1077–1157). As a proponent of *bhakti* or "devotional" Hinduism, he believed in the oneness of God and, as in Sufi or "mystical" Islam, emphasized a personal relationship with and humble submission to this God. Ramanuja's teachings of devotional Hinduism were adopted by many subsequent gurus; of these, Kabir Das (1398–1518) was probably the most famous. Kabir, who lived an unusually long life, reinforced both Hindu and Muslim beliefs and practices, so much so that both "Hindu and Muslim followers amassed for combat after his death, each side demanding to take charge of his body."[7] This debate concerning his true religious identity derived from countless verses in his poetry where he voiced sentiments such as "Let no false pride mislead you: that the Hindu and Muslim are of different family is false."[8] Though Kabir showed signs of being more of an independent thinker than being directly tied to one of these two historical religions, a tradition combining both Hinduism and Islam was emerging.

Forerunners of Guru Nanak. Guru Nanak was influenced by previous Indian thinkers, for instance, Adi Shankara, Ramanuja, and Kabir Das. Protestantism developed in a similar way. Though we often view Martin Luther as the originator of Protestantism, for example, he had many predecessors: John Wycliffe (1328–84), Jan Hus (1370–1415), and Lorenzo Valla (1407–57).

Fig. 2.1. Stained-glass window of Guru Nanak, the first Sikh Guru.

7. Linda Hess and Shukdev Singh, *The Bijak of Kabir* (Oxford: Oxford University Press, 2002), 2.
8. Ahmad Shah, *The Bijak of Kabir* 26.8 (Hamirpur: Indian Press, 1917), 66.

Things came to a head in India and the rest of South Asia with the introduction and expansion of the Mughal Empire. Although it officially lasted from the sixteenth to the nineteenth centuries, this empire had been expanding throughout the Middle Ages—and with it, tension between the Muslim minority who ruled and the Hindu majority who obeyed intensified. Sikh author Patwant Singh argues, in fact, that they were destined to crash "on a collision course."[9] Low-caste Hindus, who had nothing to lose and everything to gain, began adopting the foreign faith of Islam—the religion of the empire—in droves. As expected, many of these conversions did not immediately result in a rejection of centuries of Hindu devotion, but instead led to a sort of mixture of two seemingly contrary religions.

Guru Nanak (1469–1539)

This sentiment came to full form under the teaching of Guru Nanak, the official founder of Sikhism. Guru Nanak was born on April 15, 1469, in the city of Nankana Sahib, which is located west of Lahore, in today's Pakistani province of Punjab. Nanak actively practiced devotional Hinduism, influenced by what was called the Sant tradition, which emphasized a personal relationship with God and a rejection of the caste system. (Like all subsequent Sikh Gurus and their wives, however, Nanak was from the Khatri caste.) In fact, he later wrote, "There is no caste in the hereafter."[10] Like many other mystics, whether Hindu or Muslim, Nanak was spiritually precocious from a young age and much more interested in the sacred than the mundane. Although he married, fathered children, and worked as a storekeeper (a typical job for someone of his caste), he spent his free time composing and singing hymns, caring for and feeding the poor, and following his meditative and ritualistic practices.

And then, at thirty—the age of Jesus' call into ministry—Nanak underwent baptism in a river and received a revelation from the one true God. In this revelation, God gave Nanak ambrosia (called *amrit*) to drink, signaling initiation and immortality, and unveiled Nanak's mission: "Go in the world to pray and to teach mankind how to pray. Be not sullied by the ways of the world."[11] It was the early morning, and Nanak was taking his daily ritual bath, or *ablution*, in the Vein River when suddenly he disappeared. His family searched for his body, casting

Sikhism and the Caste System. Historically, the caste system was divided into four major classes, and each class was expected to enter a certain occupation and fraternize with and marry only within that class and occupation. For instance, Guru Nanak was part of the Khatri caste and so was pressured into a merchant profession such as bookkeeping.

9. Patwant Singh, *The Sikhs* (New York: Doubleday, 2001), 16.
10. Adi Granth 349.
11. Khushwant Singh, "The Sikhs," in *The Religious Traditions of Asia: Religion, History, and Culture*, ed. Joseph M. Kitagawa (London: Routledge, 2002), 112.

nets into the river under the assumption that he had drowned. Finding no body but instead only his clothes alongside the river, they assumed him dead. Three days later, however, he emerged from the river with a message from God: "There is no Hindu, there is no Muslim."[12] As with Buddha and the apostle Peter, this revelation compelled Nanak to leave his wife and children to preach the message far and wide. Encountering both Muslim and Hindu leaders, he shared the revelation he had received until eventually settling down in central Punjab and founding the first Sikh community. This town was called Kartarpur, located on the banks of the River Ravi.

Quite unusual for the time, Nanak wore clothing and followed customs that appealed to both Hindus and Muslims. His exuberant faith was evident to onlookers, and before long a hodgepodge of ordinary people from various religious traditions settled among his community. Nanak taught that God was reached through meditation on God's name and union with that God. And not surprisingly, his poems featured rapturous reflections on God, urging believers to "worship the name of the Lord."[13] Nanak was accompanied by a ministry partner from a Muslim background named Mardana, who excelled in music playing. When Nanak would receive divine revelation, it was to Mardana that he recited it. For the rest of his life, Nanak led the fledgling community in Kartarpur that he founded. The people offered voluntary services for the community, ate food together irrespective of caste or religion (which was extraordinarily countercultural), and gathered for worship based on the poem-songs of Nanak, who composed around a thousand hymns that would later form the nucleus of Sikhism's sacred scriptures. Before dying, Nanak appointed a human Guru to succeed him and further the message of God.

The Nine Succeeding Human Gurus (1539–1708)

The nine human Gurus who followed Guru Nanak each played a role in the expansion of Sikhism that also reflected the historical development of Greater India under the (Muslim) Mughal Empire and, later, (Christian) British Empire. The succeeding four Gurus after Nanak—Angad Dev (1504–52), Amar Das (1479–1574), Ram Das (1534–81), and Arjan Dev (1563–1606)—were poets like Guru Nanak whose hymns made their way into the Guru Granth Sahib. They did not remain in Kartarpur but

Why Did So Many Religious Leaders Arise at the Age of Thirty? Many of the most famous religious leaders of the world experienced their callings at the age of thirty. This includes Buddha, Mahavira, Jesus, and Guru Nanak. For reasons that are not clear, this was the age when they abandoned their former way of life and adopted a new one.

---

12. Pashaura Singh, "An Overview of Sikh History," in *The Oxford Handbook of Sikh Studies*, ed. Pashaura Singh and Louis E. Fenech (Oxford: Oxford University Press, 2014), 21.

13. Singh, "The Sikhs," 296.

The Term *Guru*. Although nowadays the term *guru* generally describes a teacher, in Sikhism it is capitalized and refers to the ten founding fathers of the Sikh religion as well as to the Guru Granth Sahib, the holy text venerated as a living Guru.

lived in various villages. They each developed the religious tradition in their own ways, particularly the latter two, who laid the foundation for Amritsar to become the central religious site within Sikhism (called the Golden Temple) and in which the Guru Granth Sahib would first be installed.

Guru Arjan, as I will discuss below, was the Guru who performed the sacred task of collecting and codifying the Sikh holy scriptures as well as constructing a religious temple in which to adequately house them. Guru Arjan, in fact, was even more of a prolific hymn composer than Guru Nanak, writing thousands of hymns that would be incorporated into the scriptures. The creation of the Sikh holy writings helped solidify the identity of the growing community, distinguishing it from the larger Hindu and Muslim communities. As a line from one of Guru Arjan's hymns states: "I serve the One and no other. I neither perform Hindu worship nor do I offer Muslim prayers, I have taken the formless One into my heart. I am neither Hindu nor Muslim."[14] Living during an intense time religiously and politically within the Mughal Empire, Guru Arjan was tortured and killed in the year 1606. But he left a permanent mark on the Sikh religion by means of his collection of the scriptures, establishment of the Golden Temple, and creation of important infrastructure and policies.

Fig. 2.2. The Golden Temple in Amritsar, India, is the holiest site in Sikhism.

14. Guru Dev, as quoted in Nikky-Guninder Kaur Singh, *Sikhism: An Introduction* (London: I. B. Tauris, 2011), 28.

Guru Gobind Singh (1666–1708), the Khalsa, and Combat

Guru Gobind Singh, Sikhism's tenth and final human Guru, also played a prominent role in the religion. As alluded to above, Guru Gobind Singh lived during a turbulent time in North India. As Singh writes, "it was a time of turmoil and terror, and of conquests, cruelties, and despair."[15] For example, Guru Singh's father was beheaded under the rule of the Mughal Empire, which enacted (Muslim) sharia law. In fact, death and even martyrdom befell many Sikhs, including the sixth Guru—named Hargobind (1595–1644)—as well as Singh himself. It was within this context that Singh inaugurated a new era within Sikhism. Although I will explain the clothing and conduct of Sikhism below, it is important to mention that Guru Singh was the leader most responsible for the turban, beard, clothing, and accessories of Sikhism—some of which carry military overtones. In fact, there is a specific date on which this became official. In 1699, during the harvest festival of Vaisakhi (also spelled "Baisakhi"), which inaugurates the New Year in Sikhism, Guru Singh formed a select Sikh community that was called the *Khalsa Panth*—or just *Khalsa*, meaning "pure."

The members of the Khalsa, all of whom were willing to sacrifice their lives for the religion and profess loyalty to the Guru, were baptized, embraced a rigorous code of conduct, and received new casteless last names from Guru Singh (who, until that time, had the surname Rai): *Singh* ("lion") for males and *Kaur* ("princess") for females. They also donned special clothing and accessories, often abbreviated as the *Five K's*: *kesh* ("uncut hair"), *kangha* ("comb"), *kirpan* ("sword"), *kachh* ("underwear"), and *kara* ("bangle"). At the time, this style of dress and accessories reflected historical norms as well as military gear, but beyond that, scholars continue to debate the precise origin of each of the K's and when exactly they became normative. Nowadays, at any rate, the Five K's distinguish Sikhs from both Hindus and Muslims, the two dominant religions that were practiced when Sikhism emerged, and with which Sikhism is most commonly confused by outsiders.

The Five K's

Perhaps the most distinct practice within Sikhism has to do with the Five K's. Originally designed for a smaller group within Sikhism called the Khalsa, who all drank of *amrit*, a special drink originally unavailable

---

15. Singh, *The Sikhs*, 16.

for the low caste, signaling their commitment to the Sikh cause, the Five K's are as follows:

- *Kesh* ("uncut hair")
- *Kangha* ("comb")
- *Kirpan* ("sword")
- *Kachh* ("underwear")
- *Kara* ("bangle")

It should be noted that not all Sikhs wear the Five K's.

This distinct identity bolstered the Sikh community at a time when resistance to Muslim invaders was peaking. Throughout the 1700s, for instance, Sikh armies, called *misals*, were regularly created to defend the Sikh way of life. Eventually these *misals* were united as the Sikh community gained power. Soon afterward, in the 1800s, the British took control of the land. Ruling for roughly a century (1849 to 1947), the British created a new context within Greater India and the Punjab in which the Sikhs sought greater independence and influence. For instance, the Sikhs desired greater freedoms over their religious sites, political rights, and linguistic heritage. The relationship between Sikhs and the British was mixed. On the one hand, the British ended Sikh sovereignty and encouraged Christian missionaries and institutions in the Punjab; on the other, the British favored the Sikhs over Hindus and Muslims. The complicated relationship between the Brits and the Sikhs continued until 1947, at which time the British arbitrarily partitioned the province of Punjab into the modern nations of Pakistan and India. Not surprisingly, the partition is a very sensitive and prominent topic. And despite long-standing attempts, Sikhs have never managed to create their own country. In fact, the twentieth century witnessed a long exodus of Sikhs out of India and into all regions of the world, including Asia, Africa, Oceania, Europe, and North America. In these latter two regions, it is to the United Kingdom, the United States, and Canada where most Sikhs immigrated. Today, these communities continue to grow, inculcate, and adapt.

Part 3: Religious Writings

The Guru Granth Sahib is perhaps the world's most revered religious book. Written in Gurmukhi script, the script used in the modern Punjabi language, it is sacred to all Sikhs and owes its genesis to Guru Nanak, who came from a caste specializing in accounting and therefore familiar with the written word. For centuries, the Guru Granth Sahib has been regarded by Sikhs as the embodiment of the Guru, and it is the primary focus of attention in all Sikh temples—and, in fact, what makes a Sikh temple a *gurdwara*, or "doorway to the Guru." Although we will refer to it as holy scripture, it is much more—it is actually the final Guru, the physical culmination of the Guru's teaching to humankind. In this way, it is less a book and more a living guide. And its words are timeless, mostly devoid of historical events.

Fig. 2.3. The Guru Granth Sahib, Sikhism's scripture, is lovingly kept under cloth.

The Guru Granth Sahib is one of the largest canons of scripture in any world religion, containing roughly fifteen hundred pages in modern printed volumes. It is massive and impressive to behold as scripture reciters (*granthis*) read from it on the throne (or *palki*) on which it sits. Like the Qur'an within Islam, the Guru Granth Sahib is deeply poetic, with most of the words designed to be performed in song. The book is chronological, meaning that its earliest author, Guru Nanak, is featured first. His writings, which bespeak a yearning for unity with God as well as a desire to praise and worship God, set the tone for the book.

Development of the Guru Granth Sahib

Like most other holy books, the Guru Granth Sahib was formed over the course of centuries. And its name also underwent change, since the designation *Guru* was applied to it only after the last human Guru, Gobind Singh, died in 1708. The most common name for the original version is Adi Granth, or "First Book," a term still used today to refer to all the holy scriptures—somewhat like Judaism's use of the word *Torah* to encompass both the first five books of the Hebrew Scriptures and the remaining books. And as a result, one of the common ways to refer to the Guru Granth Sahib is to use the abbreviation AG, standing for Adi Granth. Naturally, the original version did not contain all the portions in the book's present form. And even so, there are several other ways that Sikhs refer to their holy scriptures.

Each of the first five Gurus played foundational roles in the Guru Granth's composition, transmission, compilation, and dissemination. As mentioned earlier, Guru Nanak, Sikhism's initial Guru, was the first to receive divine revelation, and his roughly one thousand hymns constitute the initial portion of the text—with the opening twelve words, called the *mul mantar*, being the most famous and providing the overall introduction to the scripture as well as a daily prayer of Sikhs around the world. The next several Gurus likewise added their own compositions to the growing book as well as those of other like-minded Sikh poets. The fifth Guru, Arjan Dev, put to paper the first official volume of the Adi Granth, which was installed in the Golden Temple—the equivalent of Islam's Kaaba in Mecca or Judaism's temple in Jerusalem—in the year 1604. It is called the Katarpur Pothi, and it still resides in the same place. According to tradition, Guru Arjan decided to put the words, heretofore only in oral form, in written form in order to offer an official version in contrast to circulating rival versions that falsely claimed to be accurate.[16] This is very common among religious scriptures.

The change in the Guru Granth Sahib's status from holy scripture to living Guru occurred in 1708. In the dying words of Gobind Singh, Sikhism's last human Guru: "Whoever wishes to hear the Guru's word should wholeheartedly read the Granth or listen to the Granth being read." And this belief is repeated in Sikh prayer as follows: "Acknowledge the Guru as Granth. Acknowledge the Granth as Guru, the manifest body of the Gurus."[17]

Speaking of Guru Gobind Singh, the tenth and final human Sikh Guru, his writings were eventually incorporated into holy scripture, though they are less prominent than the original Adi Granth. Singh's compositions are called the Dasam Granth (or DG for short), and they offer insight into the religious and historical development of Sikhism

Sacred Languages. The written script for Hinduism, Islam, and Sikhism differed. Hindus spoke Hindi and used the Devanagari script (reminiscent of Sanskrit and the Vedas). Muslims spoke Urdu and used the Arabic script (reminiscent of the Qur'an). Meanwhile, Sikhs spoke Punjabi and used the Gurmukhi script (reminiscent of the Guru Granth Sahib).

---

16. Gurinder Singh Mann, "Canon Formation in the Sikh Tradition," in *Sikh Religion, Culture, and Ethnicity*, ed. Christopher Shackle, Gurharpal Singh, and Arvind-pal Singh Mandair (London: Routledge, 2014), 11.

17. Eleanor Nesbitt, *Sikhism: A Very Short Introduction* (Oxford: Oxford University Press, 2005), 38.

during the late 1600s and early 1700s. But partly because they came later historically and partly because Guru Gobind Singh's sole authorship of them has been disputed, they command only a sort of deuterocanonical status within Sikhism—similar to how the Apocrypha constitute part of the Holy Bible within Roman Catholic and Orthodox Christianity, but nonetheless do not have the same status as other books.

Living Embodiment of the Guru

The Guru Granth Sahib is the actual and physical Guru within the Sikh religion. It is not simply a series of writings recorded in lifeless ink but a living and divine guide. And because Sikhs believe that the Guru Granth Sahib is a living incarnation of the Guru, it demands that one observe a certain respect or even code of conduct in its presence. In this way, it is somewhat similar to Jewish synagogues honoring, preserving, and safeguarding Torah scrolls, which are hidden from plain sight and handled only by someone in the community entrusted with this responsibility. It is also similar to how some Christians, particularly Roman Catholic and Orthodox Christians, interact with the wine and bread of the Eucharist, believing that God is mysteriously united with the hosts. After a Roman Catholic Mass, for instance, the priest must either consume the remaining elements or store them in a locked compartment.

No matter where you are in the world, the gurdwara, or Sikh temple, places the Guru Granth Sahib as its focal point. In fact, unlike in Hindu temples, you will not typically see any other competing religious imagery, such as statues or gods. The book is safely stored under elegant fabric in a cushioned stand called a *palki*. And while it is being read from, an attendant will wave around what looks like a brush above it, akin to a horse's tail pushing flies away from its body. Historically, this was the equivalent of premodern air conditioning, but the tradition remains even in cooler climates. Like a murti or household god within Hinduism, the Guru Granth Sahib is cared for lovingly as if it were a baby in accordance with the time of day and need of the moment. For instance, at nighttime, it is tenderly put to bed, like a mother laying her infant in a crib.

Part 4: Beliefs

As is true of most religious traditions that are intimately connected to ethnicity, what it means "to be a Sikh" includes more than affirming a creed. Moreover, given its classification as a new religious movement, there is disagreement whether it is a distinct religion or an offshoot of one of its two parent religions. In this way, I value the model of Sikh scholar Eleanor Nesbitt, who identifies five distinct ways to define a Sikh. These contrary explanations define Sikhism as (1) a minor movement within Hinduism, (2) a religion deriving directly from Hinduism, (3) a mixture of Hinduism and Islam, (4) a completely distinct religion based on its own divine revelation, or (5) a nation or people group.[18] Each of these has a grain of truth, and each offers a convenient way to frame how to understand the religion. In fact, I propose a definition that combines each of these elements together, namely, understanding Sikhism as a religion that includes components of Hinduism and Islam but that nonetheless emerged as a new religious movement based on distinct revelation (scriptures), beliefs, practices, and community. But according to the Sikh Rehat Maryada, a universal code of Sikhism, a Sikh is committed to four primary things: (1) belief in the existence of God, (2) adherence to the Guru Granth and preceding ten human Gurus, (3) acceptance of the baptism taught by the tenth Guru, and (4) allegiance to no other religion. This, too, offers a great summary of Sikh beliefs.

To begin with, Sikhs believe in the existence of a timeless and formless God that goes by various names. Two of the more common names are Satnam ("true [or everlasting] name") and Waheguru ("wondrous teacher"). As Guru Nanak expressed, "There is one God, Eternal truth is His name."[19] Like Islam, but unlike Hinduism, this God has never assumed a material body on earth. In a mysterious way, God possesses all attributes, yet transcends them. Again, as Guru Nanak taught, "Though we strive to grasp [God] a hundred thousand times," "it is not through thought that He is to be comprehended."[20] In short, you may call this God what you will—Yahweh, Krishna, or Allah—but just remember that your understanding of God is as tiny as a molecule of water in the ocean. The goal of Sikhism is not necessarily to grasp this God but to join this God. Union with God, stemming from the ancient Indian religious concept of yoga as well as the ancient Sufi practice of mysticism, is what one aspires to achieve.

Besides an affirmation of the one true God, Sikhs believe in ten human Gurus as well as a scriptural Guru that are, quite mysteriously, physical manifestations of the same Guru. The human succession of Gurus lasted from 1469 to 1708, beginning the year in which Guru Nanak was born and ending the year that Guru Gobind Singh was killed. In addition, Sikhs profess several prominent Indian-based religious beliefs

---

18. Nesbitt, 4.

19. Guru Nanak, Proem, in *A World Religions Reader*, ed. Ian S. Markham and Christy Lohr, 3rd ed. (Malden, MA: Blackwell Publishing, 2009), 238.

20. Guru Nanak, Japji 1, in *A World Religions Reader*, ed. Ian S. Markham and Christy Lohr, 3rd ed. (Malden, MA: Blackwell Publishing, 2009), 238.

such as reincarnation, karma, and *mukti* (called *moksha*—"liberation"—in Hinduism). Much as Judaism, Christianity, and Islam all stemmed from a religious tradition affirming only one human life on earth, Hinduism, Buddhism, Jainism, and Sikhism grew out of a religious tradition that has always asserted that life on earth progresses from one existence to another. As Guru Nanak explained: "We do not become sinners or saints by merely saying we are. It is [previous] actions that are recorded. According to the seed we sow is the fruit we reap. By God's will . . . humans must either be saved or ensure new births."[21]

The Three Pillars of Sikhism

Sikhism generally promotes a threefold ethic that is often called the Three Pillars of Sikhism, which contrasts with the Five Pillars of Islam. This consists of (1) meditating on God by means of the Guru Granth, (2) having a (morally) respectable job, and (3) taking care of others.[22] Unlike the exclusivist religions of Islam and Christianity, but like the inclusivist religions of Hinduism and Judaism, Sikhism is a religion that does not generally attempt to inculcate outsiders. God will save people based on divine grace (called *gurparshad*), not religious denomination. Moreover, people have within themselves the ability to choose right living and make good decisions. Besides, most of us will continue living in some form in a future life as we rotate through the eternal cycle of birth, life, and death called *samsara*. In this way, Sikhism is an ecumenical religion. Multiple faiths are respected and seen as perfectly fitting for others to practice. This makes sense within the historical context of the religion. Interestingly, though, Sikhism moved away from Hinduism, Buddhism, and Jainism in one important matter. Whereas the former religions molded divisions between monastics (those who could achieve liberation upon death) and laypeople (those who could only hope to be reborn into a better station upon death), Sikhism did not. In this way, Sikhism is more closely connected to Protestantism, by which I mean that it criticizes lofty rituals, its Gurus marry and raise families, and it collapses divisions between clerics and laypeople.

Clothing and Conduct

To outsiders, the most iconic symbol of Sikhism is the clothing worn by its stereotypical practitioners, particularly the males. For

21. Guru Nanak, Japji 20, 242.
22. Nesbitt, *Sikhism*, 27.

Sikhism and Turbans. Turbans come in all colors, styles, and designs. Although there is a particular meaning behind most of them, which is lost on outsiders, the wearer has freedom to choose what kind to wear based on the occasion, circumstance, or situation.

starters, the turban is a hallmark feature of the Sikh religion, and it is perhaps the first thing that one notices. A Sikh's turban is usually made from cotton, and it is wrapped multiple times around one's head. The turban covers another important component to Sikhism: uncut hair (*kesh*). Although outsiders will rarely see a male Sikh's hair, it is traditionally long and uncut, which also corresponds to one's untrimmed beard. The lengthy hair and flowing beard of Sikh men is more than a fashion statement; it is a faith statement. At the same time, it is crucial to understand that not all Sikhs wear a turban, grow long hair, or have a beard. On the contrary, you will occasionally encounter a male Sikh who is turbanless, shorthaired, and clean-shaven. He is still a Sikh in good standing.

Fig. 2.4. Sikh man wearing turban in Delhi, India.

Part 5: Worship Practices

We can divide Sikh worship practices into both personal and corporate activities. Personal piety, of course, varies from person to person. But historically, it has been common for Sikhs to rise early in the morning, bathe, and sing from portions of the Guru Granth, which is opened at dawn and adorned in robes. In a similar way, they will end their day also singing from select hymns from the scriptures and ceremonially closing the Guru Granth. But nowadays, the internet and phone apps make this practice much easier. And the busyness of the modern person's life influences one's daily practices.

Fig. 2.5. Sikh man praying at Golden Temple in Amritsar, India.

In terms of corporate practice, specific rituals take place in the gurdwara among the community (*sangat*). As in many other religions, shoes are removed upon entry, and sitting is traditionally done on the floor (though you may encounter chairs and tables). Thus, you will want to wear comfortable and modest clothing and keep the bottoms of your feet away from the Guru Granth Sahib (in many cultures, showing the bottoms of one's feet is rude and disrespectful). Head coverings (such as a scarf or handkerchief) will also be required for both males and females, and they will be available free of charge if you do not have one. The main activity occurs in the main hall. Here Sikhs sit in the presence of the Guru Granth Sahib, accompanied by the public playing of musical instruments with great delight. The scripture is read by a *granthi*, or attendant (whether male or female), but there is not an ordained cleric who leads the service as in Christianity (though community leaders known as *sants*—traditionally always males—are highly respected). This service ends with prayers and the distribution from the *karah prashad*, which is sweetened dough (consisting of butter, flour, sugar, and water) and offered to all in attendance, regardless of whether one is a Sikh. I still remember a time when I took students to a gurdwara in Malaysia. They were shocked when offered *karah prashad* and unsure what to do until I gladly took and ate my portion, understanding that the food is more about friendliness than faith. Although guests, as on this occasion, are not judged for not knowing exact protocol, it is typical to receive the food with cupped hands and then eating it with the right hand (in many ancient cultures, the right hand is for eating and the left hand is for cleaning one's bottom).

Another central part of the worship experience at all gurdwaras is the communal meal that takes place after sitting in the presence of the Guru Granth Sahib. This meal is called *langar*, meaning "anchor," and it is a hallmark feature of Sikhism in which everyone is served a free and simple meal without regard to class, rank, or prestige. This is a time-honored and deeply meaningful experience that began during the time of Guru Nanak. Within an Indian caste-based context, the eating of a meal with those of a different caste—or no caste at all—was countercultural and reflective of a core teaching within Sikhism that all are equal and have the same value. Like communion in Christianity and iftar in Islam, the eating of a common meal together is meant to promote solidarity and fellowship, but unlike many churches that offer communion only to believers of that tradition, langar is given to everyone—whether Sikh or not. I myself have visited gurdwaras in multiple countries, and the meal is fairly standard: bread, lentils, potatoes, yogurt, and pudding. It is a filling meal but always a highlight—and surprisingly tasty. And it is also vegetarian so that everyone can partake of it in good conscience (whether Hindu, Muslim, or Christian). As with the *karah prashad*, the langar is traditionally eaten with the right hand without the use of silverware.

Are Sikhs Vegetarians? Unlike Hindus and Jains, who are strict vegetarians, and Muslims, who are traditionally carnivores (but refrain from pork), Sikhs are divided on this issue. Some are vegetarians, while others are not.

Outside India, gurdwaras also serve as community centers where much more than "religion" takes place. For instance, the gurdwara will likely contain a classroom, space for the retired community to spend time, a library that houses cultural and religious books, and a venue for Sikh marriages (married life and having children is greatly preferred over celibacy). This communal use of the gurdwara allows the Sikh community to learn elements of its faith, culture, and heritage that it would otherwise naturally imbibe if living in its historic homeland in the Punjab. The gurdwara may also be the location of festivals and celebrations throughout the year. For instance, this includes celebrations of the birthdays and deaths of each of the Ten Gurus. Baisakhi is the first day of the Sikh calendar, which commemorates Guru Gobind Singh's creation of the Khalsa order in 1699.

Part 6: Point of Contact

I have had many conversations with Sikhs in many countries in Asia. They essentially proceed in the same way. I visit their gurdwara, where they are absolutely thrilled to host me. They relish in walking me through every part of their service and explaining why they do what they do. They eagerly sit with me during the langar meal and ask me questions about what I do and why I want to learn more about Sikhism. "You are a very curious person," they say. "We do not get many visitors from the West." It is always a very enjoyable experience, and I walk away grateful for the time we spent together. Sikhs are incredibly generous and wonderfully hospitable.

Sharing my faith in Jesus Christ with Sikhs is more challenging—and it is not my standard practice to share my faith with them in their worship space unless explicitly asked. Although both Sikhism and Christianity believe in one God and we share many commonalities when it comes to morals, ethics, values, and lifestyles, it still feels like an uncrossable chasm separates our core beliefs from one another. And it is very difficult to cross that bridge. Lately, though, I have been thinking more about the Sikh doctrine of grace. It is quite beautiful. As I mentioned above, it is called *gurparshad*, which is essentially a combination of the terms *guru* and *grace*. Interestingly, this is also connected to the sweet dough that is distributed to those who visit the gurdwara. In short, Sikhs believe that God's grace will save them, and in a certain sense, the *parshad*—the sweet dough—is a token of that saving grace. And I have always appreciated how the *parshad* is lovingly distributed to everyone in the gurdwara, whether Sikh or seeker.

Within Christianity, we also believe that God will save us through grace, and we also have a visible and edible token of that grace in the form of the Lord's Supper. Just as Jesus descended to earth to show us immeasurable and unmerited favor by dying on the cross, so Christ's body is symbolically and temporarily distributed to his followers until the day arrives when we can stand in the very real presence of Christ in resurrected bodies that no longer subsist on symbols but flourish on realities. But on this point, I think the Sikh religion stops short. To be sure, it does boldly proclaim the oneness of God, it does justifiably emphasize the grace of God, and it does symbolically present the *prashad* of God. But symbols of grace are eventually meant to be replaced by realities of grace. In Sikhism, despite believing in God, leading a good life, and partaking of the elements, faithfulness is usually rewarded with another life that must be repeated, and repeated, and repeated, but never completed. In Christianity, by contrast, upon believing in God, leading a good life, and partaking of the elements, we are rewarded with life everlasting—one that we do not have to repeat, we do not have to retake, and we do not have to replay. It is not a dress rehearsal but is the actual performance, which is the real grace of God. We can subsist on symbols for only so long. Eventually we require the real thing.

Discussion Questions

1. What are the primary differences between Hinduism, Islam, and Sikhism? Of the three, which two do you think are most opposed to each other?
2. What did you learn about Sikhism that you did not previously know? How has it changed how you understand the religion?
3. Identify as many commonalities between Sikhism and Christianity as you can. How might you use one of these commonalities to share your faith with a Sikh?
4. Both Sikhism and Jainism emerged in India and out of Hinduism. Why do you think so many new religious movements arose from that religious tradition and social context?
5. Both Guru Nanak and Martin Luther lived at roughly the same time, and in fact, both became religious leaders who were famous for starting new movements that quickly spread and developed into entire religious infrastructures. Make a list of all the similarities and differences between the two figures and their movements. Which one do you think has exerted the most influence on religion? Why?

For Further Reading

Grewal, J. S. *The New Cambridge History of India*. Vol. 2, *The Sikhs of the Punjab*. Cambridge: Cambridge University Press, 1990.

Jhutti-Johal, Jagbir. *Sikhism Today*. London: Continuum, 2011.

Mandair, Arvind-pal Singh. *Sikhism: A Guide for the Perplexed*. London: Bloomsbury Academic, 2013.

Mann, Gurinder Singh. *The Making of the Sikh Scripture*. New York: Oxford University Press, 2001.

McLeod, W. H. *Sikhs and Sikhism*. New Delhi: Oxford University Press, 1999.

Nesbitt, Eleanor. *Sikhism: A Very Short Introduction*. Oxford: Oxford University Press, 2005.

Singh, Khushwant. *A History of the Sikhs*. 2 vols. New Delhi: Oxford University Press, 1992–99.

Singh, Nikky-Guninder Kaur. *Sikhism: An Introduction*. London: I. B. Tauris, 2011.

Singh, Pashaura. *The Guru Granth: Canon, Meaning, and Authority*. New Delhi: Oxford University Press, 2000.

Singh, Patwant. *The Sikhs*. New York: Doubleday, 2001.

PART 2

Muslim New Religious Movements

In this section, we discuss the two most influential religious traditions emerging out of Islam: the Baha'i Faith and the Nation of Islam. What is interesting about both these new religious movements is that they also emerged out of prior Muslim new religious movements. For instance, the Baha'i Faith arose out of the Babi religion in nineteenth-century Iran. In a similar way, the Nation of Islam developed out of the Moorish Science Temple and the Ahmadiyya Movement, which both emerged in twentieth-century America. In addition, the Baha'i Faith and Nation of Islam stem from different denominations within Islam. For example, the Baha'i Faith came from the smaller of two major Muslim denominations (called Shia Islam), while the Nation of Islam grew out of the largest Muslim denomination (called Sunni Islam). Either way, both Shia and Sunni Muslims consider both the Baha'i Faith and the Nation of Islam heretical, aberrant, and outside the bounds of orthodoxy. If you would like a refresher on Islam, be sure to read the chapter dedicated to it in my prequel, *Christianity and World Religions*.[1]

1. Derek Cooper, *Christianity and World Religions: An Introduction to the World's Major Faiths* (Phillipsburg, NJ: P&R Publishing, 2012).

chapter 3

Baha'i: The Story of Oneness

Given its impressive geographic spread as the world's most widely diffused religion in the world today (second only to Christianity), the Baha'i Faith is increasingly attracting interest.

Christopher Buck[1]

[Baha'i's] teachings revolve around the fundamental principle that religious truth is not absolute but relative, that Divine Revelation is progressive, not final. Unequivocally and without the least reservation it proclaims all established religions to be divine in origin, identical in their aims, complementary in their functions, continuous in their purpose, indispensable in their value to mankind.

Shoghi Effendi[2]

The concepts of oneness and unity are important starting points in understanding the Baha'i Faith. The Faith has often been summarized as teaching three onenesses: the oneness of God, of religion, and of humanity.

Robert Stockman[3]

---

1. Christopher Buck, *Baha'i Faith: The Basics* (London: Routledge, 2021), 2.
2. Shoghi Effendi, "Fundamental Principle of Religious Truth 4.19," in *The World Order of Baha'ullah* (Wilmette, IL: Baha'i Publishing Trust, 1991), 57–60.
3. Robert H. Stockman, *The Baha'i Faith: A Guide for the Perplexed* (London: Bloomsbury Academic, 2013), 9.

Part 1: The Beginning

The people were now in a state of ardent expectation for the Messiah. And for years, this man's teacher had been exhorting him to search and find that Messiah, the one who would succeed Islam's greatest prophet, Muhammad, exactly a thousand years after the prophet's last physical heir and descendant, the Twelfth Imam, went into occultation (or "hiding").[4] The search was not successful, however, and his teacher died before he could complete the mission assigned to him. But this all changed on a night that would make history. Mulla Husayn, the man who had been desperately in search of the Messiah or Promised One, happened upon a young man who was twenty-five years old in the town of Shiraz, Iran. Although Husayn had made plans to have evening prayers with his friends at the mosque, he was transfixed by the young man, and something deep within him told him to accept the young man's invitation to enter his home: "I was profoundly impressed," Husayn later stated, "by the gentle yet compelling manner in what that strange Youth spoke to me."[5]

As they prayed alongside each other at the prescribed time, Husayn unburdened his soul, vocalizing his failure to complete the task assigned to him: "I have striven with all my soul, O my God, and until now have failed to find your promised Messenger."[6] After prayer, their conversation turned to religious matters, and Husayn outlined a long list of attributes that he had been informed would characterize the long-awaited Messiah. And then, lo and behold, to his great astonishment, the young man replied, "All these signs are manifest in me!"[7] Husayn's mind was now darting in all directions. Concluding that the young man truly did possess all the attributes that he had been foretold, he now decided that he needed additional proof—and this proof would come in the form of two spiritual gauntlets.

First, the young man would need to explain a highly esoteric document that Husayn had composed and that no one else was able to disentangle. Amazingly, the young man swiftly read the document

---

Road Map to Baha'i Creation Story. I am narrating the origins of the Babi religion, which led to the creation of the Baha'i Faith. And we can only understand how the Babi religion came into being if we understand Shia Islam (and, specifically, a denomination within Shia Islam called the Twelvers). Besides, the Baha'i Faith does not really have a creation story.

---

4. The source of what follows comes from Nabil-i-Azam, *Dawn Breakers: Nabil's Narrative of the Early Days of the Baha'i Revelation* (Wilmette, IL: Baha'i Publishing, 1932), which was originally written in the late 1880s in Farsi and translated by Shoghi Effendi in 1932. It is important to keep in mind that Islam uses a lunar calendar, so the death of the Eleventh Imam and the emergence of the Twelfth Imam occurred in 260 AH (*Anno Hegirae*, "In the Year of the Hijra"), meaning that 1260 AH, or A.D. 1844, is the year of significance.

5. Nabil-i-Azam, 53.

6. Nabil-i-Azam, 56.

7. Nabil-i-Azam, 57.

and "unraveled all its mysteries and resolved all its problems"[8] on the spot. In fact, he even gave additional insights into truth that no other teacher had previously revealed. Deeply satisfied that he had resolved the first test, Husayn now required proof for the second, namely, that the young man would need to offer a brilliant, novel, and impromptu interpretation of one of the most demanding and difficult *surahs*, or "chapters," in the Qur'an. This surah was called *Joseph*,[9] and none of Husayn's former teachers had ever dared to offer commentary on it. Undeterred, the young man took to the task with simplicity and swiftness. He simultaneously recited and wrote a commentary on this enigmatic chapter without missing a beat. Husayn, completely astonished, uttered: "I sat enraptured by the magic of his voice and the sweeping force of his revelation."[10]

Fig. 3.1. Siyyid Ali Muhammad, otherwise known as Al-Bab, was born and worked in Shiraz, Iran.

Husayn was now spellbound and speechless, and all he could muster was to turn his eye toward a clock in the room that would forever mark the date and time of this life-changing event: May 22, 1844, at two hours and eleven minutes after sunset. Subsequently, the young man, who

---

8. Nabil-i-Azam, 59.

9. In the Qur'an, this is the twelfth chapter. It is called *Yusuf* in the original Arabic, which is the name *Joseph* in English.

10. Nabil-i-Azam, *Dawn Breakers*, 60.

from now on would be called "the Gateway," or *al-Bab*,[11] declared, "This night, this very hour will, in the days to come, be celebrated as one of the greatest and most significant of all [times]."[12] "Truly," he continued, "I am the *Bab*, the Gate of God, and you are the *Babu'l-Bab*, the gate of that Gate."[13] And at that, the Bab prophesied to Husayn that he would be the first of eighteen disciples who would independently seek, find, and believe in him, thus inaugurating his mission "to deliver the Message of God . . . and quicken the souls of men."[14] And like that, a new religion had been born, and the first convert had been made.

Baha'i Faith or Bahaism? Why don't we refer to the religion of Baha'i with an *-ism* at the end, for instance, *Bahaism*? After all, we do this with Hinduism, Buddhism, Judaism, Mormonism, and many other religions. Although you will occasionally see it in older writings, the religion of Baha'i is never called *Bahaism* today, but instead the *Baha'i Faith*.

Part 2: Historical Origin

Like a Russian doll concealing a hidden set of additional wooden dolls of decreasing size, the Baha'i Faith arose out of a splinter faith out of a majority branch out of a minority denomination out of a world religion. This splinter faith is called the Babi religion (as narrated above), the majority branch goes by the term *Twelver*, the minority denomination is named *Shia* (or *Shiite*), and the world religion is known around the globe as *Islam*. Although the Shias represent the smaller of two main denominations within Islam, which amounts to only 15 percent of the global Muslim population, it is nonetheless the predominant Islamic denomination in Iran, and not surprisingly, the Baha'i Faith first emerged in that country. The time period was in the first half of the nineteenth century, and it immediately encountered resistance because it was perceived as not only beyond the bounds of the Muslim faith but, within almost no time, beyond the bounds of the Babi religion. The intensity of the persecution that the community encountered forced its practitioners to flee to nearby lands in order to survive. How is it, then, that a faith so immediately and intensely persecuted has gone on to become one of the fastest-growing religions in the world over a span of two centuries? The answer is intimately connected to Baha'i's three most significant pioneers: the Bab, Baha'ullah, and Abdul Baha.[15]

11. For a comprehensive explanation of what the term *al-Bab* meant in its context, see Nader Saiedi, *Gate of the Heart: Understanding the Writings of the Bab* (Waterloo, ON: Wilfrid Laurier Press, 2008), 98–103.

12. Nabil-i-Azam, *Dawn Breakers*, 61.

13. Nabil-i-Azam, 61.

14. Nabil-i-Azam, 63.

15. Because these terms have been transliterated into English based on the original Arabic and Farsi, they are typically transcribed with extensive diacritical marks, for instance, *Bahá'í, the Báb, Bahá'u'lláh*, and *'Abdu'l-Bahá*. For the sake of clarity and accessibility, however, I will use simpler spellings. Likewise, although the sacred writings of the Baha'i Faith in English use antiquated language, for instance, "thou replyeth," I will modernize it to assist the meaning for the reader.

Al-Bab, "the Gateway" (1819–50)

Siyyid Ali Muhammad, who lived from 1819 to 1850, is commonly regarded as the forerunner of Baha'i and the founder of the Babi religion. He was born and raised in Iran, and the title *Siyyid* was an honorific *was a* one indicating that he was part of a special class of Muslim families. For the most part, such families had immigrated to Iran from Arab lands a couple of centuries before during the Safavid Dynasty of Islam (1501–1722) and were connected to Twelver Shi'ism, which is characterized by its belief in a series of twelve imams who descend directly from Muhammad through his daughter Fatima and her husband, Ali. Miraculously and mysteriously, Twelvers believe, the Twelfth Imam—also called the Hidden Imam and referred to as *al-Mahdi*, "the Guided One" or "Promised One"—went into occultation (or "hiding") and will return with power on the day of judgment.

Like the speculation that has ensued regarding Jesus' second coming within Christianity, ongoing speculation as well as division within Islam has been generated by this incredible event, with many different religious schools of thought emerging from it. And equally unsurprising, many have since claimed to be the Hidden and long-awaited Twelfth Imam. But what ties most directly into our conversation about Baha'i has to do with the historical era in which Siyyid Ali Muhammad lived. In short, the year that the Eleventh Imam died and the Twelfth Imam assumed office was the equivalent of A.D. 844,[16] meaning that Siyyid Ali Muhammad was raised during a time of apocalyptic speculation and heightened expectancy that the Hidden Imam would emerge during the millennium year of 1844—somewhat equivalent to how some Christians eagerly expected Jesus to physically return to earth in the year 1000 or 1033.[17]

In fact, Siyyid Ali Muhammad was actually part of a minority and heterodox movement within Twelver Shia Islam that emerged and expanded based on its belief in the imminent return of the Twelfth Imam. But unlike more mainstream Twelver Shia Islam, which expected a literal return of the Twelfth Imam who would destroy his opponents, this new movement maintained that the return of the Hidden Imam would be spiritual in nature.[18] This movement was called Shaykhism,

16. As mentioned in a previous note, keep in mind that the Muslim calendar is lunar in contrast to the Western calendar, which is solar. This explains why the dates do not perfectly align when comparing the two. Yet the same principle of a thousand years applies. In the Muslim calendar, the dates are 260 AH and 1260 AH.

17. For more about this speculation, see Derek Cooper, *Twenty Questions That Shaped World Christian History* (Minneapolis: Fortress Press, 2015), 155–71.

18. Peter Smith, *An Introduction to the Baha'i Faith* (Cambridge: Cambridge University Press, 2008), 5.

or the Shayki School, and it is still in existence today. Established in the first half of the nineteenth century in Iran, Shaykhism provided the building blocks out of which the Babi religion grew, and most converts to the Babi religion came directly from Shaykhism. In fact, scholar of Baha'i Moojan Momen went so far as to write that "it is doubtful if the Bab would have attracted so many adherents if it had not been for the Shaykhi doctrines."[19] When the leader of the Shaykhi movement died in 1844, conflict over the line of succession ensued, and a search was made to find the one about whom he had made prophecies. At this time Siyyid Ali Muhammad began publicizing his own views of himself, claiming that he was the long-awaited Promised One.[20] And so beginning in 1844, amid great apocalyptic fervor, Siyyid Ali Muhammad declared himself to be "the Gateway," or *al-Bab* (a term previously in use to describe the four representatives who had conversations with the Twelfth Imam during his so-called Minor [or Lesser] Occultation and who served as his mouthpiece until he went into total concealment during the so-called Major Occultation), not only to the Twelfth Imam, but also to God.[21]

By this time, Siyyid Ali Muhammad was in his mid-twenties, working as a merchant, and married, and his only child had just died in infancy. By all accounts, Siyyid Ali Muhammad was regarded as a holy man, respected in the community, and spiritually inclined, but he was not trained or certified as a religious cleric. From an early age, however, he had experienced visions. At the same time, it is important to understand that Iran was home to a centuries-long mystical movement within Islam called Sufism as well as a rich poetic tradition that was highly mysterious and ecstatically spiritual in nature, meaning that Siyyid Ali Muhammad's religious experiences were not too unusual or novel. For example, Ismail I (1487–1524), who reigned as Shah of the Safavid Sufi order, wrote: "My name is Shah Ismail. I am God's mystery. . . . I am the living Khidr and Jesus, son of Mary."[22]

It is from within this cultural, literary, and religious context that Siyyid Ali Muhammad composed a lengthy, rhythmically rich poem-treatise in Arabic in 1844 revealing that he was God's Messenger, Prophet,

The Occultation (or "Hiding") of the Twelfth Imam. "[T]he doctrine of the Occultation... declares that Muhammad ibn Hasan, the Twelfth Imam, did not die but has been concealed by God from the eyes of men...During his Lesser Occultation, he remained in contact with his followers through the four Babs...During the Greater Occultation... there is no longer a direct route of communication."

Momen, Introduction to Shi'i Islam, 165.

19. Moojan Momen, *An Introduction to Shi'i Islam: The History and Doctrines of Twelver Shi'ism* (Oxford: George Ronald, 1985), 231.

20. For instance, he wrote, "He Who is the Eternal Truth bears me witness [that] whoever follows this Book has indeed followed all the past Scriptures which have been sent down from heaven by God" (Qayyum al-Asma 2).

21. See, for instance, Qayyum al-Asma 3.41, in which the Bab writes, "Verily I am the 'Gate of God.'"

22. Andrew J. Newman, *Safavid Iran: Rebirth of a Persian Empire* (London: I. B. Tauris, 2009), 13–14.

Promised One, and Word.[23] Based on the style of the Qur'an, which has 114 chapters or *surahs*, this book came to be regarded as the Qur'an of the new Babi religion, which, of course, put it at odds with mainstream Islam. Consequently, whereas Siyyid Ali Muhammad had initially taught his followers to observe Shariah Islamic law, which temporarily safeguarded his fledgling movement, he soon began proclaiming that his new revelation transcended Shariah law and ushered in a new world order. Not surprisingly, this caused direct conflict with the dominant religious community and government, which resulted in a joint *fatwa*, or religious ruling on a point of Islamic law, to be issued against the Bab and his followers that declared their movement *kafir*, meaning "heretical" or "unorthodox."[24]

This was to be expected. After all, classical Islam was not only a monotheistic religion in which there was only one God, but also a one-final-prophet-only religion in which the final prophet heralding this God could be only Muhammad. As scholar of Islamic thought Catharina Raudvere writes, "Muslim tradition has not accepted revelations more recent than Islam," and so religions such as Baha'i—as well as the Babi faith—can be regarded only as "Muslim apostates."[25] This is not to imply, however, that there were not countless prophets before Muhammad who Muslims believe spoke accurately, appropriately, and authentically about God. There were. But it would require an entire reversal of historical faith to accept the teachings of the Bab, essentially the equivalent of someone in the Christian tradition claiming to be the Messiah—a claim that transports one out of mainstream Christianity into a new religious movement. In fact, the Bab claimed to be the successor not only to Muhammad, but also to Christ—and to many other significant religious figures in history. He also proclaimed himself to be *al-Mahdi* ("the Guided One") and *al-Qa'im* ("the One Who Will Arise"), which was another way of saying within a Twelver Islamic context that he was the long-awaited Messiah or Promised One.

For example, in a significant book he wrote called the Bayan, he insinuated that he was the rightful ruler of Islam, claiming that "I am the same Promised Mahdi that the Apostle of God [Muhammad] foretold,"[26] and also penning that "the fruits of Islam cannot be gathered except through allegiance to him [the Qa'im, which is the Bab's way of referring to himself] and by believing in him."[27] But as his followers grew, so, too,

23. For more about these titles, see Saiedi, *Gate of the Heart*, 93–96.
24. Momen, *Introduction to Shi'i Islam*, 136, 141.
25. Catharina Raudvere, *Islam: An Introduction* (London: I. B. Tauris, 2015), 8.
26. Bayan XI.3.
27. Bayan II.7.

did his adversaries. The government, which then constituted part of the Ottoman Empire, took the offensive. From 1847 through the remainder of his life, the Bab was imprisoned; then he was killed by firing squad in 1850. Those who continued practicing the Babi religion, as well as Shaykhism, were suppressed and forced underground. But they were guided by the hundreds of thousands of verses that the Bab had managed to compose while in prison as well as by the prophecies he pledged speaking of "Him Whom God shall make manifest."[28]

Baha'ullah, "Glory of God" (1817–92)

According to the Baha'i Faith, "the essence and purpose of the Bab's own mission . . . was to prepare the people for [a] second and greater advent" in which "another messianic figure even greater than Himself, referred to as 'He Whom God shall make manifest,'"[29] would become fully revealed on earth. This is believed to have occurred in the person of Baha'ullah.[30]

Mirza Husayn Ali was born into an aristocratic and influential family in Iran in 1817. At the age of twenty-seven, he became a follower of the Bab the same year that the Bab revealed his identity as God's Manifestation. Because of his wealth and prominence and in accordance with the times, he took three wives and sired more than a dozen children. Ali threw himself into the Bab's ministry and corresponded with him until the latter's death in 1850. While the Bab was imprisoned during the last years of his life, Ali traveled widely to spread the message about the Bab and was highly successful in making converts despite the religious persecution that this group was experiencing. In 1848, Ali led a council of believers in the nascent Babi religion in which he gave a new name to each participant under the belief that a new era of God had emerged. This is when Ali's name changed to *Baha*, "Glory," and then, upon endorsement from the Bab, to *Baha'ullah*, "Glory of God."

In due time, the persecution that Baha'ullah had previously avoided as a result of his aristocratic status and wealth came to an end when he was imprisoned in a black pit in Tehran for several months in 1852. Under the most brutal of conditions, where those imprisoned with him were regularly tortured and mutilated, he received a vision marking him as the Manifestation of God about whom the Bab had prophesied.[31]

---

28. See, for instance, Effendi, *World Order of Baha'ullah*, 100.

29. Saiedi, *Gate of the Heart*, 1.

30. His name is pronounced ba-HA-oo-LA.

31. For more, see Shoghi Effendi, "The Dispensation of Baha'ullah," in *The World Order of Baha'ullah* (Wilmette, IL: Baha'i Publishing Trust, 1991), 100.

Miraculously, this was year nine after the Declaration of the Bab, which was the year expected for the appearance of the next Manifestation of God.[32] He kept this message private, however, and revealed it only years later. In the meantime, after his release from the black pit, Baha'ullah was banished to Baghdad, where he encountered fierce opposition from his brother, who claimed to be the true leader of the Babi community. Instead of fighting, Baha'ullah fled. He set off for the mountains to pursue the life of a mystic. These were his wilderness years, similar to when Moses shepherded the flocks, David hid in the caves, and Jesus fasted in the desert. There he met Sufis, the mystical practitioners of Islam, learned much from them, and soon composed two books addressed to them called Seven Valleys and Four Valleys.

When Baha'ullah returned to Baghdad in 1856, he found the Babi religion in disarray and in need of a leader. He inspired the people, corresponded with them frequently in his writings, and managed to bridge the gap between the more traditional Shias, the more recent Babis, and the more mystical Sufis. In 1863 Baha'ullah, in an event that has been named "the Declaration in Ridvan," which provides the foundation of the ongoing Ridvan Festival in the religion today and marks the official beginning of the Baha'i Faith, revealed his identity as God's Messenger to his followers as they prepared for yet another banishment. Specifically, he made three claims: (1) that the Baha'i Faith would not use violence (or *jihad*), (2) that he would be the last Manifestation of God for a thousand years, and (3) that his message was blessed and expanding.[33]

In response to Baha'ullah's assertions, his brother claimed the same title, leading to a years-long dispute in which the Babi community divided. The vast majority accepted the claims of Baha'ullah and became Baha'is. A minority, however, sided with the brother and came to be called *Azalis*. As an exile, Baha'ullah lived the remainder of his years in Turkey and then in Israel with his family and followers until his death in 1892. During this time, the nascent Babi religion that had begun in Iran and fallen under the shadow of Shia Islam transformed into the Baha'i Faith headquartered in Israel and positioned toward the world. By the time of his death, Baha'ullah had penned more than fifteen thousand works—"now regarded by his followers as divine revelation"—claimed to be the authoritative Messenger of God whom all "the people of the world" should obey, wrote letters to monarchs and world

32. In the Baha'i Faith, the number nine represents wholeness and perfection, much as the number seven does in Judaism and Christianity. Thus, this number is used in many ways in the religion.

33. Nader Saiedi, *Logos and Civilization: Spirit, History, and Order in the Writings of Baha'ullah* (Bethesda: University Press of Maryland, 2000), 242.

leaders informing them of his identity and admonishing them to repent, and constructed the building blocks out of which the worldwide Baha'i religion would materialize.[34] In fact, when seen from the vantage point of the most prevalent religions in the Middle East at the time, Baha'ullah explicitly interpreted himself as the Messiah of, and using the texts and ideas from, each respective movement to prove his claims in six religious traditions: Judaism, Christianity, Zoroastrianism, Shia Islam, Sunni Islam, and the Babi religion.[35] For instance, Baha'ullah claimed not only to be the Paraclete that Jesus had predicted in John 14–17, but also that Baha'ullah was God the Father, whom his Son, Jesus, had concealed, since his followers were not able to receive it at this time.[36]

Fig. 3.2. The Baha'i Gardens in Haifa, Israel.

Development of the Baha'i Faith: Abdul Baha (1844–1921), Shoghi Effendi (1897–1957), and the Universal House of Justice (1963–)

Before Baha'ullah died in 1892, he explicitly appointed his oldest son, Abdul Baha, then age forty-eight, as his definitive interpreter. As he wrote, "Whoever turns to [Abdul Baha] has surely turned to God, and whoever turns away from Him has turned away from My beauty,

34. Smith, *Introduction to the Baha'i Faith*, 24, 27.
35. Christopher Buck, "The Eschatology of Globalization: The Multiple-Messiahship of Baha'ullah Revisited," in *Studies in Modern Religions, Religious Movements, and the Babi-Baha'i Faiths*, ed. Moshe Sharon (Leiden: Brill, 2004), 144–45.
36. See Baha'ullah, *The Tablets of Baha'ullah* (Wilmette, IL: Baha'i Publishing Trust, 1988), 11.

denied My proof, and is of those who transgress."[37] This took the form of a "Covenant," in which the followers agreed to the terms outlined by Baha'ullah. And within Baha'i, there are actually two kinds of covenants that Messengers can make: a "Greater Covenant" and a "Lesser Covenant." A Greater Covenant takes place when the current Prophet of God promises a new Prophet. This occurred, for example, in the case of the Bab's prophesying about the coming of Baha'ullah as "He Whom God shall make manifest." By contrast, in a Lesser Covenant, the Prophet designates a human successor (not a divine one), as was the case when Baha'ullah appointed his son Abdul Baha.[38]

Abdul Baha, or "Servant of Baha"—a clear reference to his father, Baha'ullah—was serendipitously born on the same night that the Bab declared his identity as God's Gateway, on May 23, 1844. Though he was born into luxury, his life was shaken at an early age as his father was constantly imprisoned, persecuted, hidden, or banished. As he got older, he traveled frequently with his father and was the first to hear his father's claims about himself. He personally knew all the key influencers of the brand-new Baha'i Faith and was intimately involved in it his entire life. Before his father died in 1892, he was established as the successor and interpreter of his father's writings. Amid deep division within the community, however, Baha'ullah also made it clear that Abdul Baha was a mere servant of his father (hence his name) and not an actual Manifestation of God like his father, Baha'ullah, or like the Bab. Although division did not immediately end, Abdul Baha proved himself a capable ambassador of the Baha'i Faith.[39] For instance, he traveled extensively throughout the Middle East, Europe, and North America as an evangelist of the religion, serving as the first Baha'i person that the international men and women he encountered had ever met. As he did so, he articulated the vision of the Baha'i Faith as a religion offering a solution to the ills of the world at large, and he adeptly responded to all kinds of questions that people had about God, the prophets and religions of old, and how Baha'i was similar to and different from them.[40] Like his father, Abdul Baha was a prolific author, and he penned thousands of documents

---

37. Baha'ullah, *Baha'i World Faith: Selected Writings of Baha'ullah and Abdul Baha* (Wilmette, IL: Baha'i Publishing Trust, 1976), 205.

38. Buck, *Baha'i Faith*, 71.

39. See Robert Weinberg, *The Ambassador to Humanity: A Selection of Testimonials and Tributes to Abdul Baha* (Oxford: George Ronald, 2020). Weinberg provides primary records of all the various people that Abdul Baha met on his extensive travels around the world in service to the faith.

40. To see the vast number of topics he covered, see Shoghi Effendi, *Some Answered Questions*, https://www.bahai.org/library/authoritative-texts/abdul-baha/some-answered -questions/1#610118851, which is a collection of talks by Abdul Baha from the first decade of the 1900s in response to questions by outsiders.

that possess an authoritative (though not divine) status in the canon of Baha'i writings. Among those, one of the most important was *Will and Testament*, a book that outlined foundational beliefs, practices, and polity that guide the Baha'i Faith to this day. In it, Abdul Baha instituted what are essentially infallible interpreters and enforcers of the Baha'i Faith: twin pillars of the religion that he called the "Guardianship" and the "Universal House of Justice."

Fig. 3.3.
Entrance into the shrine of Baha'ullah, Baha'i's most revered figure, located in Akko, Israel.

The "Guardian" that Abdul Baha appointed as he neared his death in 1921 was his oldest grandson, Shoghi Effendi (1897–1957). This was a controversial appointment within the religion, and so the language he used was unequivocal: "He that obeys [Shoghi Effendi] not, has not obeyed God; he that turns away from him has turned away from God, and he that denies him has denied the True One."[41] Like his grandfather,

41. Abdul Baha, *The Will and Testament of Abdul Baha* (Wilmette, IL: Baha'i Publishing Trust, 1990), 21.

Effendi was reared in the faith and enjoyed unrivaled access to the key influencers of the movement. Also like his grandfather, he was appointed as a human interpreter of the Baha'i Faith, not an actual Manifestation of God like the Bab or Baha'ullah. The transition of leadership from Abdul Baha to Shoghi Effendi marked a significant transition for the Baha'i Faith. First, the Ottoman Empire, which had targeted the Baha'i Faith for as long as it had existed, was crumbling at the time of Abdul Baha's death. Meanwhile, the British, who immediately took custody of the Holy Land, were very friendly to the religion and allowed it to enlarge. This enabled Effendi to expand and beautify the headquarters of the religion in Haifa in such a way as to make it an international destination. Second, Effendi was a polyglot who wrote and spoke not only the Middle Eastern languages of Arabic, Farsi, and Turkish, but also the European languages of English and French. Such fluency led him to translate key Baha'i writings into European languages for the first time. This was incredibly important for the religion's expansion. Finally, Effendi was an able administrator. Not possessing the magnetic personality of his grandfather and great-grandfather, he led with his strengths: writing, translation, administration, and institution-building.

When Effendi died rather unexpectedly in 1957, he had put in place the institutional structures of the Baha'i Faith that characterize it to this day. And these structures, rather than one authoritative individual, provide leadership to the religion. These structures manifest themselves primarily at the local, national, and international levels. At the local level, each congregation is to consist of a Local Assembly of nine elected members who make decisions on behalf of their community and generally organize and oversee congregational life and outreach. At the national level, Effendi called for a National Spiritual Assembly that would "concentrate their minds upon those measures that will conduce to the welfare and happiness of the Baha'i Community."[42] This also consists of nine elected members, with one of their most important roles being to elect members at the highest order. At this international level, Effendi expanded the role of the Universal House of Justice. Although the institution itself had been created by his great-grandfather Baha'ullah, no members had yet been elected. This changed after Effendi's death. From 1963 onward, the Baha'i Faith would be officially led by nine members, elected every five years. Headquartered in Haifa, Israel, the Universal House of Justice serves as a sort of supreme court for all matters pertaining to doctrine and practice within the Baha'i Faith.

The Most Diverse Religion in the World? Baha'i is an extremely diverse religion. In fact, in America, it is ten times more multiracial than Christianity. For instance, whereas only around 5 percent of American churches are multiracial, American Baha'i congregations are more than 50 percent multiracial.

Mike McMullen, *The Baha'is of America: The Growth of a Religious Movement* (New York: New York University Press, 2015), 1.

42. Shoghi Effendi, "Letter of March 12, 1923," in *Baha'i Administration*, https://www.bahai .org/library/authoritative-texts/shoghi-effendi/bahai-administration/3#904837722.

One of the many ways that the Universal House of Justice guides the Faith is through its distribution and publication of writings. Of these, one of the more significant ones was composed in 1985. Titled "The Promise of World Peace," this document outlines the primary aim of the Baha'i Faith: world peace. In short, in order for the Baha'i Faith to help the world achieve world peace—far more than simply ending war—the following issues must be resolved: discrimination, racism, prejudice, child exploitation, world hunger, opposition to technology and science, socioeconomic disparity, unbridled nationalism, religious strife, oppression of women, lack of universal education, and the absence of an international language.[43] In this way, what arose out of a small movement within Twelver Islam in nineteenth-century Persia has grown into a religion commending a global vision and new social order in which the entire planet must actively, mutually, and jointly engage.

Part 3: Religious Writings

The corpus of Baha'i writings is incredibly extensive, most of which has never been translated and a good deal of which was stolen or lost.[44] What is more, the sheer number of documents penned demonstrates the unswerving commitment of Baha'is to literacy and the written word even though both Manifestations of God within Baha'i—the Bab and Baha'ullah—were educated mostly at home. Additionally, unlike other religions in which revelation always occurred orally before later being written down, the Baha'i Faith was written down first—and by the actual figures regarded as Manifestations of God. Their most foundational books include the writings of the four earliest leaders of the religion: the Bab, Baha'ullah, Abdul Baha, and Shoghi Effendi. But only writings from the first two are sacred; the latter two are authoritative but not of divine origin. Among these four, there are tens of thousands of written documents recorded primarily in Arabic and Farsi (Persian), but also, when it comes to the writings of Shoghi Effendi, in Turkish, English, and French. These documents include many genres: poems, treatises, manuals, laws, and instructions. But most are letters, usually called *tablets*, many of which are quite lengthy.

We can begin with some of the most important writings of the Bab, but we must also keep in mind that he wrote thousands of works that we will by no means exhaust. Scholar of Baha'i Nader Saiedi has

---

43. *The Promise of World Peace: A Letter by the Universal House of Justice to the Peoples of the World* (College Park: University of Maryland Press, 2015), 8–9.
44. Saiedi, *Gate of the Heart*, 40.

conveniently classified the Bab's writings into three periods: (1) an interpretive stage (1840s–1846), (2) a philosophical stage (1846–47), and (3) a legislative stage (1847–50), which roughly correspond to the stages in which the Bab first revealed himself and then dived deeper into the mysteries, before then offering more instructions on living.[45] When taken all together, most of the Bab's writings have to do with offering thought-provoking interpretations of the Qur'an, much in the same way that Jesus offered interpretations of the Hebrew Bible. This makes complete sense historically because, just as Jesus' religious and political context was that of Judaism and the interpretation of the Hebrew Bible, so the Bab's was that of Islam and the interpretation of the Qur'an. And to be even more precise, Jesus typically spoke from the context of Pharisaic Judaism in the same way that the Bab spoke from the context of Shia Islam.

We can begin with the writing in 1844 in which he first claimed to be *al-Bab*, "the Gateway," as well as the Promised One and the successor to Muhammad. This writing goes by the name *Qayyum al-Asma* ("the Self-Subsisting Lord of All Names"), but it is also called *Tafsir-i-Suriy-i-Yusuf* ("Commentary on the Surah of Joseph"), since it contains the Bab's interpretation of the twenty-second chapter of the Qur'an. It is modeled after the structure of the Qur'an and so contains 114 chapters or *surahs*. In this important writing, the Bab discusses the principle of progressive revelation and discloses both his identity and that of the next Manifestation (who will be Baha'ullah). Here are some key quotes from this book:

> We have, of a truth, sent down this divinely inspired Book unto our Servant. . . . Ask then Him Who is Our Remembrance [the Bab] of its interpretation, inasmuch as He, as divinely ordained and through the grace of God, is invested with the knowledge of its verses.[46]

> If you are truly faithful to Muhammad, the Apostle of God and the Seal of the Prophets, and if you follow His Book, the Qur'an, which is free from error, then here is the like of it—this Book, which We have, in truth and by the leave of God, sent down unto our Servant. If you fail to believe in Him, then your faith in Muhammad and His Book which was revealed in the past will indeed be treated as false in the estimation of God. If you deny Him [the Bab, you will have] denied Muhammad and His Book.[47]

45. Saiedi, 29–36.
46. Qayyum al-Asma 3.
47. Qayyum al-Asma 4.

Another writing is called *Kitabu'r-Ruh* ("Book of the Spirit"), which the Bab wrote in 1845 on his way back from his pilgrimage in Mecca, where he publicly proclaimed his identity in the holiest place on earth for Muslims. Approximately seven hundred chapters long and also modeled after the style of the Qur'an, in it the Bab identifies himself with Jesus and the Holy Spirit. Finally, I will mention the *Bayan* ("Utterance"). Written in 1847, it comes to us in two forms: one in Farsi (Persian) and the other in Arabic. The one in Farsi is more comprehensive, and it contains nineteen chapters. This book is one of the most important in Baha'i because it teaches progressive revelation, the nature of God, the transcendence of Baha'i over Islam, the constitution of society, and the creation of a new religion.

Next, we have the writings of Baha'ullah. Like the Bab, he wrote thousands of documents in Farsi and Arabic, most of which have never been translated. Also like the Bab, he penned his writings with great rapidity, as if in a trance and with no indication that he premeditated what he was going to write. Naturally, there are far too many of his writings to mention. Some influential ones include The Four Valleys (1856), which is a mystical treatise describing the four "valleys" or approaches that one takes to reach God: self, reason, love, and heart. This is closely related to The Seven Valleys (also 1856), which is a spiritual writing focused on reaching God through the valleys of search, love, knowledge, unity, contentment, wonderment, and nothingness. Another prominent book is the Book of Certitude, which he wrote in 1861 in response to someone who questioned his legitimacy as a Manifestation. Finally, *Kitab-i-Aqdas* ("The Most Holy Book") is an important writing that he composed in 1873 to offer guidance regarding the development of the Baha'i Faith. It covers many topics, including the creation of the Universal House of Justice.

Part 4: Beliefs

The Baha'i Faith is traditionally summarized as teaching three core doctrines that center on oneness or unity: the oneness of God, the oneness of humanity, and the oneness of religion. These are the cornerstones of the faith. As Shoghi Effendi writes, the oneness of God is "the pivot round which all the teachings of Baha'ullah revolve."[48] In short, everything you might encounter with this religion—its architecture, prayers, structures, and practices—centers on the cardinal belief that just as God is one, so, too, is humanity and religion. And by implication,

48. Effendi, *World Order of Baha'ullah*, 42.

the root error or "problem" with this world is division: division about God, division of humankind, and division about religion.

Fig. 3.4. Oneness is very important to Baha'i, symbolized by diversity and the number nine.

To begin with, Baha'is believe that God is one. In this way, the Baha'i Faith is a monotheistic religion. There is only one deity. At the same time, this one God is revealed only through Messengers whose messages seem to appear different from one another. This oneness is a paradox summarized in a verse stating, on the one hand, that "the Unseen can in no wise incarnate His Essence and reveal it unto men," while, on the other, that "I have manifested Myself unto men."[49] Such a paradox can best be described as meaning that although God is transcendent, unified, and ultimately unknowable, God is nonetheless compassionate enough to send down Divine Messengers that we call "Manifestations of God" who speak to people in their own languages and in ways that they can understand. This is why the Baha'i Faith validates and does not undermine religions that precede it. On the contrary, the Baha'i Faith believes that the different Manifestations that came in times past reflect God's overarching oneness to people on earth.

Second, once we assume that God is one, it only follows that humanity is also one. Just as the apostle Paul used the metaphor of the different parts of the church constituting the one body of Christ in 1 Corinthians 12, so the Baha'i Faith understands all of humanity—not just a single nation

49. Baha'ullah, *Gleanings from the Writings of Baha'ullah*, 20, https://www.bahai.org/library/authoritative-texts/bahaullah/gleanings-writings-bahaullah/1#529444114.

or region of the world—as one, unified, and sharing the same substance. In this way, the Baha'i Faith is not only intrinsically global in orientation; it is also planetary. In short, its aim is to unite all on earth—not just one region, demographic, or nationality. As Baha'ullah wrote (similar to what we also find in Genesis 1): "We created you all from the same dust. . . . Since We have created you all from one same substance it is incumbent on you to be even as one soul."[50] From its earliest days, the Baha'i Faith repudiated slavery, promoted the equality of women, condemned bigotry and economic disparity, and included people from all ethnic, racial, geographic, and social backgrounds. This is ultimately based on the oneness of humankind. All are regarded as equal. What is more, this doctrine explains why there are no clergy in Baha'i. There is no need for human intermediaries, and instead everyone should play an active role in his or her own spirituality. This also explains why Baha'i events start with prayer, which is an intentional act designed to bring unity and oneness among all the people present. Finally, on a larger scale, the oneness of humanity urges everyone to have a voice in how society is structured. Rather than dividing people into classes that separate them, Baha'i teaches that the world will truly know itself and accomplish its purposes only after being united and understanding itself as one people—as one planet.

Finally, Baha'is believe that religion is one. More to the point, the only religion that exists is the one religion of God. But God does not give people more than they can bear or understand at the time. Human civilization, after all, is constantly evolving, and so God works incrementally, progressively, and successively. For example, as Abdul Baha wrote, "From the days of Adam until today, the religions of God have been made manifest, one following the other, and each one of them fulfilled its due function."[51] These religions and their prophets, though developing at different times and among different people, demonstrate how "the religion of God is one religion, but it must be ever renewed."[52] Or, to use the words of Baha'ullah, although those who "are made manifest unto the peoples of the earth [are] the Exponents of a new Cause and the Revealers of a new Message . . . [they] are regarded as one soul and the same person." Consequently, "if you call them all by one name and ascribe to them the same attributes, you have not erred from the truth."[53] In a word, the Baha'i Faith teaches that the Manifestations of old—whether

Who Was the Bab, Really?
The Bab could be described as (1) cult leader splintering out of Twelver Islam, (2) mouthpiece of the Twelfth Imam, (3) head of the Shaykhi movement, (4) founder of the Babi religion, (5) forerunner of the Baha'i Faith, or (6) the Eighth of Nine Manifestations of God. In Baha'i, he is the last three.

---

50. Baha'ullah, *The Arabic Hidden Words*, 68, https://www.bahai.org/library/authoritative-texts/bahaullah/hidden-words/2#439014978.

51. Baha, *Selections from the Writings of Abdul Baha*, 23, https://www.bahai.org/library/authoritative-texts/abdul-baha/selections-writings-abdul-baha/1#324741256.

52. Baha, 23.

53. Baha'ullah, *Gleanings from the Writings of Baha'ullah*, 21.

Krishna, Zoroaster, Abraham, Moses, Buddha, Jesus, Muhammad, the Bab, or Baha'ullah—all teach the same message, since they are actually one soul that merely reflects the unity of God. Such Manifestations have appeared since the beginning of time in accordance with what people needed and could process at that time. And in this present era, the Manifestation representing the will of God is Baha'ullah, and the message he is proclaiming is the Baha'i Faith.

Fig. 3.5. The Lotus Temple in New Delhi, India, one of Baha'i's most beautiful shrines.

Still, all these Manifestations are bound by their contexts and so seem to reflect some differences. This is properly referred to as *progressive revelation*. As civilization advances, so, too, does the message it receives. "In this respect," writes Baha'ullah, "each Manifestation of God has a distinct individuality, a definitely prescribed mission, a predestined revelation, and specially designated limitations. Each one of them is known by a different name, is characterized by a special attribute, fulfills a definite mission, and is entrusted with a particular Revelation."[54] For this reason, the different prophets and religions of the world "appear to diverge and differ," but "in the eyes of them that are initiated into the mysteries of Divine wisdom, all their utterances are, in reality, but the expressions of one Truth."[55] In other words, while Christians and Muslims, for instance,

54. Baha'ullah, 21.
55. Baha'ullah, 21.

believe that their religion is unique, distinct, and true, Baha'is recognize them for what they truly are: contextualized Manifestations of the one God that, when properly understood, teach the same eternal principles. Accordingly, Baha'is emphasize what different religions have in common rather than what they have in disagreement. Will someone eventually succeed Baha'ullah and update the Baha'i Faith? The answer is yes, but that will not happen for a thousand years.[56]

Part 5: Worship Practices

The Baha'i Faith is a religion sharing practices with many others, such as prayer, devotion, service, outreach, discernment, and togetherness. Yet these practices can proceed quite differently than they do in other religions. In this section, we will discuss some of the distinctives of Baha'i worship practices.

First, it is important to note that there are no clergy, no sacraments, no sermons, no altars, no proselytization, no local temples, and no real rituals. Although it may seem strange for a religion not to have and use these things, it is not if you recognize that the Baha'i Faith considers itself to be an evolved religion that is best suited for our current day. Consequently, most of the elements just mentioned have their genesis in religions centuries old that developed before the advent of the modern, scientific, and technological age of today. Moreover, because the Baha'i Faith is in its infancy, it cannot yet support the infrastructure that it hopes to build in the centuries to come. Rather than these traditional religious components, perhaps the most basic worship practice within the Baha'i Faith is simply the reading of select prayers accompanied by song, which can be done anywhere, at any time, and with anyone you want. And there are also study circles that are akin to Bible studies. With no real local temples, however, most Baha'is do not attend an actual place of worship but instead meet in homes; in fact, in the United States, there is only one house of worship, which is located in suburban Chicago.

Second, the numbers nine and nineteen play an important role in one's devotional life. The number nine, for instance, not only is the highest integer, but represents completeness, perfection, and unity within diversity. In terms of numerology, it is the value of the word *Baha*, "Glory." You will see this number displayed in many ways in Baha'i. For instance, it is traditionally believed that there are nine Manifestations of God, a nine-pointed star is the symbol of the religion, houses of worship contain

---

How Many Manifestations Have There Been?
In the Baha'i Faith, there is no complete list of all the Manifestations of God. Instead, as Baha'ullah states, "the names of some of them are forgotten and the records of their lives lost." Of those usually acknowledged, there are nine: Krishna, Zoroaster, Abraham, Moses, Buddha, Jesus, Muhammad, the Bab, and Baha'ullah.

Baha'ullah, 174.

---

56. See Baha'ullah, *The Kitab-i-Aqdas*, 37, https://www.bahai.org/library/authoritative-texts/bahaullah/kitab-i-aqdas/1#824700177.

nine sides, and there are often nine features surrounding them: gardens, gates, fountains, ponds, and the like. Also, the Feast of Ridvan, commemorating when Baha'ullah declared his identity, is a nine-day holiday. The number nine is related to another important number: nineteen. Historically, for example, the Bab originally gathered nineteen followers (like Jesus' twelve disciples), and nineteen years transpired between the Bab's and Baha'ullah's declarations (1844 and 1863). The Baha'i Faith also teaches that one year comprises nineteen days of nineteen months, the last month of which is reserved for fasting during the day as with Ramadan in Islam. In house congregations, meetings occur every nineteen days, a period that corresponds to the beginning of each month in Baha'i.

Third, we can turn to a foundational worship practice within Baha'i called *consultation*. As Baha'ullah once wrote, "in all things it is necessary to consult," and "it is one of the explicit ordinances of the Lord."[57] Indeed, with so many authoritative writings to select, interpret, and understand, one of the immediate challenges that Baha'is face when discerning direction, looking for guidance, or interpreting the scriptures is deciding which passages to apply and how to understand them. As Shoghi Effendi writes, "God's will is best attained through consultation."[58] This has led to a process in which a person or group of people attempt to seek out the application of scripture or the making of a decision by cultivating a humble, detached, selfless, and prayerful disposition. Although "the ideal of Baha'i consultation is to arrive at a unanimous decision,"[59] it is acceptable to take a majority vote, but all must support the decision.

Part 6: Point of Contact

According to Baha'i, the Bab and Baha'ullah are the two latest revelations of God for humankind. Although this does not mean that previous revelations are necessarily abrogated or refuted, it does imply that God offers revelation in a progressive, sequential, and timely way. More to the point, Baha'is believe that revelation must be updated, modified, and revised. Or, to use language within the Baha'i Faith itself, God has made a Greater Covenant with humankind to provide direction through various Manifestations, numbered to be nine: Krishna, Zoroaster, Abraham, Moses, Buddha, Jesus, Muhammad, the Bab, and Baha'ullah. But

Every Religion Has Its Seasons. Baha'i teaches that religions are like seasons. For instance, God sends a Manifestation in the spring, but it is not until summer that it becomes ingrained. By the fall, the people have replaced the message with superstition. And by winter, they have all but buried it under the snow.

---

57. Baha'ullah, in *Consultation: A Compilation*, 5 and 13, respectively, https://www.bahai.org/library/authoritative-texts/compilations/consultation/1#249611345.

58. Shoghi Effendi, in *Consultation: A Compilation*, 29, https://www.bahai.org/library/authoritative-texts/compilations/consultation/3#668166237.

59. Baha'ullah, in *Consultation: A Compilation*, 44.

God also made a Lesser Covenant, in which the Baha'i Faith will provide "definitive guidance" forever.[60]

I resonate with this concept in Baha'i. That is because I must admit that I sometimes struggle with the Christian conviction that God has revealed himself only in selective, isolated, and exclusive ways. Consequently, something inside me really appreciates how Baha'i tries to, on the one hand, celebrate the theological compassion of an omniscient God and, on the other, safeguard the integrity of each world religion. After all, having studied religions for so many years and having met so many welcoming and wonderful people who practice them, I do not find it easy to criticize the entire structure on which their world hangs as if it were completely worthless. It isn't. On the contrary, it would be much easier to simply praise elements of their religion that I enjoy and then walk away in peace.

There are many challenges with this line of thinking of the Baha'i Faith, however, and in this section, I will list four. The first challenge is that such thinking begs the question: If, say, Islam is too dated to warrant learning about how God may have been revealed to Arabs in the seventh century, why spend so much time learning about how God may have been revealed to Iranians in the nineteenth century? From the perspective of history and geography, is there really a difference? After all, the historical, social, linguistic, and religious context at that time is crushingly inaccessible to the vast majority of people alive today—as well as back then. For instance, hardly any scholars of religion today—let alone "ordinary" people—can read Farsi, are familiar with Shia Islam, and know the complex history of Iran. In fact, most of the writings of the Baha'i Faith have never even been translated. All things the same, in other words, would it not make more sense for people to simply study the religion in which they were raised, since they speak that language, understand that history, and take part in that culture? If so, it would mean that there is very little reason to learn about Baha'i.

The second challenge of Baha'i's desire to be religiously inclusive is that the implication is that the revelation given to humankind in successive stages is universal and applicable to all people at that time. In truth, however, all world religions emerge out of a very specific, local, and geographically isolated context. For instance, Judaism arose in an ancient Near Eastern context in the Middle East among a small group of people who spoke Hebrew. Likewise, Sikhism arose in an Indian context in the Punjab among a tiny group of people who spoke Punjabi. The same could be said for many other religious traditions.

60. Stockman, *Baha'i Faith*, 22.

Third, if all previous world religions are valid, why do we not hear more about prophets and religions in regions of the world that are historically overlooked, marginalized, and disregarded? For example, although ancient religious systems were lovingly practiced for millennia across Africa, Latin America, and Oceania, why is there no discussion about the message that these prophets revealed? Instead, only select prophets from Hinduism, Zoroastrianism, Judaism, Buddhism, Christianity, Islam, and Baha'i are regarded as true Manifestations. That is quite a blow to the majority of the population today that does not live in Asia or the Middle East.

Finally, the most challenging conviction presented by the Baha'i Faith is that the messages of the prophets of old were the same. Sure, there were slight differences based on what people could understand at that time, but the basic teachings were very similar. The truth is, though, that they weren't. It is one thing to make a claim about what, say, Zoroaster may have taught, since the historical data is almost non-existent, but that is decidedly not the case with what Moses, Buddha, Jesus, Muhammad, Baha'ullah, and others taught. I have given my life, for instance, to studying what these religious leaders were all about. And believe me, they were not all about the same thing. To be sure, they may have, say, used the same alphabet, but their language, their vocabulary, and their meanings differed radically. Jesus was not Buddha, Krishna was not Baha'ullah, and Moses was not the Bab. To say otherwise is to make beliefs and practices—indeed, the very enterprise of religion itself—meaningless. And it is also to misrepresent what these figures gave their lives to and for. They deserve better.

Discussion Questions

1. What is the Baha'i Faith? What are its most distinct features?
2. What is the difference between Baha'ullah and the Bab? How were their messages similar, and how were they different?
3. Why do you think the Baha'i Faith is so appealing to people today around the world?
4. The Baha'i Faith is a huge proponent of world peace, and it actively encourages believers to pursue it. Do you think human civilization is capable of achieving world peace? What would need to happen for it to occur?
5. If you were sharing your Christian faith with a Baha'i, what would you emphasize as a way to connect to his or her beliefs and practices? What do you think would be most off-putting to that person?

For Further Reading

Buck, Christopher. *Baha'i Faith: The Basics*. London: Routledge, 2021.

McMullen, Mike. *The Baha'is of America: The Growth of a Religious Movement*. New York: New York University Press, 2015.

Saiedi, Nader. *Gate of the Heart: Understanding the Writings of the Bab*. Waterloo, ON: Wilfrid Laurier Press, 2008.

Smith, Peter. *An Introduction to the Baha'i Faith*. Cambridge: Cambridge University Press, 2008.

Stockman, Robert H. *The Baha'i Faith: A Guide for the Perplexed*. London: Bloomsbury Academic, 2013.

chapter 4

Nation of Islam: The Story of Reeducation

Islam played a significant role in the reconfiguring of the relationship between race, religion, and progress among a significant minority of African Americans who earnestly appropriated…Islamic names, symbols, rituals, and concepts in an effort to participate in America's prosperity and modernity.

Kambiz GhaneaBassiri[1]

Although Islam and the African American Experience share a long tradition, the [Nation of Islam] was a "homegrown religion" with strong connections to the Ahmadiyah [and] the Moorish Science Temple.

Ula Yvette Taylor[2]

Part 1: The Beginning

Sixty-six trillion years ago, the first peoples of the earth walked the planet. Though called by many names today, the original name of their tribe was Shabazz, their skin color was black, their language was Arabic, and their religion was Islam. This "Nation of Islam," as we may call them, has no beginning and no ending, and yet it is older than the sun and the stars. The Nation was ably ruled by twenty-four leaders referred to as *scientists*, but who were essentially deities, one of whom served as the supreme God. Together, they judged the earth for eons.

1. Kambiz GhaneaBassiri, *A History of Islam in America* (Cambridge: Cambridge University Press, 2010), 196.
2. Ula Yvette Taylor, *The Promise of Patriarchy: Women and the Nation of Islam* (Chapel Hill: University of North Carolina Press, 2017), 2.

But, alas, one catastrophic event occurred that would one day lead to the Nation's eventual departure out of paradise and entrance into the hardships of servitude and indoctrination. This took place around the year 4600 B.C., and the event had been prophesied thousands of years earlier. The scientist responsible for this catastrophe was named Yakub, and he was intent on engineering a devilish race devoid of color and pigmentation—white. At last, after hundreds of years of experimentation, Yakub succeeded, creating a white race that had initially been taken from the Black and superior Nation of Islam. For thousands of years, this colorless and white race eked out a living among the caves of Europe. They were specialists in "tricknology," the slyest of all races.

Although Allah sent prophets to this devilish race to share the truth of Islam, the savages rejected it and clung to their superstitious ways. This endured for centuries until the 1500s, when the white race captured the Black nation, sent them as slaves to the Americas, foisted their false religion of Christianity upon them, stripped them of their language, and uprooted memories of their noble past. This was in fulfillment of prophecy about the "man of lawlessness" in 2 Thessalonians 2, inaugurating an era in which the white race would rule the Black nation until 1914. In due time, Allah was manifested in the person of W. D. Fard in Detroit on July 4, 1930. Henceforth, whoever embraces Fard's message will overcome the lies of the white man, the shams of his Christian god, and the wiles of his ways. At some point in the near future, a Mothership will appear from the sky, escaping the sight of whites but appearing in plain sight to followers of Fard. This Mothership will bring judgment on the white race while vindicating the original Black Nation of Islam.[3]

Road Map to Nation of Islam Creation Story. This is how the Nation of Islam understands how everything came into being. Dominant themes include stereotyping of races, the assumption that Allah and Islam have always existed, a disregard for historical precision, animosity toward Christianity, and the nontraditional Islamic belief that Allah would materialize as a person.

Part 2: Historical Origin

Although Islam represents only around 1 percent of the American population, African Americans comprise 20 percent of that number. And among them, 50 percent are converts.[4] These statistics give testimony to a significant yet sorely neglected and misunderstood story of religion in America that illustrates what happened when the world's second-largest

---

3. This origin story is based on Elijah Muhammad's own teaching on this matter, as outlined in *The Supreme Wisdom: Solution to the So-Called Negroes' Problem* (Chicago: University of Islam, 1957), and *Message to the Blackman in America* (Phoenix: Secretarius Memps Publications, 1973). The specific time periods and language used come directly from Elijah Muhammad.

4. Besheer Mohamed and Jeff Diamant, "Black Muslims Account for a Fifth of All U.S. Muslims, and about Half Are Converts to Islam," Pew Research Center (January 17, 2019), https://www.pewresearch.org/fact-tank/2019/01/17/black-muslims-account-for-a-fifth-of-all -u-s-muslims-and-about-half-are-converts-to-islam/.

religion was reinterpreted by America's second-largest ethnicity. What emerged were a series of united yet separated, similar yet different, and succeeding yet overlapping new religious movements that differed radically from traditional Islam. The three primary movements that formed are the Ahmadiyya Movement, the Moorish Science Temple, and the Nation of Islam. Their members have come to be referred to as *Black Muslims in America*.[5]

This phrase was coined by C. Eric Lincoln, a sociologist of religion who wrote the first book on these movements and whose use of the phrase has endured. As he wrote in his seminal study more than fifty years ago, "The Black Muslims are probably America's fastest growing raci[al] sect,"[6] underscoring their significance in the history of religion. These new religious movements did not emerge in a vacuum, however, and they can be understood only within the religious, social, and historical contexts of the nineteenth and twentieth centuries in America. The Nation of Islam went on to become the largest and most influential of these religious movements—and it will be the sole focus of this chapter—but it is essential to understand that it followed and paralleled the Ahmadiyya Movement and the Moorish Science Temple of America.

W. D. Fard (Dates Unknown)

W. D. Fard, known by countless aliases and whose year of birth and death are disputed, is one of the most enigmatic figures in American religious history. Every aspect of his life—his identity, background, and nationality—has come under intense scrutiny. Although his followers claim that he immigrated to the United States from Mecca, others believe that he arrived in Detroit via Chicago after jail time in California—all of which possibly occurred after leaving his hometown of Portland, Oregon, where he either was born or moved to after arriving from overseas.[7] No one knows for sure.

Whatever his exact origins, W. D. Fard forged a new life for himself in the automotive capital of the world during very turbulent times in the early twentieth century. Presenting himself as a purveyor of fine silks, he ingratiated himself into the homes of Black families and used his sales tactics to inculcate them into his exotic yet engaging new religion.

Influences. A variety of factors led to the creation of African-American Muslim movements. Most significant were slavery, segregation, racism, traditional African religions, the Great Migrations, Jim Crow laws, clandestine rituals of the Freemasons (and Shriners), new religions among white communities, anti-immigration laws of foreigners from Muslim countries to the United States, and enduring injustices of African Americans.

---

5. One of the seminal books using this term is C. Eric Lincoln, *The Black Muslims in America* (Boston: Beacon Press, 1961). It was Lincoln, in fact, who coined the term *Black Muslims* in 1956. See his explanation of it in Lincoln, iv.

6. Lincoln, 19.

7. Common places of origin for Fard are proposed to be New Zealand and Afghanistan, but no one knows for sure. For more, see Judith Weisenfeld, *New World A-Coming: Black Religion and Racial Identity during the Great Migration* (New York: New York University Press, 2016), 68–69.

By the time he arrived in Detroit in the summer of 1930, migration of African Americans from the South was in full swing during the Great Migrations. From 1910 to 1920, for instance, "the black population in Detroit increased 611 percent, and the overall black population in the North increased from 75,000 to 3 million."[8] It was this demographic that Fard targeted. With Jim Crow laws in place and discrimination everywhere apparent, Fard's teachings centered on three things: "Allah is God, the white man is the devil, and the so-called Negroes are the Asiatic Black people, the cream of the planet earth."[9] This teaching was opportune, effective, and fruitful, and his depiction of a "black divinity" as superior to the blue-eyed God of the white race resonated with those who had been beaten down by white Christian America.[10] After three and a half contested but effective years of ministry, in which he attracted "roughly eight thousand converts, nearly all of them from southern migrant backgrounds,"[11] Fard disappeared. Last seen at a Chicago airport in 1934 after having been expelled from Detroit by the police, he uttered these final words: "I will be back to you in the near future to lead you out of this hell."[12]

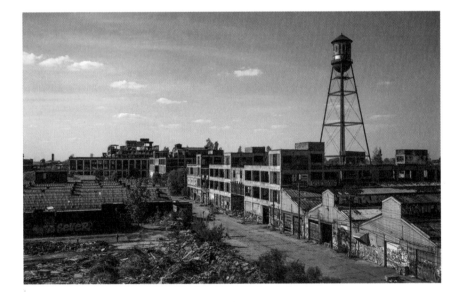

Fig. 4.1. The Nation of Islam started in 1930 in Detroit, Michigan, the center of the automotive industry.

8. Clifton E. Marsh, *The Lost-Found Nation of Islam in America* (Lanham, MD: Scarecrow Press, 2000), 24–25; Herbert Berg, *Elijah Muhammad and Islam* (New York: New York University Press, 2009), 24–25.

9. As quoted in Marsh, *Lost-Found Nation of Islam*, 37.

10. Louis A. DeCaro, *On the Side of the People: A Religious Life of Malcolm X* (New York: New York University Press, 1996), 24.

11. Michael Knight, "Converts and Conversions," in *The Cambridge Companion to American Islam*, ed. Juliane Hammer and Omid Safi (Cambridge: Cambridge University Press, 2013), 91.

12. DeCaro, *On the Side of the People*, 25.

Elijah Muhammad (1897–1975)

Though the most viable successor to Fard's so-called Lost-Found Nation of Islam, Elijah Muhammad was also deeply indebted to the Moorish Science Temple, which was the first Black Islamic society in America, formed in New Jersey in 1913 by Drew Ali (1886–1929).[13] As historian Edward Curtis explains, "Elijah Muhammad would adopt Drew Ali's . . . formula for understanding Islam and turn it into the most well-known tradition in the history of African-American Islam."[14] But unlike predecessors and influencers such as Edward Blyden (1832–1912), Drew Ali, and Marcus Garvey (1887–1940), Elijah Muhammad drew much closer connections between race and religion, maintaining that to be Black was to be Muslim—and, by extension, that to be white was to be Christian. As he taught: "Christianity is not for black people. . . . Christianity is only for the white people."[15] This was a ratcheting up of a concept that proved to be distinctive with the Nation of Islam. Although Elijah Muhammad grew up in the Christian South, and his father had been a Baptist preacher, he tired of cooperation with white America, going so far as to reject the civil rights movement and the likes of Martin Luther King Jr. (1929–68) on the basis that Black participation with whites only strengthened white America. By contrast, Muhammad was an avowed separatist who believed that the only way for African Americans to move forward was by boycotting white businesses and institutions and, in their place, creating independent and Black-owned establishments, schools, and factories.

Muhammad became a prominent figure in America, writing, recording, and lecturing as much as possible. His most famous teaching was *Message to the Blackman in America*, which he wrote in 1965. This book engaged many topics, including religion, race, history, biblical and Qur'anic interpretation, prayer, and ethics. Muhammad argued that Christianity was "the religion of slavery" in contrast to Islam, which "recognizes complete equality."[16] Moreover, the "dead Jesus" of the white Christians was ineffective compared to Allah, the God of Black men and women. As he wrote:

> Allah (God) loves us, the so-called Negroes (Tribe of Shabazz) so that He will give lives for our sake today. Fear not, you are not more forsaken.

13. The original movement was called the Moorish Temple of Science, or simply Canaanite Temple, before becoming the Moorish Science Temple of America. It was founded in 1925 and incorporated as a legal entity in Chicago a year later.

14. Edward E. Curtis IV, *Islam in Black America: Identity, Liberation, and Difference in African-American Islamic Thought* (Albany: State University of New York Press, 2002), 62.

15. Muhammad, *Supreme Wisdom*, 19.

16. Muhammad, 36.

God is in person, and stop looking for a dead Jesus for help, but pray to Him whom Jesus prophesied would come after Him. He who is alive and not a spook.[17]

Muhammad referred to white people as "devils." For instance:

[White people] are really the devils whom the righteous (all members of the black nation) should shun and never accept as truthful guides of God. . . . But the time has at last arrived that Allah (God) will put an end to their persecuting and killing the righteous (the black nation).[18]

Although much of this language was common among his predecessors, Muhammad also taught unique concepts related to the origins of the Black race (which I will discuss below). He also advanced highly contested teachings about Islamic practices, history, and language even though he had never visited orthodox mosques in the Middle East, studied the writings of prominent Islamic figures, or learned Arabic. Instead, to the dismay of his mounting number of opponents, he manufactured his own version of Islam that seemed to suit his own context and that differed radically from the mainstream. Although this mattered little to Elijah Muhammad's most ardent followers, it became a breaking point for his most famous disciple.

Malcolm X (1925–65)

Malcolm X, born Malcolm Little, became a member of the Nation of Islam while in a Massachusetts prison in 1947. Upon his parole in 1952, he became its most famous spokesperson, speaking across the country to enthralled audiences. Malcolm X's presence in the movement skyrocketed the religion's appeal and made it a household term. For instance, he helped start *Muhammad Speaks*, a newspaper published by the Nation of Islam that operated from 1961 to 1975. Transcending an exclusively Muslim audience, this newspaper went on to become "the best-selling black newspaper in the nation, claiming a circulation of 600,000 copies every other week."[19] Malcolm was also featured in a documentary in 1959 called *The Hate That Hate Produced*, which cast a different light on a movement that had previously been interpreted as militant and anti-white.

17. Muhammad, *Message to the Blackman in America*, 3.
18. Muhammad, 280.
19. GhaneaBassiri, *History of Islam in America*, 243.

Fig. 4.2.
Malcolm X was probably the most famous former member of the Nation of Islam.

It was also at this time that Malcolm was experiencing his own doubts about the authenticity of Elijah Muhammad's moral character and actual knowledge of historic Islam. These doubts became overwhelmingly apparent when Malcolm went on pilgrimage in 1964 to Mecca and Medina, the Holy Land of Islam. This is when the anti-white rhetoric and aberrant doctrine that he had been taught by Elijah Muhammad dissolved as he witnessed, experienced, and interacted with people of all races and ethnicities who joined together in equality and fellowship under orthodox Islam. As he wrote in his autobiography:

> My pilgrimage broadened my scope. It blessed me with a new insight.
> . . . I saw all *races*, all *colors*—blue-eyed blonds to black-skinned Africans—in true brotherhood. . . . In the past, yes, I have made sweeping indictments of *all* white people. I never will be guilty of that again—as I know now that *some* white people are truly sincere, that some truly are capable of being brotherly toward a black man. The true Islam has shown me that a blanket indictment of all white people is as wrong as when whites make blanket indictments against blacks. Yes, I have been convinced that *some* American whites do want to help cure the rampant racism which is on the path to *destroying* this country.[20]

20. Malcolm X, *The Autobiography of Malcolm X: As Told to Alex Haley* (New York: Ballantine Publishing Group, 1973), 369.

Malcolm officially left the Nation of Islam that same year (1964) in favor of mainstream Islam but was assassinated only a few months later by Nation of Islam radicals.

W. D. Muhammad (1933–2008)

The Five Percenters. Malcolm X and W. D. Muhammad were not the only ones to leave the Nation of Islam in the 1960s. "Allah the Father," previously called Clarence 13X, created the "Five-Percent Nation" or simply "Five Percenters," in which 10% know the truth but keep the 85% in ignorance, while 5% are righteous and enlighten the 85%.

For more on the Five Percenters, see Wakeel Allah, *In the Name of God: A History of Clarence 13X and the Five Percenters* (Atlanta: A Team Publishing, 2007).

Malcolm X was not the only member of the Nation of Islam who questioned the validity of the movement and the integrity of its leader. Born immediately before W. D. Fard disappeared, W. D. Muhammad was one of many sons born to Elijah Muhammad, the so-called Messenger of the Nation of Islam. Although he was raised inside the movement, he, for the same reasons Malcolm had, began entertaining serious doubts about it in the 1950s and early 1960s, eventually rejecting his father's religion in favor of Sunni Islam before later repenting of his ways and returning to the Nation of Islam in the 1970s. By the time his father died in 1975, he was in position to lead the movement away from a more novel sectarian Islam to a more mainstream Sunni Islam. This was bolstered by W. D. Muhammad's early education in the Qur'an and Arabic, which, unlike what his father had experienced, naturally predisposed him toward traditional Islamic interpretations, practices, and beliefs. Quite controversially, he even permitted white people to enter the previously Black-only community. Speaking to an audience in 1975, W. D. Muhammad said: "There will be no such category as a white Muslim or black Muslim. All will be Muslims."[21] Soon thereafter, the new leader also changed the name of the organization to the World Community of al-Islam in the West (WCIW)—and later, to the American Muslim Mission (AMM). He also renamed all religious buildings—formerly called *temples*—to *masjids*, or *mosques*, and he referred to himself as an *imam*, the traditional Islamic title for a community leader. He called this change the "Second Resurrection."[22]

Louis Farrakhan (b. 1933)

W. D. Muhammad encountered vigorous pushback from members of the Nation of Islam who favored the teachings of the former leader Elijah Muhammad. This is seen most clearly in the eventual successor to the Nation of Islam, Louis Farrakhan, who had been excommunicated by W. D. Muhammad in 1977. Originally joining the movement under the

---

21. As quoted in Curtis, *Islam in Black America*, 115.
22. Edward E. Curtis IV, *Black Muslim Religion in the Nation of Islam, 1960–1975* (Chapel Hill: University of North Carolina Press, 2006), 176.

direct influence of Malcolm X, Farrakhan rose in the ranks and became a trusted disciple of Elijah Muhammad. But after experiencing how the movement was transitioning from a focus on Black nationalism to mainstream tolerance, he reconstituted the Nation of Islam according to its historical beliefs and practices.[23] Farrakhan's leadership of the movement solidified over time, and he has become one of the most celebrated religious leaders in America, particularly among the African-American community. A frequent author, speaker, and media personality, he has mediated his style between the separatism of Elijah Muhammad and the traditionalism of W. D. Muhammad. Although his rhetoric has softened over the decades, his leadership has maintained what seems to be the original separatist and Afrocentric aims of the movement.

Part 3: Religious Writings

The Nation of Islam makes use of sacred writings that can be divided into two groups: (1) the holy books from Christianity and Islam (as interpreted by the Nation of Islam) and (2) original religious books developed by the founders of the movement. I will start with the sacred texts among Christians and Muslims.

Fig. 4.3. The Qur'an in English is used by members of the Nation of Islam.

As imaginative as the Nation of Islam is in connecting to people in their unique context, it still preaches and evangelizes from previous

23. Vibert L. White Jr., *Inside the Nation of Islam: A Historical and Personal Testimony by a Black Muslim* (Gainesville: University of Florida Press, 2001), 211.

religious writings. In short, the Bible and Qur'an are the religious and textual bedrock of the movement—but with a clear preference for the Qur'an. Elijah Muhammad, for instance, drew heavily from the Bible in his teachings, pamphlets, ethical principles, and rituals even while criticizing it. This phenomenon elicited a paradox. On the one hand, Muhammad repudiated the Bible, calling it a "poison book,"[24] and he used it only because it was the text that his people were familiar with. On the other hand, Muhammad repeatedly used the Bible as a prop to offer novel interpretations and validations of his ministry, allowing him to have his cake and eat it, too. Muhammad's engagement with the Qur'an, however, was more complicated. While he taught that the Qur'an "is not from a prophet but direct from Allah,"[25] both he and his movement were less familiar with it. This had the effect of Muhammad's not being able to offer as much insight from it as from the Bible, though he never failed to reinforce that "I have the Keys of God to your (so-called Negroes') problems," meaning that he was the definitive source of interpretation when it came to both the Bible and the Qur'an.[26] To this day, you will hear leaders within the Nation of Islam use either holy book, but the preference is clearly the Qur'an.

In addition to the Bible and Qur'an, the Nation of Islam has generated its own writings that are the anchor of its beliefs. As Elijah Muhammad cryptically said, for example, "Both the present Bible and the Holy Quran must soon give way to that holy book which no man as yet but Allah has seen."[27] We can start with the movement's founder. W. D. Fard taught his followers very intricate and secret knowledge about mathematics, cosmology, mythology, geography, and history that were interwoven into two pamphlets that he transmitted only orally: *Teachings for the Lost-Found Nation in a Mathematical Way* and *Secret Ritual of the Nation of Islam*. Although not published, Elijah Muhammad immediately oversaw "the perpetuation of [Fard's] teaching . . . after Fard disappeared."[28] Of Muhammad's many writings, perhaps the two most influential are *The Supreme Wisdom* (1957) and *Message to the Blackman in America* (1965).[29] These writings articulate standard beliefs about the Nation of Islam, namely, that it represents the original people and religion of the world, that it has been corrupted by white "devils" that have foisted their false Christian religion upon Black civilization, and that liberation can be

Corrupt Bible?
Elijah Muhammad wrote, "From the first day that the white race received the Divine Scripture they started tampering with its truth to… blind the black man. It is their nature to do evil and the book cannot be recognized as the pure and Holy Word of God. The Bible is now being called the poison book by God Himself."

Muhammad, 59.

24. Muhammad, *Supreme Wisdom*, 59.
25. Muhammad, 66.
26. Muhammad, 62.
27. Muhammad, 15.
28. Lincoln, *Black Muslims in America*, 15.
29. Marsh, *Lost-Found Nation of Islam in America*, 37.

achieved by those who live by the beliefs and practices of the Nation of Islam (discussed more fully below).

Part 4: Beliefs

The Nation of Islam has many distinct religious beliefs. All these, however, either were directly drawn from or ran parallel to the beliefs of African-American Muslim groups such as the Moorish Science Temple that arose at the same time. For instance, Kambiz GhaneaBassiri's explanation of Drew Ali's beliefs shows them to be almost identical to those within the Nation of Islam: "In Ali's teachings, Islam became a means by which black Americans could strip themselves of the stigma associated with the color of their skin so that they could play a greater role in society. Through Islam, Ali 'de-negrofied' his followers."[30] Patrick Bowen expands on this description by including elements beyond race: "The Nation of Islam taught ideas that seem to have blended black folk traditions, black nationalism, [and] Eastern Islamic teachings . . . along with a deep knowledge of history, science, esotericism, various forms of Christian fundamentalism, and a profound desire to resist white racist violence."[31]

Deity

The Nation of Islam teaches that W. D. Fard was Allah incarnate. There are several reports, for instance, of W. D. Fard's claiming, "I am God Himself."[32] These are further reinforced by Elijah Muhammad's clear teaching on this matter in which he asserts in one of his most foundational works: "Master W. Fard Muhammad, our God and Savior, the Great Mahdi, Almighty God Allah in Person."[33] Indeed, as scholar Judith Weisenfeld states, "The presence of God on earth as a living human being is a central element of the [Nation of Islam's] theology."[34] In fact, the very first thing that Elijah Muhammad said to W. D. Fard was: "I know who you are, you're God himself." Fard's response paralleled that of Jesus to his disciples when they made the same deduction: "That's right, but don't tell it now. It is not yet time for me to be known."[35]

W. D. Fard Materialized as Allah. In a Nation of Islam confessional statement titled "What the Muslims Believe," the last of twelve articles is as follows: "We believe that Allah (God) appeared in the Person of Master W. Fard Muhammad, July, 1930; the long-awaited 'Messiah' of the Christian and the 'Mahdi' of the Muslims."

Muhammad Speaks, April 21, 1972, as quoted in Marsh, *Lost-Found Nation of Islam in America,* 47.

---

30. GhaneaBassiri, *History of Islam in America,* 196.

31. Patrick D. Bowen, *A History of Conversion to Islam in the United States,* vol. 2, *The African American Islamic Renaissance, 1920–1975* (Leiden: Brill, 2017), 14.

32. As quoted in Weisenfeld, *New World A-Coming,* 67.

33. Muhammad, *Supreme Wisdom,* 12.

34. Weisenfeld, *New World A-Coming,* 124.

35. *Muhammad Speaks,* Special Issue, April 21, 1972, as quoted in Marsh, *Lost-Found Nation of Islam in America,* 39.

However central this teaching is to the Nation of Islam, what is essential to note is that traditional Islam—whether Sunni or Shia—holds to a completely different belief, making it clear in no uncertain terms that Allah is above creation and will never materialize in the form of a man. To instruct otherwise was and is heretical, punishable, and unpardonable. Classically articulated, it is *shirk*, the cardinal sin within Islam that seeks to ascribe something to God—in short, what Christians are guilty of, according to mainstream Islam.

Fig. 4.4. Male members of the Nation of Islam at rally dressed in common style of bow ties and suits.

Dress and Diet

The Nation of Islam is renowned for its strict dress code. While men are instructed to wear suits, women are supposed to dress in modest Muslim clothing that includes head coverings. In particular, men are known for wearing suits with bow ties. This expectation of clothing, scholar Judith Weisenfeld explains, "disciplined the body, separating adherents from their false identity, and purifying them to assume their restored and true religio-racial identities."[36] In fact, within the Nation of Islam, clothing, and the sexual propriety befitting it, is a serious matter. The male organization within the Nation of Islam, called the Fruit

36. Weisenfeld, *New World A-Coming*, 67.

of Islam, enforces male clothing and searches all male attenders for weapons and illicit paraphernalia upon entry into the mosque, while its female counterpart, the Muslim Girls Training and General Civilization Class, monitors very closely what women are allowed to wear and also searches them as they enter. In truth, members of the Fruit of Islam cling to a much grander vision. They are an elite militaristic force that holds to a higher standard of physical, mental, and spiritual maturity, illustrated by their dapper appearance, physical prowess, and devotional zeal. This stress on a proper dress code is reinforced in dietary practices. Members of the Nation of Islam are instructed to avoid pork, alcohol, drugs, tobacco, and other items harmful to their health.

Superior Black Civilization

The original Black Muslims of America were united in their belief that the Black race was superior to that of the white race and that it was heir to a mighty and beautiful civilization before the white race buried this truth. This idea was popular in the late nineteenth century and early twentieth centuries. For instance, it appears, to some extent, in the writings of prominent Black intellectuals such as Edward Blyden (1832–1912) and W. E. B. Dubois (1868–1963)—both of whom differed from the figures mentioned in this chapter both because they remained in the Christian tradition and because they were intellectuals who walked in different circles.[37] It also manifests itself in the speeches of Marcus Garvey (1887–1940). For instance, Garvey said, "Every student in history . . . knows that the Negro ruled the world, when white men were savages and barbarians living in caves."[38] Likewise, "I am the equal of any white man; I want you to feel the same way."[39]

This concept was embraced and fully incorporated into both the Moorish Science Temple and the Nation of Islam. Their writings and teachings are framed in racial categories in which the Black civilization is described as original and superior to that of the white and devilish race. This is why African-American Islam, as interpreted by its founders, was originally only for Blacks and not whites. As Elijah Muhammad explains: "The only people born of Allah is the Black Nation of which the so-called Negroes are descendants. That is why Islam is offered to them." It is not, in other words, offered to the whites because "the white

Marcus Garvey? Marcus Garvey (1887–1940) founded the Universal Negro Improvement Association (UNIA) in 1914 to improve the lives of Black men and women and repatriate them in a back-to-Africa movement. His movement paralleled the development of the National Association for the Advancement of Colored People (NAACP), which was founded in 1909.

---

37. Curtis, *Islam in Black America*, 17–18.

38. As quoted in Mary Lefkowitz, *Not out of Africa: How Afrocentrism Became an Excuse to Teach Myth as History* (New York: Basic Books, 1997), 132.

39. As quoted in GhaneaBassiri, *History of Islam in America*, 195.

race cannot be righteous unless they could be born again (grafted back into the black man)," which is, of course, impossible.[40]

Reeducation

The Nation of Islam rejects the political, educational, and religious systems built by whites. Instead, it has chosen to construct its own curricula, organize its own community centers, and send its kids to its own schools where they can be taught the truth of who they are and thus be reeducated rather than brainwashed by the white agenda. In this way, writes historian Ula Yvette Taylor, the Nation of Islam is "deliberately out of step with mainstream black America."[41] Although Farrakhan has softened on this issue—and he was the architect of the famous Million Man March in 1995—the Nation of Islam follows its own path. Its first attempt at wholesale education and separatism came through the creation of what was called the University of Islam (later renamed the Clara Muhammad School). The children attending this school receive an education covering not only basic subjects taught in public schools but also religious teachings and the Arabic language. The Nation of Islam still operates independent schools.

Focus on the Here and Now

The Nation of Islam emphasizes the present over the future. In contrast to Christianity, for example, which promises an eternal life of blessedness to those who put their faith in Jesus Christ, the Nation of Islam is more this-worldly than otherworldly, arguing that liberation is meant to be achieved now rather than later. In this configuration, physical resurrection to live in an afterlife is not the goal; it is instead to undergo "mental" resurrection, in which one realizes the truth of the world and follows that teaching. As Elijah Muhammad wrote, those who accept his new teaching "will begin enjoying . . . [the] Hereafter life here [and] now!" Consequently, there can be no hell. As Elijah Muhammad again wrote, "They (the so-called Negroes) should know that if anything has led or will lead them to hell, it's the white (devil) race and their false religion (Christianity)."[42] Practically speaking, this focus on the here and now is attested in a well-known nine-pointed description of what the Nation of Islam seeks to attain, titled "What Muslims Want." All nine points listed

40. Muhammad, *Supreme Wisdom*, 51–50.
41. Taylor, *Promise of Patriarchy*, 2.
42. Muhammad, *Supreme Wisdom*, 40–42.

have to do with things being accomplished "immediately," for instance, freedom, justice, opportunity, dignity, and education in this lifetime.[43]

Fig. 4.5. Women wear head coverings in the Nation of Islam.

Entrepreneurship, Self-Sufficiency, and Business Ventures

One of the hallmark features of the Nation of Islam is its emphasis on forming businesses and organizations founded, possessed, and managed by African Americans. This can be traced to Booker T. Washington's Tuskegee Institute and his book *Up from Slavery*. The Nation of Islam followed suit. As Ula Yvette Taylor explains, "Schools, grocery stores, dry cleaner, restaurants, a newspaper, a clothing factory, and a host of small entrepreneurial ventures cluttered the landscape near each . . . temple."[44] This ability to create independent and Black-owned institutions was made possible historically only by the ending of slavery a couple of generations before. Providing a great boon to the movement, it generated a Black middle class that came from poverty and government assistance. In Robert Dannin's estimation, it was this "Bookerite fortitude" that gave dignity to its disciples and money to its movement.[45] Most pointedly, this mindset allowed for its Messenger, Elijah Muhammad, to preside "over a multimillion-dollar business empire which consisted of a printing press,

43. Muhammad, *Muhammad Speaks*; Marsh, *Lost-Found Nation of Islam in America*, 47.
44. Taylor, *Promise of Patriarchy*, 2.
45. Robert Dannin, *Black Pilgrimage to Islam* (Oxford: Oxford University Press, 2002), 46–47.

farms, restaurants, a meat packing plant, homes, apartments, trucks, a clothing factory, and a small bank."[46]

Part 5: Worship Practices

I have already alluded to many practices within the Nation of Islam in my discussions of its history and religious writings, so I will isolate only a couple of practices to discuss in more depth below.

New Name, New Identity

Conversion to the new religious movements connected to African-American Islam has been so transformative and reconfiguring that it has resulted in the creation of identity cards, the changing of names, and the donning of new clothes. For instance, the most famous members of the Nation of Islam throughout the twentieth century are known more for their new postconversion names given by the movement than their natural names given by their parents, for instance, Elijah Muhammad (rather than Elijah Poole), Malcolm X (rather than Malcolm Little), Muhammad Ali (rather than Cassius Clay), and Louis Farrakhan (rather than Louis Walcott).

Prayer and Other Rituals

Despite the novelty of rituals introduced by the Nation of Islam, it still relies heavily on the bedrock worship practice in traditional Islam of *salat*, or "prayer," even if it is practiced differently. For instance, although there is ample evidence that this was not promoted in the initial years of the Nation of Islam,[47] eventually followers were encouraged to pray five times a day from the first chapter of the Qur'an called *al-Fatiha*. This is standard within Sunni Islam. But what was completely aberrant about the practice within the Nation of Islam was doing so in any language other than Arabic, and Elijah Muhammad originally ordered Nation of Islam followers to say the prayer in English. Also, rather than observing Ramadan, which is the most important month within Islam, through communal fasting from sunup to sundown, the Nation of Islam originally had members pray during the Christmas season, which was an obvious attempt to cast aspersions on the Christmas season of Advent, at which time, Muhammad once said, "you used

---

46. Curtis, *Black Muslim Religion in the Nation of Islam, 1960–1975*, 4.
47. Curtis, 132.

to worship a dead prophet by the name of Jesus."[48] This changed only when W. D. Muhammad took over the movement, pushing the Nation of Islam to observe Ramadan at the prescribed time according to the Muslim calendar.

Fig. 4.6. Nation of Islam mosque in Chicago, Illinois.

Part 6: Point of Contact

I have had countless conversations with believers in the Nation of Islam, and they have each taken the same tone. The initial conversations usually revolve around race, particularly regarding Blacks versus whites. These are heated topics, and I will be honest: I cannot help but sympathize with the Nation of Islam in terms of its perception of American Christianity as creating or condoning centuries of racial bigotries, dehumanizing laws, unjust systems, and economic imbalances. This perception is based on historical fact, and all these degrading actions have greatly disadvantaged African Americans—not to mention greatly damaged the witness of the body of Christ. Not a day goes by, for instance, in which the specter of these racial practices and prejudices does not make an appearance in our neighborhoods, in our social media platforms, and in our institutions. In this way, I humbly and sympathetically grieve with members of the Nation of Islam as they voice their frustrations, resentments, and pains as Black Muslims in America. In my conversations with members of the Nation of Islam, in particular, I do not contest their experiences. I am willing to listen to them as long as they like, which is usually over several interactions.

48. GhaneaBassiri, *History of Islam in America*, 231; Curtis, *Black Muslim Religion in the Nation of Islam, 1960–1975*, 133–34.

Eventually, I prefer to move the conversation away from positioning white versus Black or Europe versus Africa, and instead to illustrating the nature, origins, and development of worldwide Christianity. For example, as I argue in my book *Introduction to World Christian History*, "Christianity, from its earliest days, has nurtured a grander vision that encompasses all political empires and all people groups."[49] And the New Testament is replete with verses confirming this. In fact, one could even argue that "Christianity was born in biblical Africa."[50] Not only, after all, was "the majority of the Bible . . . penned on African soil,"[51] but eight of the most influential Christian theologians of all time lived, ministered, and died in Africa.[52] Therefore, it is a lie, it is a myth, and it is a travesty to advance the long-disproved argument that Christianity is a white religion, or a European religion, or a religion of slavery. To be sure, Christianity has a large white population, European Christianity has exerted a disproportionate influence over the world, and certain Christians have practiced and promoted slavery for centuries. At the same time, one could easily argue exactly the opposite, namely, that Christianity is a Black religion, that African Christians have been practicing the Christian faith since the first century, or that Christianity is a freeman's religion.

All this is to say that the Nation of Islam's framing of Christianity is woefully wide of the mark. And in my latest conversations with members of the Nation of Islam, I have adopted a new approach to engage this. Here is what I say: "Don't take my word on the matter. All I ask is that you take Elijah Muhammad's advice on one point." For instance, in his foundational book *Supreme Learning*, Muhammad wrote this:

> Learning is a virtue. The education and training of our children must not be limited to the "three Rs" (reading, 'riting and 'rithmetic) only. It should instead include the history of the black nation, the knowledge of civilizations of man and the Universe, and all sciences. It is necessary that the young people of our nation learn all they can. Learning is a great virtue, and I would like to see all the children of my followers become possessors of it. It will make us an even greater people tomorrow.[53]

49. Derek Cooper, *Introduction to World Christian History* (Downers Grove, IL: InterVarsity Press, 2016), 16.

50. Keith Augustus Burton, *The Blessing of Africa* (Downers Grove, IL: IVP Academic, 2007), 111.

51. Burton, 111.

52. Cooper, *Introduction to World Christian History*, 48–49.

53. Muhammad, *Supreme Wisdom*, 58.

To this I say Hallelujah and Amen. My prayer for my friends who are part of the Nation of Islam is that they take up this charge and examine the global history of Black Christianity, investigate the Black origins of civilization, and discover what Black scientists teach about the nature of our past. That is because real learning not only teaches virtue, but tells truth. And here is the truth: Christianity is not one man's partisan interpretation of history, but instead one people's public interpretation of it. As Christians, we have nothing to lose from learning the truth—and everything to gain. But the same cannot be said for the Nation of Islam.

Discussion Questions

1. Why do you think so many new religious movements among African-American Muslims emerged at the same time? What did they have in common?
2. What do you think happened to W. D. Fard? What do you think he really taught?
3. What was the nature of W. D. Muhammad's and Malcolm X's disagreement with Elijah Muhammad? Who do you think was closer to the truth?
4. What did you learn in this chapter that you want to study in more depth?
5. If you were sharing your faith with a person from the Nation of Islam, where would you start? Are there any topics that you would want to focus on or avoid? Which ones?

For Further Reading

Curtis, Edward E., IV. *Black Muslim Religion in the Nation of Islam, 1960–1975*. Chapel Hill: University of North Carolina Press, 2006.

Farrakhan, Louis. *A Torchlight for America*. Chicago: FCN Publishing, 1993.

Felber, Garrett. *Those Who Know Don't Say: The Nation of Islam, the Black Freedom Movement, and the Carceral State*. Chapel Hill: University of North Carolina Press, 2020.

Gardell, Mattias. *In the Name of Elijah Muhammad: Louis Farrakhan and the Nation of Islam*. Durham, NC: Duke University Press, 1996.

Haddad, Yvonne Yazbeck, and Jane I. Smith, eds. *Muslim Communities in North America*. Albany: State University of New York Press, 1994.

Lee, Martha F. *The Nation of Islam: An American Millenarian Movement*. Lewiston, NY: Edwin Mellen, 1988.

Lincoln, C. Eric. *The Black Muslims in America*. Boston: Beacon Press, 1961.

Marsh, Clifton E. *The Lost-Found Nation of Islam in America*. Lanham, MD: Scarecrow Press, 2000.

Muhammad, Elijah. *Message to the Blackman in America*. Phoenix: Secretarius Memps Publications, 1973.

———. *The Supreme Wisdom: Solution to the So-Called Negroes' Problem*. Chicago: University of Islam, 1957.

Taylor, Ula Yvette. *The Promise of Patriarchy: Women and the Nation of Islam*. Chapel Hill: University of North Carolina Press, 2017.

X, Malcolm. *The Autobiography of Malcolm X: As Told to Alex Haley*. New York: Ballantine Publishing Group, 1973.

PART 3

Christian New Religious Movements

In this section, we discuss the two most influential new religious movements emerging out of Christianity in the last two centuries: Mormonism and the Jehovah's Witnesses. As you read about these religions in the two chapters that follow, consider what makes them different from mainstream Christian denominations such as Lutheranism and Presbyterianism. After all, these also emerged centuries after Christianity came into being. In short, what exactly puts Mormonism in a different theological category from Methodism? Why is the former traditionally considered an actual Christian offshoot while the latter is historically regarded as an authentic Christian denomination?

chapter 5

Mormonism: The Story of Restoration

Mormonism's understanding of itself as a restoration movement began with the belief that the Church of Jesus Christ was removed from the earth when direct communication between divinity and humanity ceased at the end of the apostolic age.

Jan Shipps[1]

Will everybody be damned, but Mormons? Yes.

Joseph Smith[2]

Mormonism is to Christianity as Christianity is to Judaism. Both Mormonism and Christianity established themselves by reinterpreting a preceding faith. Christianity built on Judaism but emphasized the death and resurrection of Jesus Christ; Mormonism began with Christianity but accepted a new revelation through a modern prophet.

Richard Bushman[3]

The Church of Jesus Christ of Latter-day Saints, the Mormons, will soon achieve a worldwide following comparable to that of Islam, Buddhism, Christianity, Hinduism, and the other dominant world faiths. . . . Indeed, they stand on the threshold

---

1. Jan Shipps, "The Reality of the Restoration and the Restoration Ideal in the Mormon Tradition," in *The American Quest for the Primitive Church*, ed. Richard T. Hughes (Urbana: University of Illinois Press, 1988), 183.

2. Joseph Smith, as quoted in Joseph Fielding Smith, *Teachings of the Prophet Joseph Smith* (Salt Lake City: Deseret News Press, 1958), 119.

3. Richard L. Bushman, *Mormonism: A Very Short Introduction* (Oxford: Oxford University Press, 2008), 62.

of becoming the first major faith to appear on earth since the Prophet Mohammed rode out of the desert.

Rodney Stark[4]

Part 1: The Beginning

Road Map to Mormon Creation Story. The Mormon version of creation differs from traditional Christianity in many ways, for instance, Elohim is God, Jehovah is Jesus, and Michael is Adam. Lucifer lived among all of them as a deity in the celestial kingdom, the highest heaven, before the "organization"— not "creation"— of all things on our planet, the telestial kingdom.

In the beginning, the head of the Gods decided to organize a new world called the telestial kingdom. Countless other worlds had, of course, been organized before, but this one was special. The assembly of Gods included Elohim, Jehovah, and Michael, but Elohim was clearly the leader. Elohim commanded Jehovah and Michael to begin their work and "organize it into a world like unto the worlds that we have hereunto formed." The two lesser Gods obeyed and went down from the celestial kingdom in which they were assembled. These two Gods completed every task Elohim had commanded them, each time returning back to the celestial kingdom to inform Elohim that their orders had been executed. Over the course of five days, the telestial kingdom had been organized, the waters and dry land had been divided, the light and the darkness had been separated, the seeds had been planted, and the animals had been multiplied.

Eventually the sixth day arrived, and there were no human beings to inhabit the kingdom that the Gods had organized. Unlike the previous days, Elohim personally joined Jehovah and Michael to organize the first human being. Michael volunteered himself, and he was transformed. Upon awaking from a deep sleep caused by Elohim and Jehovah, Michael had his name changed to Adam. Formed from dust, Adam became the leader of the human race, the holder of the keys of salvation, and the priest of the earth. Elohim and Jehovah organized a woman for Adam, and Adam called her Eve. Elohim and Jehovah gave Adam and Eve strict rules to follow before they returned to the celestial kingdom.

As soon as they had departed, however, Lucifer appeared. "Well, Adam," Lucifer stated, "you have a new world here." Adam was dumbfounded. "Yes," Lucifer reiterated, "a new world, patterned after the old one where we used to live." Adam replied, "I know nothing about any other world." That is because Elohim and Jehovah had erased his memories when they transformed him from Michael to Adam. "Oh," Lucifer realized, "I see, your eyes are not yet opened. You have forgotten

4. Rodney Stark, "The Rise of a New World Faith," *Review of Religious Research* 26, no. 1 (September 1984): 18–19.

everything. You must eat some of the fruit of that tree." Before long, Eve appeared, and Lucifer told her to do the same thing, claiming that "I am your brother." Lucifer persuaded her to eat the forbidden fruit, which she then gave to Adam. Upon doing so, Eve recognized the one talking to them as Lucifer, who had been thrown out of Elohim's celestial kingdom. Amid the conversation, Elohim and Jehovah stood before them and demanded to know what was going on. Lucifer replied, "I have been doing that which has been done in other worlds." Elohim then banished Lucifer, Jehovah stationed cherubim at the entrance, and Adam and Eve were expelled from the garden, but not before Elohim promised that a Savior would one day redeem them.

The decades on earth went by, but three years before Adam died, he assembled all the sons of the earth that he had begat into the Valley of Adam-ondi-Ahman. Jehovah joined them there, and they blessed Adam, calling him "Michael, the prince, the archangel." This assembly established the Quorum of the Twelve, who were entrusted to perpetuate the Priesthood from generation to generation, including establishing the High Priest to oversee them, for no one could lead the church unless established in this Priesthood. In the end times, Adam will reappear with Jehovah in this place, which is located in Missouri. This will be during the second coming. In the meantime, there is only one man to whom these great truths were revealed, and his name was Joseph Smith.[5]

Part 2: Historical Origin

The Church of Jesus Christ of Latter-day Saints, also known as Mormonism, has grown from six followers in 1830 to a membership of more than 16 million today to an anticipated 260 million within the next few decades.[6] Originally part of a much larger movement within American Christianity in the nineteenth century that sought to repristinate the church's faith, "its adherents regard it as a restoration of ancient

---

5. This creation story is assembled from various parts of the Doctrine and Covenants (especially 107 and 116), the Pearl of Great Price, and the creation script used in Mormon temples. See also Latayne C. Scott, *The Mormon Mirage: A Former Member Looks at the Mormon Church Today*, 3rd ed. (Grand Rapids: Zondervan, 2009), 212–14. Let me clarify the possible confusion about this story by offering some needed context. As Mormon theologian Bruce McConkie explains: "Elohim is the plural of the Canaanite El . . . ; consequently, its literal meaning is Gods. Accordingly, as the Prophet [Joseph Smith] pointed out, such Old Testament passages, as 'In the beginning God (Elohim) created the heaven and the earth' (Gen. 1:1), should more properly be translated, 'In the beginning the head of the Gods brought forth the Gods,' and they created the heavens and the earth." Bruce R. McConkie, *Mormon Doctrine* (Salt Lake City: Bookcraft, 1966), 162.

6. Rodney Stark, a noted sociologist of religion, estimated that Mormonism would increase at a 30 percent growth rate per decade until at least the year 2080, meaning that there will be more than 260 million by that time. See Stark, "Rise of a New World Faith," 23.

Christianity."[7] In this way, Mormonism is restorationism. In fact, the very name *Church of Jesus Christ of Latter-day Saints* indicates this belief and interprets its "saints"—its members—to be agents of Jesus' restored gospel. As this church teaches, "The Lord inspired the Prophet Joseph [Smith] to restore truths to the Bible text that had been lost or changed."[8] At the same time, Mormonism is completionism. After all, its founder, Joseph Smith, "did not [exclusively] think of himself as going back to a primordium of true Christianity," but instead of "completing a work that had never been perfectly realized."[9] Consequently, the term *Latter-day Saints* also reflects the apocalyptic flair of Mormonism, indicative of the belief that the last days were imminent, and so we are living in the "latter days." To be sure, this twin story of restoration and realization is centuries old within Christianity, but it developed in endlessly unique ways within Mormonism.

Joseph Smith (1805–44)

Joseph Smith grew up in upstate New York during an era in which religious fervor, curiosity, and experimentation were widespread. The region that Smith called home is referred to as the "burnt district,"[10] a name attesting to the spiritual fire that emblazoned it during the Second Great Awakening. As Jan Shipps explains, this area "favored the creation of new religious movements . . . [and] produced an atmosphere of experimentation."[11] This culture engulfed Smith and explains his fascination with the occult, magic, and denominationalism. For at this time magical practices, glass-looking, and treasure-seeking were widely practiced, and Smith was even legally found guilty of it.[12] In fact, it is very telling that the first thing the fourteen-year-old Joseph Smith asked God and Jesus Christ when they physically appeared to him in 1820 was "which of all the sects is right?" Not surprisingly, they replied that "all were wrong," that "their creeds were an abomination," and that their followers "were all corrupt."[13] Instead, a completely new "sect" had to be created.

---

7. Bushman, *Mormonism*, 1.

8. Gospel and Principles 10.

9. Bushman, *Mormonism*, 5.

10. Charles Finney (1792–1875), a contemporary of Joseph Smith who lived in the same region, was the first to use this wildly popular phrase.

11. Jan Shipps, *Mormonism: The Story of a New Religious Tradition* (Urbana: University of Illinois Press, 1985), 7.

12. Jon Butler, *Awash in a Sea of Faith: Christianizing the American People* (Cambridge, MA: Harvard University Press, 1990), 243.

13. Pearl of Great Price, History 1:18–19.

Fig. 5.1. Joseph Smith is the founder of Mormonism.

Golden Plates. Emma Hale, Smith's first wife, said: "I frequently wrote day after day, often sitting at the table close by him [Joseph Smith], he sitting with his face buried in his hat, with the stone in it and dictating... He had neither [manuscript] nor book to read from. If he had anything of the Kind [sic] he could not have concealed it from me."

Emma Smith Bidamon, "Interview with Joseph Smith III, February 1879," in *Early Mormon Documents*, ed. Dan Vogel (Salt Lake City: Signature Books, 1996), 1:539.

Joseph Smith's "First Vision" was followed up three years later with the "Second Vision" in 1823 in which the angel Moroni revealed the location of a sacred book made of gold plates. It would take four years, however, before Smith obtained the plates and began translating them with the assistance of his first wife, Emma, who transcribed what Smith dictated while he intuited the translation through seer stones he observed in a hat.[14] It was also during this time, in 1829, that John the Baptist appeared to Smith and reinstituted the Aaronic Priesthood, an event followed up by visitations from Peter, James, and John, who reinstituted the Melchizedek Priesthood.[15]

By the time Smith organized the Latter-day Saints in 1830, he was the target of ongoing criticism, he was tainted by scandal, and he was the recipient of death threats. Not surprisingly, both he and his followers were regularly on the move and constantly encountering opposition—both verbally and physically. Still, Smith's movement grew. As it did, his appetite for expansion—whether political, economic, sexual, or spiritual—enlarged with it. After escaping prison in Missouri, Smith founded a city in Illinois that he named Nauvoo. This became Mormonism's new Zion, with Latter-day Saints moving there to establish a new city set on a hill. But dissent from within and hostility from without engulfed the

---

14. Initially, Smith had used Martin Harris as his scribe, but while they were in Harris's possession, the 116 pages of the heretofore-uncompleted translation were lost. For more on this interesting development, see Shipps, *Mormonism*, 13–20.

15. Doctrine and Covenants 13.

town, and Joseph Smith was shot to death by an angry non-Mormon mob while under arrest in the county jail in 1844.

Fig. 5.2. The angel Moroni, the last prophet from the Book of Mormon and the one who appeared to Joseph Smith, stands atop many Mormon temples.

The source of much (but not all) of this antagonism, both inside and outside the movement, was Smith's controversial institution of plural marriage. Naturally, there is no end to the speculation that has ensued, to the scholarship that has emerged, and to the scandal that has endured related to this topic. What was Smith's motivation? Did he think he was following the examples of the Old Testament patriarchs? Did he believe that God had actually commanded him to marry dozens of women? Or did he simply want to assert his authority or satisfy his sexual cravings by taking advantage of the opposite sex? All we know is that Smith began privately entering into plural marriage as early as the 1830s. And he continued doing so until his death in 1844, by which time he had entered more than thirty marriages with females in the community—a third of whom were already married. Smith also scandalously authorized around thirty other male leaders (never women) in his community to follow his lead and marry multiple wives.[16] So ingrained did plural marriage become within Mormonism, in fact, that it persisted for a half-century before the religion was forced to cede the practice in 1890 as a prerequisite for Utah to become a state in the United States (though Mormon fundamentalists practice it to this day).[17]

16. Richard L. Bushman, *Rough Stone Rolling: A Cultural Biography of Mormonism's Founder* (New York: Vintage Books, 2007), 440, 443.

17. Bushman, *Mormonism*, 90–99.

Brigham Young (1801–77)

Brigham Young was campaigning for Joseph Smith in New England in the latter's bid to become President of the United States when he heard that Smith had died in the Illinois jailhouse shootout. As the senior member of the Quorum of the Twelve Apostles, Young returned home, assumed leadership of the movement, and began the trek westward toward Utah under banishment orders from the government. Young's taking of the mantle was not without controversy, however, since many claimants clamored to succeed Mormonism's first prophet.

Brigham Young's leadership differed drastically from Joseph Smith's. While Smith was all about idea creation, Young was all about institution-building. As Douglas Davies observes: "Brigham possessed a spirituality that was concerned as much with agriculture and social welfare as with building temples and practising their rites. He also had a prevailing sense of where the Saints should go and a real intimation of when they had arrived there."[18] Young established Latter-day communities all across the West and made Utah synonymous with Mormonism. He founded settlements, created institutions, oversaw immigration, erected infrastructures, started companies, and governed territories. He was a gifted leader. But he was not without his faults. As his biographer writes, "Young was no less controversial than his predecessor, and non-Mormons routinely accused him of ecclesiastical tyranny, licentiousness, and even murder."[19]

Young clashed strongly both with government officials and with critics of his movement, and he was not above using violence to achieve his ends. Under his watch, Mormonism became known for cultivating a peculiar people, whose controversial practices, revolutionary tendencies, mysterious rituals, and theocratic leanings bristled against mainstream American culture. Again, as his biographer explains, "Within a Protestant America dedicated to monogamy, monotheism, and Jacksonian democracy, Young advocated a plurality of wives, a plurality of gods, and a unity of power."[20] In fact, for many critics, it was the former that provoked the greatest wrath. Young, after all, became an even more notorious polygamist than his predecessor, possessing more than fifty wives and siring even more children.[21] But by the time of his death in 1877, he had laid the groundwork for Zion, the Jerusalem of Mormonism, in the most unexpected of places: the Salt Lake Valley of Utah.

Mormon Divisions. After Joseph Smith's death, his first wife, Emma Hale, remarried, moved to Missouri, and with her sons and descendants led the Reorganized Church of Latter Day Saints (now called Community of Christ), which rejected controversial practices such as polygamy and the secret temple rituals. Smith's direct lineage led this denomination until the 1990s.

---

18. Douglas J. Davies, *An Introduction to Mormonism* (Cambridge: Cambridge University Press, 2003), 117–18.
19. John G. Turner, *Brigham Young: Pioneer Prophet* (Cambridge, MA: Belknap Press, 2012), 3.
20. Turner, 4.
21. Turner, 374–85.

Fig. 5.3. Salt Lake City, Utah, is the headquarters of Mormonism.

Mormon Denominations. There is no one or unified Mormonism. Mormon denominations include, e.g., the Community of Christ, Recognized Church of Jesus Christ of Latter Day Saints, Council of Friends, Apostolic United Brethren, Fundamentalist Church of Jesus Christ of Latter-day Saints, the Church of Jesus Christ in Zion, the Restored Branch of Jesus Christ, and dozens of others.

Mormonism Today

Since Utah became a state in 1890, Mormonism has forged a unique identity. Although Salt Lake City—and Utah in general—is the Mecca of the movement, it has always aspired to worldwide representation. Wherever Mormons lived, wards—the official name for local Mormon congregations—became identity markers, and communities intentionally sought to maintain the religion's distinct identity from the world, that is, from the "Gentiles." This has proved difficult, especially given Mormonism's deep ties with whites and its historical prejudice against Blacks, leading to more than a century of Black men being prohibited from entering the Priesthood based on Joseph Smith's identification of "the Indians of the Americas as the 'Lamanites,' the cursed, dark-skinned descendants of the wicked who had wiped out the righteous Nephites" in the Book of Mormon.[22]

Today, Mormonism is a global faith, practiced around the world by people from all ethnicities, languages, and backgrounds. Missionary activity outside the United States had begun, in fact, when Joseph Smith was still alive, and by the time he died in 1844, the twenty-five thousand members of the faith included a "significant" percentage from the United Kingdom.[23] This missionary thrust is deeply ingrained within the movement. Not only was it one of the primary impetuses behind the religious community's regularly moving westward in its earliest days, but Smith's ordination of missionaries dating back to the first congregation in 1830

22. Bushman, *Mormonism*, 111; Turner, *Brigham Young*, 209.
23. Bushman, *Mormonism*, 10.

proved pivotal to the growth it experienced. The expectation of young men and women to perform two years of missionary service after high school remains strong, as does emphasis on participation in one's local Mormon chapel, including tithing and service, as well as the nurturing of the family unit for the furtherance of the community. This is all situated within the continued belief that the Latter-day Saints alone possess and transmit the truth, that the movement is sustained by a prophet (also called *president*) who is able to speak on behalf of God, and that this God desires to be worshiped across the globe. In comparison with many much older yet much smaller religions, Mormonism "is still an extremely young institution," which—it is hoped by its followers—has "many miles to travel, and many vestures to change, before its vision of Zion is realized."[24]

Part 3: Religious Writings

The Church of Jesus Christ of Latter-day Saints contains four bodies of sacred writings referred to as the Standard Works: (1) the Bible, (2) the Book of Mormon, (3) the Doctrine and Covenants, and (4) the Pearl of Great Price.

First, the Bible has always been used by Mormons as sacred writing. In fact, Joseph Smith claimed that the most famous figures in the Bible—Elohim, Jehovah, Michael, Moses, John the Baptist, Peter, James, and John—all personally visited him in different locations across New York, Pennsylvania, Missouri, and Illinois. Although Smith did attempt his own biblical translation (even though he did not know any of the original languages), it was never finished; and what was attempted was not published during his lifetime. Instead, the King James Version has become the standard translation used among Latter-day Saints. This is not to say that Mormons have not used other translations, but the King James has been preferred for many reasons, not least because it was used by Smith and because he emulated the wording and rhythm of the King James in his own writings, thus creating a literary symmetry when paired with Smith's Book of Mormon, Doctrine and Covenants, and Pearl of Great Price.[25] Still, an uneasy tension exists between the King James Version and the Latter-day Saints given the repeated Mormon teaching that the Bible has been corrupted and not translated correctly.

What about the Apocrypha? In 1833, Joseph Smith wrote: "Verily, thus saith the Lord unto you concerning the Apocrypha—There are many things contained therein that are true, and it is mostly translated correctly. There are many things contained therein that are not true, which are interpolations by the hands of men… [I]t is not needful that the Apocrypha should be translated." (Doctrine and Covenants 91:1–6)

24. Davies, *Introduction to Mormonism*, 254.
25. Philip L. Barlow, *Mormons and the Bible: The Place of the Latter-day Saints in American Religion* (New York: Oxford University Press, 2013), 162–98.

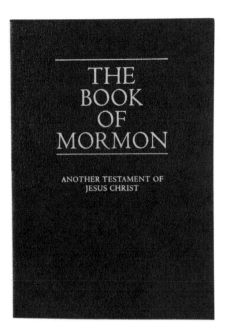

Fig. 5.4.
The Book of
Mormon is part
of the Standard
Works, a canon
of four Mormon
scriptures.

Second, the Book of Mormon "was Joseph Smith's calling card to the world."[26] Though panned by critics, it provided the foundational narrative and evidence of miraculous feats for the religion of the Latter-day Saints. Significantly, it also contained Jesus' reiteration of the promise from Malachi that another prophet would come *after* Jesus (3 Nephi 24:1; 25:5)—instead of *before* Jesus, which mainstream Christians have always interpreted as John the Baptist—setting the scene for Joseph Smith to assume that role. Published in 1830, the Book of Mormon contains fifteen books and recounts the captivating history of an Israelite family that migrated from the Holy Land to the Americas before the tribes of Israel were dispersed during the Babylonian exile in approximately 600 B.C.

In the Americas, in some unknown yet debated location, since not a shard of archaeological, genetic, or textual evidence has ever materialized to support it,[27] this Israelite family eventually divided into warring tribes called the Lamanites and Nephites—the latter of whom prevailed and whom Jesus Christ visited and preached to in person after his resurrection. Centuries later, a prophet by the name of Mormon (after whom Mormons are called) collected the writings of the Nephites on plates made of gold and entrusted them to his son, Moroni, who buried them in upstate New York in the A.D. 400s before he died. Twelve

26. Bushman, *Mormonism*, 23.
27. David Johnson, "Archaeology," in *Encyclopedia of Mormonism*, vol. 1, *The History, Scripture, Doctrine, and Procedure of the Church of Latter-day Saints*, ed. Daniel Ludlow (New York: Macmillan, 1992), 62.

centuries later, in the 1820s, a divinized Moroni revealed the location to Joseph Smith, who translated the plates from a language that Smith called "reformed Egyptian" into King Jamesian English. Upon completion, Smith returned the plates to Moroni, who took them away, evidently to the celestial kingdom where he lives.

Book of Mormon People Groups

People Group	Location in Book of Mormon	When They Entered Americas	Where They Lived
Jaredites	Book of Ether	After Tower of Babel incident; died out around 600s B.C.	Mexico?
Nephites	Books of Nephi, Mosiah, Jacob & Mormon	Left Jerusalem c. 600 B.C.; destroyed by Lamanites c. A.D. 385	Central America?
Mulekites	Book of Omni	In 580s B.C. after Mulek, Zedekiah's only surviving son, escaped Babylonian destruction of Jerusalem	Central America?
Lamanites	Books of Nephi	Left Jerusalem c. 600 B.C.; turned into "American Indians"	Americas

Third, the Doctrine and Covenants is a collection of 138 chapters, called *sections*, that contain revelations, policies, and prophecies almost exclusively from Joseph Smith. Originally published in 1833, it was revised and expanded in 1835 to complement the Book of Mormon as scripture, and since then, a few revelations from past Mormon presidents (also called *prophets*) have been included (with the possibility of more in the future). The title of this document is noteworthy. It conveys not only the importance of new doctrines that the church teaches but also the promises that its members are required to make in response to it (which I will discuss below). For example, one of the important doctrines that Mormons are taught in this document is that Joseph Smith was given the keys of God's kingdom (which refers to his reinstating the so-called Aaronic and Melchizedek Priesthoods), and Smith is portrayed as the true restorer of the gospel.

Fourth, the Pearl of Great Price is another collection of writings from Joseph Smith. It contains the book of Moses (with retellings of the lives of Adam to Noah), the book of Abraham (a novel interpretation of

Abraham's life supposedly translated from an Egyptian text but proved to have been made up[28]), Smith's revised translation of Matthew 24, a personal history of faith (in which Smith narrates how both Elohim and Jehovah appeared to him in bodily form), and the Articles of Faith. Many of these books and events are taken directly from the Bible itself, and they all belie their dependence on it in one form or another. For instance, the Articles of Faith offer a list of thirteen beliefs. These correspond closely to traditional Christianity, with the exception of Article 8: "We believe the Bible to be the word of God as far as it is translated correctly; we also believe the Book of Mormon to be the word of God." As noted above, Mormon distrust of previous Bible translations is complicated by the fact that it almost exclusively uses the King James Version, which, of course, would be implicated in the charge of mistranslation.

Part 4: Beliefs

Although there are many similarities between the Latter-day Saints and mainstream Christianity, I will highlight some of the key distinctions in order to draw out the differences more clearly.[29]

"Mormonism Is Christianity"

In my interactions with Mormons, I have encountered a phenomenon that "puzzles Latter-day Saints more than any other criticism," namely, the charge that they are not Christians.[30] This is truly mystifying to Saints. Rather than seeking to reject Christianity, they maintain that they have sought only to restore it. As Bruce McConkie, a noted Mormon theologian and author of a classic Latter-day doctrinal text, unequivocally asserts, "Mormonism is Christianity; Christianity is Mormonism; they are one and the same, and they are not to be distinguished from each other in the minutest details."[31] Like Martin Luther (1483–1546) and the Protestant Reformation, which attempted to realign the beliefs and practices of the church with historic Christianity rather than reinvent them, so, too, Joseph Smith and the Latter-day Saints assert that they

---

28. When the scroll that Smith purportedly translated from was discovered in 1966, Egyptologists found that it did not correspond in the least with what Smith had claimed to be the actual translation. See Bushman, *Mormonism*, 70.

29. As a standard reference and compilation of doctrines, I will be drawing mostly from a manual called *Gospel Principles*. Originally published in 1989, it has undergone several editions over the years. I will be using the 2009 edition: *Gospel Principles* (Salt Lake City: Church of Jesus Christ of Latter-day Saints, 2009).

30. Bushman, *Mormonism*, 3.

31. McConkie, *Mormon Doctrine*, 363.

are attempting only to restore the church to its original purity. After all, Mormons argue, they believe that Jesus Christ is the Son of God who died on the cross to save us from our sins and who was resurrected from the dead.

Ongoing Revelation

Perhaps the most significant doctrine within Mormonism is its belief in ongoing revelation. Simply put, no ongoing revelation, no Latter-day Saints. As Richard Bushman explains, "No single doctrine distinguishes Mormonism more sharply than the belief in direct revelation."[32] This foundational doctrine manifests itself in three primary ways: (1) its writings, (2) its leadership, and (3) its common beliefs. First, as explained above, Joseph Smith founded this movement under the conviction that he was receiving a new revelation and that the writings he composed were made possible only by his belief that revelation is ongoing and not complete. Second, the pattern that Smith set has been followed for centuries by prophet-presidents who offer occasional yet official revelation to the church at large. For example, as God states in the Doctrine and Covenants, "I [God] have given [Joseph Smith] the keys of the mysteries, and the revelations which are sealed, and I shall appoint unto them another in his stead."[33] Although Smith was the initial prophet of God's revelation, the movement continues to be guided by these prophet-presidents who speak on behalf of God. Finally, everyday believers are taught to pray and ask God to confirm spiritual truths. In Mormon circles, this language has been immortalized in Smith's assertion that God would "cause your bosom to burn" as a way to establish the veracity of the faith.[34] This same concept is used to verify the truth of the Book of Mormon as expounded at the end of the book.[35]

God and the Trinity

Although the concept of the Trinity exists within Mormonism, it is not the Trinity as maintained in historic Christianity. On the contrary, Mormonism is a polytheistic religion, and I will describe how each member of the Mormon Trinity differs from classic Christianity. In fact, as

32. Bushman, *Mormonism*, 3.
33. Doctrine and Covenants 28:7.
34. Doctrine and Covenants 9:8.
35. "And when ye shall receive these things, I would exhort you that ye would ask God, the Eternal Father, in the name of Christ, if these things are not true; and if ye shall ask with a sincere heart, with real intent, having faith in Christ, he will manifest the truth of it unto you, by the power of the Holy Ghost" (Moroni 10:4).

Dan Vogel argues, "Mormonism was never trinitarian."[36] And Mormon scholars concede that the Mormon Trinity "is obviously at variance with much of traditional Christianity."[37] Instead, a novel configuration emerged that expanded and conflated the roles of the Godhead, maintaining that each of the three members of the Trinity is a separate person—and that, moreover, countless humans have also gone on to become divinities. The configuration of the Mormon Trinity maintains (1) that Elohim is the supreme God—who is sometimes rendered in the singular and sometimes in the plural; (2) that Yahweh (who is also called *Jehovah* in Mormonism) is Jesus; and (3) that the Spirit is the Holy Ghost. These three Gods represent the Mormon Trinity, and they are the ones worshiped. As I alluded to, however, "in addition there is an infinite number of holy personages, drawn from the worlds without number, who have passed on to exaltation and are thus gods."[38]

To briefly describe each of the members of the Trinity: Joseph Smith openly taught, "The Father has a body of flesh and bones as tangible as man's."[39] As he elaborated, "God himself was once as we are now, and is an exalted man."[40] This God is called Elohim or Heavenly Father, and though not recorded in the Standard Works, Mormons teach that Heavenly Father is married to Heavenly Mother, who begat spirit children.[41] Next, Mormons assert that Jehovah (or, more properly, Yahweh) is Jesus (and not God the Father, as consistently maintained in historic Christianity). As Mormon theologian McConkie explains, "Christ is Jehovah; they are one and the same Person."[42] Similarly, as James Talmage teaches, "Among the spirit-children of Elohim the firstborn was and is Jehovah or Jesus Christ."[43] According to Mormon theology, Jesus was first created in the spirit world by Heavenly Father and Heavenly Mother; but on earth, when he was born a man, he became the son of Heavenly Father and Mary.[44] Jesus also married and sired children, and was possibly married to multiple wives, giving witness to the polygamous nature of the Godhead

36. Dan Vogel, "The Earliest Mormon Concept of God," in *Line upon Lion: Essays on Mormon Doctrine*, ed. Gary James Bergera (Salt Lake City: Signature Books, 1989), 17.

37. Robert L. Millet and Shon D. Hopkin, *Mormonism: A Guide for the Perplexed* (London: Bloomsbury Academic, 2015), 43.

38. McConkie, *Mormon Doctrine*, 282.

39. Doctrine and Covenants 130:22.

40. Joseph Smith, "How God Came to Be God," in *Joseph Smith: Selected Sermons and Writings*, ed. Robert L. Millet (New York: Paulist Press, 1989), 131.

41. McConkie, *Mormon Doctrine*, 366; see also Scott, *Mormon Mirage*, 168–69.

42. McConkie, *Mormon Doctrine*, 282.

43. James E. Talmage, *The Articles of Faith: A Series of Lectures on the Principal Doctrines of the Church of Jesus Christ of Latter-day Saints*, 51st ed. (Salt Lake City: Church of Jesus Christ of Latter-day Saints, 1974), 471.

44. Millet and Hopkin, *Mormonism*, 48.

(and so the precedent for plural marriage).[45] Finally, the Holy Spirit is called the *Holy Ghost* within Mormonism. McConkie explains that the Holy Ghost "can be in only one place at one time and he does not and cannot transform himself into any other form or image than that of the Man whom he is, though his power and influence can be manifest at one and the same time through all immensity."[46] This articulation of the Holy Ghost as possessing a body and being limited to one location at a time stands in direct contrast to the classical Trinitarian confession of God the Holy Spirit as fully God, without a body and not bound by human limitations.

Exaltation: How to Become a God

Although similar language is used, the plan of salvation within Mormonism differs radically from that of mainstream Christianity. First, the divine being that we refer to as God was previously a human being who progressed to divinity over eons. As McConkie writes, "All men in pre-existence were the spirit children of God our Father, an exalted, glorified, and perfected Man."[47] This belief explains why human beings are capable of becoming gods in their own right. Again, as McConkie states, "In a future eternity, spirit children will be born to exalted, per-fected glorified couples for whom the family unit continues."[48] This is the method Jesus followed in becoming divine or "exalted." For instance, Jesus was the son of Heavenly Father and Heavenly Mother, and it was decided millennia ago that Jesus would be able to have a body and become the Savior on earth. Other spirit beings, for instance, Adam and Eve, followed suit on their path toward exaltation. But unlike traditional Christianity, which interprets Adam and Eve's eating of the forbidden fruit as negative, Mormons regard it as positive, since it paved the way for them to have physical children, who could then go on to attain a divine status. Finally, for Mormons, Jesus' atonement for sin does not cover all sins; and what is more, his atonement was achieved when he cried in the garden of Gethsemane and not when he died on the cross or was physically resurrected three days later. In fact, the Church of Jesus Christ of Latter-day Saints does not endorse the cross, and you will not see it represented in its art, buildings, or symbols. As with the Jehovah's Witnesses, the cross plays no part in Mormonism.

God Was Once a Man. Joseph Smith wrote: "God himself was once as we are now, and is an exalted man, and sits enthroned in yonder heav-ens!...We have imagined and supposed that God was God from all eternity. I will refute that idea...[God] was once a man like us; yea, that God himself the Father of us all, dwelt on earth, the same as Jesus Christ did; and I will show it from the Bible."

Joseph Smith, "Teachings," 345, as quoted in McConkie, *Mormon Doctrine*, 229–30.

---

45. See Christopher Blythe, "Was Jesus Married?," *BYU Studies Quarterly* 60, no. 3 (2021): 75–84.
46. McConkie, *Mormon Doctrine*, 256.
47. McConkie, 523.
48. McConkie, 523.

The Afterlife

Mormonism teaches that a deceased person will enter one of three destinations upon death: (1) the celestial kingdom, (2) the terrestrial kingdom, or (3) the telestial kingdom.[49] This is, in part, based on the Mormon interpretation of John 14:1–2, where Mormons believe that Jesus made it "obvious [and] self-evident to anyone that life hereafter consists of more than merely a heaven and a hell."[50] First, the celestial kingdom is reserved for Mormons in good standing,[51] and it contains "three heavens or degrees."[52] This is the highest and most blessed destination, and it is only for those who receive ordination into the Priesthoods (or are sealed to someone who is) and who die as faithful members of the Mormon church. These men and women will receive the same body they had on earth but in a more glorified state. Next comes the terrestrial kingdom, which is reserved for those who die before the advent of Christ or who are generally good people who never embrace Mormonism. Unlike the celestial kingdom, in which one basks in the glory of Elohim and Jehovah, the terrestrial kingdom allows one to see only Jehovah, that is, Jesus. Finally, the telestial kingdom is the worst place of all. Although there are different degrees, it is where we all currently live, and Lucifer is currently lord of this world, though he will eventually be banished. Most people will end up in the telestial kingdom, which, confusingly, is sometimes interpreted as being here on earth and sometimes as being located elsewhere.

Part 5: Worship Practices

In this section, I will focus our attention on Mormon worship practices, which include visits to Latter-day places of worship as well as missionary methods.

Temples and Wards

Places of worship within Mormonism go by several names: temples, chapels, churches, congregations, wards, and branches. There are two categories. The first is a *temple*, often referred to as a "House of the Lord."[53]

---

49. Doctrine and Covenants 88:1–31. There is also a fourth, which is essentially the equivalent of hell, and below the telestial.

50. Millet and Hopkin, *Mormonism*, 125.

51. It also includes space for those who would have received the truth if they had heard it and those who died before the age of accountability. See Doctrine and Covenants 137.

52. Doctrine and Covenants 131:1.

53. McConkie, *Mormon Doctrine*, 545.

As Bushman states, "The temples represent the culmination of Mormon life as well as Mormon worship."[54] The next category comprises chapels called *wards* or *branches*. Generally speaking, a local chapel of fewer than three hundred is called a *branch*, and one of more than three hundred is referred to as a *ward*. A cluster of branches constitutes a *district*, while a cluster of wards makes up a *stake* (essentially a bishopric or diocese).[55] Importantly, the ward and branch are public venues, and these are the only worship spaces that outsiders such as me are allowed to visit. By contrast, a temple is reserved only for members in good standing inside the Church of Jesus Christ of Latter-day Saints. There is an exception, however, and I have visited a couple of Mormon temples. In short, when a new temple is built, "Gentiles"—the name for non-Mormons—are welcome to visit and learn more about Mormon practices; once the temple is officially dedicated, however, it is off-limits to all but insiders. In fact, not even members of a Mormon chapel can visit it without a "temple recommend."

Fig. 5.5. Mormon temple in La Jolla, California. Temples do not allow outsiders to visit.

Within the private place of worship, that is, the temple, all rituals performed are not only sacred but secret. Mormons are prohibited from sharing details about this experience upon pain of excommunication and damnation. But ex-Mormons have provided ample testimony, which

54. Bushman, *Mormonism*, 58.
55. Danny L. Jorgensen, "The Latter-day Saint (Mormon) Religion in America," in *World Religions in America: An Introduction*, ed. Jacob Neusner, 3rd ed. (Louisville: Westminster John Knox Press, 2003), 283.

has been consistently corroborated. In fact, many of the rituals can be directly attributed to secret Masonic rites that Smith learned when he joined the Freemasons in Nauvoo in 1842 and immediately began instituting in his endowment rituals.[56] As mayor and representative of the people in that town, Smith was fast-tracked in the Freemasons over the course of one single day, progressing from Entered Apprentice to Fellow Craft to Master Mason—what would take ordinary members years or decades to accomplish.[57] The secret rituals he learned were only slightly modified to accommodate his temple ordinances.

The importance of the temple cannot be overestimated, for Joseph Smith believed that he had recovered the Priesthood, and none of the most distinct and important rituals within Mormonism can be performed anywhere else than in the temple. To begin with, before any member can enter, he or she must have what is called a *temple recommend*, an official invitation that is granted only to those in good standing—in short, those who are performing all their duties, contributing 10 percent of their income to the church, following community guidelines, and actively involved in service. These members must wear white clothing specifically designed for temple use, and their first visit to the temple involves receiving ordinances, what are called *endowments*. These are special instructions that help one reach the celestial kingdom, that is, the highest heaven. Effectively, this means receiving special undergarments (the sacred temple garment required to be worn for the rest of one's life, separate from the outerwear worn during a temple visit), learning the true creation of the worlds and their division into the celestial, terrestrial, and telestial kingdoms (which I described in the opening of this chapter), and being taught insider information such as secret handshakes and phrases (called *tokens*) necessary to enter the highest realm of heaven, as well as making solemn and unbreakable vows called *covenants*. Married couples also "seal" their marriages, meaning that they are eternally bound together not only in this life, but in the celestial one with their spouses and children.

Finally, future visits to the temple involve what is called *baptism of the dead* or *proxy baptism*, in which young Mormon members are baptized (sometimes dozens of times in one session) on behalf of a dead relative— or, more commonly, anyone alive who never had the opportunity to accept the truth of Mormonism. The member being baptized on behalf of the dead is then "dunked" by a priest "in the name of the Father, and of the Son, and of the Holy Ghost." This emphasis on baptism—some

56. Davies, *Introduction to Mormonism*, 222.
57. Bushman, *Rough Stone Rolling*, 450.

might even say radical obsession—stems from the Mormon belief that baptism is necessary for exaltation, and great lengths have been taken by the Mormon church to search for, identity, and document those who died before Joseph Smith restored the faith. Because baptism of the actual individual being dunked would have already taken place at a local ward in the baptismal font, baptism of the dead is made vicariously on behalf of the deceased.

In contrast to secret temple practices, public places of worship, generally called *chapels*—but more specifically *wards* or *branches*—are overseen by male bishops who volunteer their time and do not receive financial remuneration. Mormon chapels are typically devoid of artwork, painting, and statues, but there is a font for baptisms, which are usually performed around the age of eight (understood to be the age of accountability). Wards assemble on Sunday mornings. The main elements consist of a sacrament meeting, Sunday school, and an additional class. The sacrament meeting resembles a Christian service. There are greetings and announcements, songs from a hymnbook, teachings, testimonies, prayers, and the passing of the sacraments of bread and water. I have attended several of these, and they are not too different from nonliturgical Christian church services. But you should dress up when attending (for instance, suit and tie for men and modest dress for women), since the attire is more formal. Regarding the sacrament, the bread and water are available to everyone—including children and visitors—and there is no hint of transubstantiation, in which Christ's body is mystically changed into the elements. Instead, the sacrament represents a pledge between the communicant and Christ. It is about remembrance. Finally, the Sunday school lessons and meetings are divided by age and gender, and they follow a specific curriculum published by headquarters. Members progress through the various Mormon documents.

Evangelism, Priesthood, and Family

The missionary thrust of Mormonism stemmed from Joseph Smith, who regularly commissioned missionaries to propagate the faith. This practice continues to this day, most famously in the two-year missionary service that Mormons are expected to complete. Typically, this missionary service is performed after high school. Teams are formed in twos (always the same gender), the location is chosen by Mormon leaders, and expenses are financed by the parents. Discipline is of utmost importance during missionary service. Not only are there strict requirements when it comes to dress code, social habits, and moral propriety, but missionaries are required to study for hours a day and evangelize door-to-door without any guarantee of success. The missionary service is a rite of passage in which young members transition into fully committed, dedicated, and mature believers.

Fig. 5.6. Mormons are traditionally encouraged to do a two-year missionary service after high school. They follow a strict dress code and schedule.

By the time of their missionary service, Mormon males in good standing have already undergone two Priesthood ordinations: the Aaronic and Melchizedek Priesthoods. (Females are not ordained and do not possess official leadership roles.) These Priesthoods authorize males to administer ordinances such as baptism, the sacrament, and confirmation (the gift of the Holy Ghost). As I mentioned above, the Aaronic Priesthood was instituted by John the Baptist, while the Melchizedek— which is the higher order—was instituted by Peter, James, and John. Typically, boys are ordained to the Aaronic Priesthood as deacons at the age of twelve and as priests by sixteen, with the Melchizedek Priesthood being conferred around the age of eighteen. The expectation of faithful Mormon males is that they will undergo the Priesthoods, perform their missionary service, maintain good standing within the church, marry, have children, and fuse their family together for eternity in a temple "sealing." In Mormonism, after all, "family is the highest way of life."[58] It is the greatest human bond, and Mormons around the world are known for their family devotion.

58. Bushman, *Mormonism*, 58.

Part 6: Point of Contact

I have been in dialogue with Mormon believers for more than twenty-five years. This began in high school when I had several friends who were part of the Latter-day Saints, and it has continued over the years through visits I have had at both Mormon chapels and temples as well as through conversations I have had with Mormon leaders during interreligious dialogues. To be sure, there is not one singular approach I take with all Mormons, but I have learned the hard way that attacking the credibility of Joseph Smith, lampooning the practice of polygamy, or ridiculing Mormon writings makes them resistant to engage. I eventually moved away from these strategies; instead, I have returned to two points of contact over the years.

The first is the notion of church apostasy. As Elohim and Jehovah purportedly told Joseph Smith the first time that they appeared to him in 1820, no faithful church traditions were left on earth. Following the death of the twelve apostles, everyone in the church was wrong and part of an apostate religion. Having myself been raised in a Restorationist denomination known as the Stone-Campbell Movement, which formed at exactly the same time and in exactly the same place as Mormonism did, I resonate with the notion that humankind can get in the way of God's plans and that we have all fallen short in our practice of faith and expression of love. In fact, as someone now within the Protestant Reformation tradition, I recognize the value of Reformers such as Martin Luther and John Calvin in helping the church recover a more biblically centered gospel. In fact, as both Luther and Calvin clearly taught, it is one thing to encourage the church to return to the gospel already entrusted to the church, but it is altogether different to re-create a new gospel under the assumption that the previous one was insufficient. Mormonism maintains, for instance, that the gospel was entirely corrupted, that God had completely abandoned the church, and that not a single person could be numbered among the faithful from the death of the last apostles to the revelation unveiled to Joseph Smith in 1820. This is a startling claim, and it stands barrel-chested in the face of historic Christianity. Do we really think that lowly of God's power, Jesus' love, or the Holy Spirit's ministry? It does not correlate with Scripture to suggest that Christ would plant, water, and nurture his church only to immediately curse it, leaving it to wither and die.

Second, one of the other most frequent conversations I have with Mormons has to do with their secret rituals. As I have alluded to above, Mormonism teaches one set of doctrines in public and another in private.

Publicly, the Latter-day Saints market themselves as Christians centered on Jesus Christ. Sure, they have additional writings, but they affirm the major tenets of the Christian faith, such as the Trinity, the sacraments of baptism and the Lord's Supper, and salvation through Jesus Christ. Privately, however, a secret narrative is unveiled. This narrative involves multiple worlds, various gods, and furtive handshakes. We learn that God used to be a man, that Jesus was created, and that the highest heavens are reserved only for those who perform rituals learned behind closed doors. But here is the problem. Christianity is a public faith. We do not openly publish doctrines to outsiders while covertly revealing secrets to insiders. Instead, what you see on Sunday morning is what you get on Wednesday afternoon. And what you read in your Bible at home is what you hear preached from the pulpit. Christ's death, after all, tore the temple curtain so that we could step inside the truth without fear that what is made public is different from what is made private. Gnostic Christianity, in which only insiders get the goods while the outsiders remain in ignorance, has no place in the church. It has no place in Christianity. And it should have no place in Mormonism.

Discussion Questions

1. What are the primary differences between mainstream Christianity and Mormonism?
2. If you could go back in time and meet with Joseph Smith, what questions would you ask him? What do you think he would say?
3. What ideas, beliefs, or practices most surprised you about Mormonism? Having read this chapter, do you conclude that Mormonism is closer to or further from mainstream Christianity than what you previously thought?
4. Have you ever read any of the Standard Works within Mormonism? If you were to begin reading one of the books, which one would you start with?
5. Explain in your own words what the Mormon belief in the Trinity is. How is it similar to and different from the classic understanding of the Trinity within Christianity?

For Further Reading

Barlow, Philip L. *Mormons and the Bible: The Place of the Latter-day Saints in American Religion*. New York: Oxford University Press, 2013.

Bushman, Claudia Lauper, and Richard Lyman Bushman. *Building the Kingdom: A History of Mormons in America.* New York: Oxford University Press, 2001.

Bushman, Richard L. *Mormonism: A Very Short Introduction.* Oxford: Oxford University Press, 2008.

———. *Rough Stone Rolling: A Cultural Biography of Mormonism's Founder.* New York: Vintage Books, 2007.

Givens, Terryl. *By the Hand of Mormon: The American Scripture That Launched a New World Religion.* New York: Oxford University Press, 2002.

———. *People of Paradox: A History of Mormon Culture.* New York: Oxford University Press, 2007.

Hardy, Grant. *Understanding the Book of Mormon: A Reader's Guide.* New York: Oxford University Press, 2010.

Shipps, Jan. *Mormonism: The Story of a New Religious Tradition.* Urbana: University of Illinois Press, 1985.

Turner, John G. *Brigham Young: Pioneer Prophet.* Cambridge, MA: Belknap Press, 2012.

Vogel, Dan, ed. *Early Mormon Documents.* 5 vols. Salt Lake City: Signature Books, 1996–2003.

———. *Joseph Smith: The Making of a Prophet.* Salt Lake City: Signature Books, 2004.

Webb, Stephen H. *Mormon Christianity: What Other Christians Can Learn from the Latter-day Saints.* New York: Oxford University Press, 2013.

chapter 6

Jehovah's Witnesses: The Story of Biblicism

Jehovah's Witnesses are unique; they have preached millenarianism longer and more consistently than any major sectarian movement in the modern world.

M. James Penton[1]

There are few people in the West who have not encountered the Jehovah's Witnesses. Their persistent house-to-house evangelism has brought them to the doors of most households. . . . Yet, despite being one of the best-known religious organizations, they are probably one of the least understood.

George Chryssides[2]

Jehovah's Witnesses do not consider themselves Protestants. In fact, they are quite critical of Protestants, and even more critical of Catholics. To Witnesses, both traditions have fallen away from the true teachings of the Bible and actually are working in ways contrary to God.

Dell deChant[3]

1. M. James Penton, *Apocalypse Delayed: The Story of Jehovah's Witnesses*, 3rd ed. (Toronto: University of Toronto, 2015), 7.
2. George D. Chryssides, *Jehovah's Witnesses: Continuity and Change* (London: Routledge, 2016), 5.
3. Dell deChant, "Apocalyptic Communities," in *World Religions in America: An Introduction*, ed. Jacob Neusner, 3rd ed. (Louisville: Westminster John Knox Press, 2003), 196.

Part 1: The Beginning

Road Map to Jehovah's Witnesses Creation Story. Jehovah's Witnesses maintain that God's name is Jehovah, that the spirit of the archangel Michael was transferred to the physical body of Jesus when the latter was born, that only a literal 144,000 believers will reign in Heaven with Jehovah, and that all other Jehovah's Witnesses will live in a restored Earth.

In the beginning, there was only Jehovah. Jehovah was and is without rival, having no equals, no partners, and no co-creators. The first thing Jehovah created was another spirit being who lived in heaven and was called Michael. But in the future, his name would be changed to Jesus when it was his appointed time to live on the earth. Eventually Jehovah's power, or what we might call Jehovah's holy spirit or force, created the heavens and the earth, including the angels, light, land, vegetation, and animals, before finishing with the creation of human beings. It is not possible to know exactly how long it took Jehovah to create everything. People sometimes maintain that it was six literal twenty-four-hour days, but plain reason, the Hebrew language, and the findings of modern science show this idea to be misguided. It was probably much longer, perhaps billions of years in total. Who knows?

The first human being was called Adam. Though it is not possible to know with certainty, he was likely created in the year 4026 B.C. Adam was created as a perfect son of Jehovah, but his failure to abide by Jehovah's laws resulted in a great punishment. Both he and his wife, Eve, were banished from Paradise. The human descendants of Adam and Eve lived, multiplied, expanded, and received Jehovah's laws. Unfortunately, they largely ignored Jehovah and corrupted the ways in which Jehovah was to be remembered and worshiped. But Jehovah left testimony in the scriptures. At long last, Jehovah was ready to ransom humankind from suffering and death. To do so, Jehovah transferred the spirit life of Michael, who was living in heaven alongside him, into the womb of a young Jewish maiden in the Middle East named Mary by means of holy spirit. The baby's name was Jesus, and he lived a perfect life on earth and died on a torture stake to make possible everlasting life. (So-called Christians say that he died on the cross, but they are wrong.) At death, the spirit of Jesus was restored by Jehovah, and he placed Jesus at Jehovah's right hand. Then in 1914, Jehovah gave Jesus, who then resumed his old name, Michael, the power to rule. Although Jesus now reigns in heaven with 144,000 literal followers, his earthly rule is imminent. In fact, we are perhaps mere seconds or minutes away from the moment when he will return to earth to destroy evildoers, inaugurate his millennial rule, and reward those who faithfully follow the laws of Jehovah.[4]

---

4. This Jehovah's Witness worldview is pieced together from various pamphlets published directly by the Jehovah's Witnesses.

Part 2: Historical Origin

The Jehovah's Witnesses were ignited from the embers of nineteenth-century American revivalism to become one of the most outspoken, apocalyptic, and countercultural religious movements in the world. Fastidious about door-to-door evangelism, enamored of biblical prophecy, and notorious for separatist tendencies, the Jehovah's Witnesses have grown into a community of more than thirteen million strong with representation around the globe and among diverse people groups. Their consistent, unswerving, and driving conviction that the end of the world is upon us has led them to build an empire of print whose faithful *publishers*, otherwise known as *members*, promulgate the message of "the truth" door to door, city to city, country to country.

Adventism and Millerism (Antecedents to the Jehovah's Witnesses)

The Jehovah's Witnesses are a branch that sprouted from a larger tree that can variously be called Adventism or Millerism. Before we discuss the Jehovah's Witnesses, therefore, we must first understand how these others came into being. Although millenarianism, or the radical expectation of an imminent end of the world in which Jesus will reign (either literally or figuratively) for a thousand years, can be traced back to the early days of the church, it reached a crescendo in nineteenth-century American revivalism. Partly a product of the Second Great Awakening, countless new denominations and new religious movements emerged that believed that the end of the world would occur immediately. To them, it was more than a pipe dream; it was a certitude. One of the most well-known movements that reflects this mindset was Millerism, which was based on the teachings of a man named William Miller.

William Miller (1782–1849)

Though not trained theologically, Miller became a serious student of the Bible after serving in the military and later becoming a farmer. Based on his investigation of the prophetic and apocalyptic books in Scripture, such as Daniel and Revelation, he concluded that the end of the world "will be accomplished" in 1843.[5] But when that did not happen, he emended the year to 1844. This is when Jesus' Second Advent, that is, his second coming, was supposed to arrive, at which time Christ would establish

---

5. William Miller, *Evidences from Scripture and History of the Second Coming of Christ about the Year 1843 and of His Personal Reign of 1000 Years* (Brandon: Vermont Telegraph Office, 1833), 38.

his millennial kingdom and destroy evildoers. Unfortunately for Miller, the dates he predicted came and went. Nothing happened. Meanwhile, as many as a quarter of a million people had embraced his teaching, some of whom lost their fortunes and properties.[6] This was called the Great Disappointment. And the movement split into many factions, some of which assembled into opposing churches that came to be referred to as Adventism given their shared emphasis on Jesus' Second Advent.

Among the various churches within Adventism that formed, the largest was called the Seventh-day Adventist. This denomination maintained that Jesus had indeed returned in 1844; his return was to the sacred temple in heaven, however, not to an earthly abode in America. Adventism's interest in the Old Testament also led it to institute a practice established among the Seventh-day Baptists in which they worshiped on Saturdays rather than Sundays, and before long Adventists were preaching that the fourth commandment regarding the keeping of the Sabbath was to be practiced on the Jewish Sabbath, not the Christian Sunday. This was confirmed by the divine revelations of Ellen White (1827–1915), who assumed leadership of the Seventh-day Adventists. According to one of her revelations, White had a vision in which Jesus appeared with the Ten Commandments, and the fourth commandment (about the Sabbath) was illuminated more than the others. Not all Adventists were convinced, however. And Adventism continued to splinter into dozens of denominations and movements. Yet its influence expanded and went on to forever change the trajectory of one man's life—and the millions who have since followed his teachings: Charles Taze Russell.

Charles Taze Russell (1852–1916)

Charles Taze Russell grew up in Pennsylvania during the height of the Civil War and lived his last days during World War I. Receiving only a minimal education, he became a partner in his father's clothing business at a young age and grew quite wealthy. Spiritually curious from childhood, he preferred studying the Bible and reflecting on the theological topics that he learned while attending a Presbyterian church and then, later, a Congregational one. He underwent a crisis of faith while at the Congregational church, but his doubts were overcome at the age of eighteen when he first encountered the teachings of Adventism under the preaching ministry of Jonas Wendell (1815–73), a former follower of William Miller. Rather than joining that denomination, though, Russell immersed himself in Scripture, using the Adventist framework he had

Adventist Denominations. There are dozens of Adventist denominations, all of which share common histories and doctrines but differ in other areas. Some of the more well-known Adventist denominations are the Seventh-day Adventists, Advent Christian Church, Christadelphians, Church of God, Life and Advent Union, Primitive Adventist Church, World Wide Church of God, and Abrahamic Faith.

---

6. Gary Land, *The A to Z of the Seventh-day Adventists* (Lanham, MD: Scarecrow Press, 2009), 3.

just learned. He agreed with other Adventist interpreters such as Nelson Barbour (1824–1905) who believed that Jesus would invisibly return in 1874. So contagious was his interest in interpreting the Bible that Russell began to assemble a group to study the Bible in depth. Though it would not be called by the name for several more decades, what developed in that Bible study was the beginnings of a new movement: the Jehovah's Witnesses.

By the age of thirty, Russell had sold his father's business for the modern equivalent of a million dollars.[7] This money allowed him to focus his time and energies on the Bible. As he did so, he fretted about the end times, he ruminated on global news, he engrossed himself in perplexing doctrines, and he obsessed over biblical chronologies. The system he developed was typical of American white males at the time who had their Bibles in one hand and news reports in the other. It essentially consisted of scrutinizing the Bible through a prism of dispensational theology, millenarian expectation, creedal aversion, world events, common-sense realism, and unquestioned individualism. It was not long before Russell concluded that only the method of interpretation he presented offered "the truth"—the rest being erroneous at best or apostate at worst.[8]

In 1879, Russell established a magazine that would later come to be called *Watchtower*, which has been in continuous publication ever since. Two years later, he founded what would eventually be named the "Watch Tower Bible and Tract Society of Pennsylvania," nicknamed "the Society." A collection and revision of Russell's writings culminated with the publication of a six-volume series on biblical interpretation called *Studies in the Scriptures*.[9] Unlike Joseph Smith, however, Russell never claimed personal visits from the Godhead or private revelations from Jehovah. Rather than relying on supernatural experiences, Russell's authority rested on rigorous study of the Bible. Despite not knowing the biblical languages of Hebrew and Greek or the ecclesial language of Latin,[10] Russell in his six-volume magnum opus offered the definitive plan of salvation that had yet eluded theologians and ministers of the past. As he wrote in the preface of his first volume: "Few realize that from the time creed-making began, A.D. 325, there was practically no Bible study for 1260 years. . . . Few realize that real Bible study, such as was practiced in the early Church in the days of the Apostles, has only

Invisible Second Coming?
Adventist interpreters believe the Greek word παρουσία, used two dozen times in the New Testament, is more accurately translated as "presence" or "being alongside" rather than the more traditional translation of "coming" or "arrival." From this reasoning, they concluded that Christ's παρουσία, "presence," was invisible.

Jerry Bergman, "The Adventist and Jehovah's Witness Branch of Protestantism," in *America's Alternative Religions*, ed. Timothy Miller (Albany: State University of New York Press, 1995), 36.

7. Andrew Holden, *Jehovah's Witnesses: Portrait of a Contemporary Religious Movement* (London: Routledge, 2002), 17.

8. Chryssides, *Jehovah's Witnesses*, 271.

9. Charles Taze Russell, *Studies in the Scriptures*, 7 vols. (1886; repr., Brooklyn, NY: Watchtower Bible and Tract Society, 1916).

10. Holden, *Jehovah's Witnesses*, 18.

now come back to Bible students."[11] Not surprising given his remarks, Russell's deep dive into Scripture and disdain for creedal confessions led him to publicize a variety of unorthodox Christian teachings, for instance, that there was no Trinity, that there was no hell, that Jesus was a created being, and that his second coming would be invisible.[12]

Fig. 6.1.
Jehovah's Witnesses believe that Jesus' second coming occurred invisibly in 1914.

Joseph Rutherford (1869–1942)

Charles Taze Russell's commonsense approach to Scripture resonated with the self-reliant disposition of America that was so pervasive throughout the nineteenth and twentieth centuries. Joseph Rutherford, for instance, a self-made, scrappy man from the Midwest who had come under the influence of the Jehovah's Witnesses while practicing law in Missouri in 1894, aligned with the movement given its focus on logical, precise, and individual interpretations of an authoritative text. Upon purchasing and reading the existing volumes of Russell's *Studies in the Scriptures*, Rutherford embraced the teachings offered and was baptized in 1906. He quickly made a name for himself because of his profession as a lawyer and his ability to legally defend both Russell and the burgeoning movement.

When Russell died in 1916, a fight for succession ensued, and Rutherford's legal training secured his leadership. There was ongoing conflict, however, and a large percentage left as Rutherford sought to organize, systematize, and centralize the movement under his authority—going so

11. Charles Taze Russell, *Studies in the Scriptures*, vol. 1, *The Plan of the Ages* (Brooklyn, NY: Watchtower Bible and Tract Society, 1916), iii–iv.

12. George D. Chryssides, *The A to Z of Jehovah's Witnesses* (Lanham, MD: Scarecrow, 2009), xxxiii.

far as to call it a "theocratic" kingdom. Like his predecessor, Rutherford thought it best to reach people with his life-changing message through print. He took eagerly to the pen, writing a book a year for the remainder of his life. Also like his predecessor, Rutherford had a penchant for revising prophetic dates and altering theological doctrines. In 1920, he wrote *Millions Now Living Will Never Die*, in which he confidently asserted:

> We … prove … that the social order of things, the second world, legally ended in 1914, and since that time has been and is passing away; that the new order of things is coming in to take its place; that within a definite period of time the old order will be completely eradicated … and that these things shall take place within the time of the present generation and that therefore there are millions of people now living on earth who will see them take place, . . . [who] will never die.[13]

This event, of course, never happened. But Rutherford died before this failed prophecy could embarrass him. Yet that would not be the case for his next prophecy in which he doubled down by claiming the following:

> In the fall of the year 1925, . . . Scriptures definitely fix the fact that there will be a resurrection of Abraham, Isaac, Jacob, and other faithful ones of old, … fully restored to perfect humanity and made the visible, legal representatives of the new order of things on earth.[14]

When this event failed to happen, Rutherford admitted that he had "made an ass of himself," but that did not stop him from purchasing a mansion in San Diego where he believed the biblical patriarchs would dwell.[15] When that also never happened, he comforted himself by making it his winter residence. And it is also where he died.

In addition to biblical date-setting, Rutherford was also heavily involved in centralizing the new organization and instituting many of the policies and practices that are associated with it to this day. For example, Rutherford made door-to-door evangelism mandatory for elders, labeled as "Pagan" the celebration of holidays and birthdays, forbade saluting a flag, and prohibited blood transfusions. Most significant, however, was the name change he made to the organization. In an attempt to distance it from the splinter groups that favored Russell's teachings (called *Russellites* or *Bible Students*), Rutherford unveiled a new name for the organization

13. Joseph Franklin Rutherford, *Millions Now Living Will Never Die* (Brooklyn, NY: International Bible Students Association, 1920), 12.

14. Rutherford, 88.

15. Chryssides, *A to Z of Jehovah's Witnesses*, xvi–xviii.

in 1931: the *Jehovah's Witnesses*. This change coincided with an increasing emphasis on using the name *Jehovah* to refer to God. In fact, in 1934 Rutherford wrote an entire book on the topic, titled *Jehovah*, in which he explained that "Jehovah will cause all of his creatures to know his name and its meaning."[16]

Fig. 6.2.
Jehovah's Witnesses are expected to do door-to-door evangelism on a regular basis.

Nathan Knorr (1905–77)

Nathan Knorr succeeded Joseph Rutherford at the latter's death in 1942. Knorr had been a faithful servant of the organization, working his way up to the top of the vocational ladder since joining it in 1923. Recognizing the need for better educational standards, Knorr established an institution called the Gilead School that trained Jehovah's Witnesses in biblical interpretation, doctrinal matters, and missionary strategies. And like those of his predecessors, Knorr's publications were circulated around the world under the arm of the organization's inexhaustible publishing house. These publications coincided with the continual development of the movement outside the United States. But Knorr instituted a novel practice that characterizes the Society to this day: author anonymity. Unlike Russell and Rutherford, who were prolific writers, Knorr was not, and it has been argued that Knorr "wanted to hide his own inadequacy [as a writer] by having practically all Watchtower literature published anonymously."[17] This practice exists to this day.

16. Joseph Franklin Rutherford, *Jehovah* (Brooklyn, NY: Watchtower Bible and Tract Society, 1934), 29.
17. Penton, *Apocalypse Delayed*, 106.

But perhaps the most significant accomplishment under Knorr's leadership was the translation and publication in 1961 of the New World Translation, which has become the official biblical translation of the Jehovah's Witnesses. Like other documents published by the Society, this work did not include the names of its translators, and non–Jehovah's Witness Bible scholars have routinely questioned the integrity of the New World Translation. Although panned by its critics for being biased and tendentious, the translation continues to be used by the members of the Jehovah's Witnesses. Unfortunately, this translation has been overshadowed by one of the most disastrous years in the history of the Witnesses that fell under the tenure of Knorr: the failed prediction of the end of the world in 1975. The organization experienced a crisis, losing perhaps 20 percent of members, indicating that change was needed.[18]

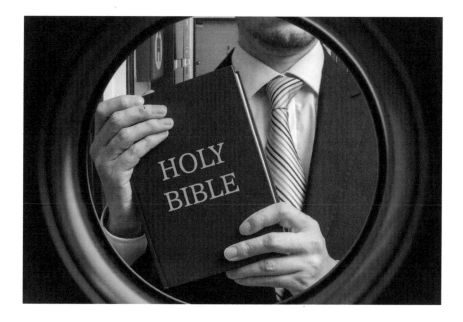

Fig. 6.3. Jehovah's Witnesses use the Bible alone for their scripture, but only their translation: the New World Translation (NWT).

Watchtower Society Today

The Jehovah's Witnesses have gradually moved away from being a one-man religious operation that publicizes its leader's meticulous biblical meanderings into pamphlets and magazines toward becoming a highly structured, centralized, and hierarchical organization led by a group of male leaders called the Governing Body who discern God's voice and then proclaim it to their followers anonymously. This proclamation is very efficiently heralded by means of the Society's massive printing empire.

18. Penton, 130.

The literature distributed permeates every aspect of Jehovah's Witnesses' lives: what they are to believe, how they are to act, and how they should interact with outsiders. Significantly, there are no independent Jehovah's Witnesses theologians or scholars. Unlike mainstream Christianity, in which individuals are free to research and publish across virtually all disciplines, including religion, the Governing Body alone determines and publishes doctrines and practices. In fact, as the leaders advise their members, "Avoid independent thinking . . . [which would lead to] questioning the counsel that is provided by God's visible organization."[19]

This countercultural mindset characterizes the Society to this day. Ironically, in fact, although the Jehovah's Witnesses believe themselves to be the sole vehicle of truth that offers salvation to the world, the world that they so desperately seek to save often perceives them more for what they are against than for what they are for. As scholar Jerry Bergman explains, they have amassed a very long list of separatist practices, which prohibit "saluting the flag, becoming part of the armed forces, voting, running for office, any patriotic display, involvement in the sale or manufacture of weaponry, using tobacco, accepting blood transfusions, using most blood products, using pornography, celebration of birthdays, Christmas and all other holidays, [and] membership in organizations [ranging from civic groups to sports]."[20]

Part 3: Religious Writings

The religious writings of the Jehovah's Witnesses consist of two major kinds: (1) the Bible and (2) literature published by the Society.

First, Jehovah's Witnesses maintain that the Bible alone is the Word of God and the only infallible revelation to humankind. In their words, it is not only "scientifically accurate," but also "historically accurate."[21] Like mainstream Protestantism, Witnesses affirm sixty-six books in the Bible and reject the Apocrypha as nonscriptural. Unlike traditional Christianity, however, the Jehovah's Witnesses believe that much of the Bible has been corrupted and mistranslated. This is the reason for the publication of the New World Translation, completed in both the Old and New Testaments in 1961. This is the official translation of the Society, and all other biblical translations must be filtered through this one. Ironically, however, for a translation claiming to have corrected the errors of all others in history,

19. *Watchtower*, January 15, 1983, 22.

20. Bergman, "Adventist and Jehovah's Witness Branch of Protestantism," 37.

21. *What Does the Bible Really Teach?* (Brooklyn, NY: Watchtower Bible and Tract Society, 2005), 20–21.

its only translator with any knowledge of the biblical languages had a few semesters of college Greek and no formal training in Hebrew.[22]

There are several distinctives of the New World Translation. To begin with, as would be expected from an organization called the Jehovah's Witnesses, the name for God has been changed to *Jehovah* in more than seven thousand instances in the Bible. And although biblical scholars have long since proved that the correct transliteration of the name of the God of the Hebrew Bible is closer to *Yahweh* (YHWH) than *Jehovah* (JHVH), Jehovah's Witnesses have ignored this and persist in calling their God by that name. Next, most of the biblical verses implying or downright declaring the divinity of Christ have been retranslated. Below are some of the most prominent examples. These are offered alongside the English Standard Version, which is representative of mainstream Christian Bible translations.

Translation of Prominent Verses Compared (Bold Added for Emphasis)[23]

English Standard Version (Mainstream Christian)	New World Translation (Jehovah's Witnesses)
"In the beginning was the Word, and the Word was with God" (John 1:1).	"The Word was in the beginning with God and **was a god**" (John 1:1).
"For by him all things were created, in heaven and on earth . . .—all things were created through him. . . . And he is before all things" (Col. 1:16–17).	"By means of him all **other** things were created in the heavens and on the earth. . . . All **other** things have been created through him. . . . Also, he is before all **other** things" (Col. 1:16–17).
"For in him the whole fullness of deity dwells bodily" (Col. 2:9).	"Because it is in him that all the fullness of the **divine quality** dwells bodily" (Col. 2:9).
"Waiting for our blessed hope, the appearing of the glory of our great God and Savior Jesus Christ" (Titus 2:13).	"While we wait for the happy hope and glorious manifestation of the great God **and of** our Savior, Jesus Christ" (Titus 2:13).
"To those who have obtained a faith of equal standing with ours by the righteousness of our God and Savior Jesus Christ" (2 Peter 1:1).	"To those who have acquired a faith as precious as ours through the righteousness of our God **and [of]** the Savior Jesus Christ" (2 Peter 1:1).

Second, in addition to the Bible, the Jehovah's Witnesses rely heavily on official literature that comes directly from headquarters. In fact,

22. Raymond Franz, *A Crisis of Conscience: The Struggle between Loyalty to God and Loyalty to One's Religion* (Atlanta: Commentary Press, 1983), 50n15.

23. Bruce M. Metzger, "The Jehovah's Witnesses and Jesus Christ: A Biblical and Theological Appraisal," *Theology Today* 10, no. 1 (1953): 65–85.

literature published by the Society plays a far greater role in the life of a Jehovah's Witness than acknowledged. Officially, the organization asserts that the Bible alone determines all doctrine and practice. Practically, however, I have never attended a service with, studied with, or been evangelized by a Witness who did not always possess and repeatedly consult literature published by the organization. My experience perfectly echoes what Andrew Holden writes: "Despite the Witnesses' claim that the Bible is their only source of authority, they make constant use of a huge welter of both hard and paperback publications, tracts, [digital apps], and *The Watchtower* and *Awake!* magazines. . . . [They] are almost as significant to the Witnesses as the Bible."[24] Relative to other Christian traditions, this is not an unusual practice. Virtually all Christian traditions that derive ultimate authority from the inspired Bible also appeal to human-written theologians, ecclesial policies, and faith-forming documents. The difference is, however, that the Jehovah's Witnesses emerged as a movement based entirely on the conviction that all previous religious traditions were wrong because they did not use and interpret the Bible alone for all doctrine and practice. For instance, as Charles Taze Russell stated in the preface to his first significant work: "It will be noticed that its references are to Scripture only. . . . The testimony of modern theologians has been given no weight, and that of the so-called Early Fathers has been omitted."[25]

Part 4: Beliefs

Although the Jehovah's Witnesses share commonalities with other new religious movements in many ways (some of which I discussed above), they are also characterized by several distinctives. In this section, I will focus on what distinguishes them from other groups, particularly from mainstream Christianity.

The Godhead: There Is No Trinity

The Jehovah's Witnesses have always rejected the classic Christian belief of the Trinity in which God the Father, God the Son, and God the Holy Spirit are one God in three persons. Instead, the Witnesses teach that there is only one God, and that this God is named Jehovah. According to Witnesses, Jehovah does not have any equal members. As they explain, "Jehovah God has no beginning or end."[26] Next, Jesus, also named Christ,

---

24. Holden, *Jehovah's Witnesses*, 67.
25. Russell, *Plan of the Ages*, A12.
26. *What Does the Bible Really Teach?*, 218.

was originally a spirit being named Michael. As the Society teaches, "the Bible indicates that Michael is another name for Jesus Christ, before and after his life on earth."[27] Jesus, that is, Michael, was Jehovah's first creation. But he is not divine—at least not in the same sense that Jehovah is. In fact, Jesus "never even considered trying to be equal to his Father. The Bible clearly teaches that the Father is greater than the Son (John 14:28; 1 Corinthians 11:3)."[28] When Jesus was raised after dying on a "torture stake" (not a cross), only his spirit was resurrected—not his humanity. In this way, Witnesses believe that "Jesus resumed the name Michael on his return to heaven in 1914, establishing the connection with his prehuman existence."[29] In short, in his preexistent and heavenly state, Jesus is Michael; but when incarnated on earth, he is Jesus. Finally, according to Witnesses, the Holy Spirit is not divine but simply Jehovah's "active force or agenda. It is not a person." Consequently, it is always spelled in lowercase and without the article—hence "holy spirit" rather than "the Holy Spirit."[30]

Apocalypse Now: The End Is Nigh

Another belief that has been taught by the Jehovah's Witnesses since their inception is that we are living in the last days. In fact, they argue, the end of the present world could happen today. This obsession with the end times has resulted in Jehovah's Witnesses' proposing a flurry of end-time dates, none of which has materialized. Historian M. James Penton goes so far as to describe this as one of the Witnesses' most "peculiar" features, arguing that there is no way that the movement would have grown to become a worldwide religion had it not consistently asserted the end of the world. As Penton states, "No major Christian sectarian movement has been so insistent on prophesying the end of the present world in such definite ways or on such specific dates as have Jehovah's Witnesses."[31] For example, "The years of 1874, 1914, 1918, 1925, and 1975 were all earmarked, to a greater or lesser extent, as times for the Second Coming of Christ, yet all brought bitter disappointment."[32]

End-Time-Date Misses of the Jehovah's Witnesses

The Jehovah's Witnesses have predicted each of the following dates as the end of the world, the end of the ages, the return of Christ, or some

27. *What Does the Bible Really Teach?*, 218.
28. *What Does the Bible Really Teach?*, 41–42.
29. Chryssides, *A to Z of Jehovah's Witnesses*, 92.
30. Chryssides, 73.
31. Penton, *Apocalypse Delayed*, 3.
32. Holden, *Jehovah's Witnesses*, 1.

new epoch, age, jubilee, or harvest. Each time the date comes and goes, though, they revisit and reinterpret it.

- 1874
- 1878
- 1881
- 1910
- 1914
- 1918
- 1920
- 1925
- 1975[33]

Four Classes of Afterlife: Heaven, Paradise, Annihilation

One of the distinct beliefs of the Jehovah's Witnesses going back to the time of Russell is their rejection of predestination, the immortality of the soul, and hell (that is, everlasting torment). For Jehovah's Witnesses, free agency is essential and not to be superseded. Everyone has the ability to decide for himself or herself whether to accept the clear teachings of scripture about who Jehovah is and what Jehovah expects. Unfortunately, the Jehovah's Witnesses have revised their teachings on this matter so many times that the following is a summary of what appears to be the majority view today.[34] In short, Witnesses believe that there are three eternal destinations: (1) heaven, (2) paradise, and (3) annihilation. The first of these two are for Jehovah's Witnesses, while the last is for those who are not part of the Witness community.

Destination of Three Classes of Human Beings

Name	Description	Destination
Anointed Class (also called Elijah Class, Bride of Christ, Remnant, Heavenly Class, Little Flock, or Faithful and Discreet Slave)	Literal 144,000 individuals from all biblical eras who have already died physically but have been resurrected as spirit beings now reigning in heaven with Christ	Reigning in heaven; already resurrected in spirit bodies

33. Penton, *Apocalypse Delayed*, 4.
34. Penton, 98, 281.

Great Crowd (also called Great Multitude, Other Sheepers, Jonadabs, Elisha Class, or Earthly Class)	Virtually all Jehovah's Witnesses living today who will experience the equivalent of soul sleep upon death until the millennial reign of Christ in which they will be resurrected in bodies to live on Paradise-Earth	Paradise on earth; currently in Hades (in soul sleep) but will be resurrected in actual bodies and will live in Paradise-Earth
Nonbelievers (also called Pagans, Apostates, Worldly People, or Evildoers)	Individuals who have rejected Jehovah's message and lifestyle and who either will experience oblivion at death or will be in Hades (in soul sleep) where they will one day be resurrected to choose to either accept Jehovah and live on Paradise-Earth or reject him and be annihilated	First will go either into oblivion (cease to exist) or into temporary Hades

The first class consists of 144,000 literal individuals who will reign with Christ in heaven as spirit beings. They are saved by faith. The size of this class has only recently been "sealed," implying that only a handful from historic Christianity were included. In fact, there is no other logical way to get around this fact, since "the Society has resolutely rejected any suggestion that the number 144,000 is symbolic rather than literal."[35] This incredibly small number of the anointed class also indicates that virtually all Jehovah's Witnesses today are excluded and so can be part of only the second class of believers. This second class, called the Great Crowd, consists of present believers in Jehovah. They are saved by works.[36] Rather than their reigning with Christ in heaven as spirit beings, their reward is eternity on a restored earth in resurrected bodies. While they await this event, their souls are sleeping in an unconscious state often called Hades, which is not to be confused with hell (a concept that Witnesses reject). The third class is the most confusing. This group comprises the majority of the present and past world. If Armageddon happens when they are alive, they will be destroyed. If they die before Armageddon, however, they will cease to exist upon death if wholly evil or, if not wholly evil, will be temporarily stationed in Hades until the final resurrection. If resurrected, they will be able to choose to either follow Jehovah (and so be allowed to live on Paradise-Earth) or reject Jehovah (in which case they will be annihilated). It should be noted that all who were disfellowshipped,

---

35. Chryssides, *Jehovah's Witnesses*, 270.
36. Penton, *Apocalypse Delayed*, 274–75.

that is, officially excommunicated from the Jehovah's Witnesses, will not enjoy any rewards in the afterlife.

Pagan Christianity: Apostate Christendom

Jehovah's Witnesses believe that Christianity is Pagan and that their organization "is the sole means of salvation."[37] They maintain that virtually all Christian practices, rituals, and beliefs derive from Paganism. For instance, the cross is regarded as a Pagan symbol, and Jesus was not put to death on one. Instead, all the references to the "cross" (σταυρός) in the New Testament have been changed to either "stake" or "torture stake" in their Bibles and literature. For example, the New World Translation writes that Simon Cyrene was compelled to carry Jesus' "torture stake" (Matt. 27:32). In Witness literature, Jesus is never depicted as dying on a cross; instead, he is always portrayed as dying on a stake. Consequently, there are no crosses or crucifixes anywhere in kingdom halls. Next, Witnesses believe that all creeds are human-made and corrupt. They offer no insight as to what the Bible actually teaches. Finally, as mentioned above, Witnesses consider all Christian celebrations, such as Christmas and Easter, to be Pagan in orientation. In short, Witnesses do not honor or participate in any days from the Christian calendar—let alone personal birthdays, national holidays, or civic obligations.

Part 5: Worship Practices

The Jehovah's Witnesses follow practices that appear like mainstream Christianity. What is distinct, however, is the specific beliefs associated with them. To begin with, Jehovah's Witnesses spend more time trying to convert people to their religion than actually worshiping their God. As historian Zoe Knox explains, their "time and energy is largely directed towards proselytism rather than revering Jehovah."[38] In a similar way, Witnesses emphasize study. In fact, according to sociologist of religion Holden, the term *study* better describes what Jehovah's Witnesses do than *worship*. As he explains in detail:

> Since becoming a respectable Witness involves reading large amounts of textual information in preparation for a never-ending series of

---

37. Chryssides, *Jehovah's Witnesses*, 12.
38. Zoe Knox, *Jehovah's Witnesses and the Secular World: From the 1870s to the Present* (London: Palgrave Macmillan, 2018), 108.

meetings, studying is a more appropriate term for describing their weekly activities than *worship*. Glossolalia [speaking in ecstatic language], creed recitation, even periods of silent meditation are so far removed from the Witnesses' activities that someone claiming to have had an experience of a transcendental nature would be most unlikely to find solace in a Kingdom Hall. At no point in meetings is time made available for individual prayer. Unlike charismatic movements, spontaneous prayers and prayers by invitation are absent. . . . In a modern age in which social movements articulate expressive identities, the Witnesses stand out as staid and conservative.[39]

This confirms my decades-long experiences visiting kingdom halls, talking with Witnesses who were coworkers, and observing the way in which they have attempted to convert me in door-to-door evangelism. Kingdom halls more closely resemble schools than sanctuaries. Although there are certain rituals you take to become a member of the organization, the first and most important step is studying the Bible with an experienced Witness, who will explain key passages and doctrines, which must be accepted and cannot be questioned. As it was once explained to me when I visited a kingdom hall, believing in Jehovah parallels the story of Philip and the Ethiopian eunuch in Acts 8 in which Philip read the Scripture to the eunuch, the eunuch accepted the teaching, and then he was baptized. "Three things," he said: "we study the scriptures, we believe in the scriptures, we get baptized based on the scriptures."

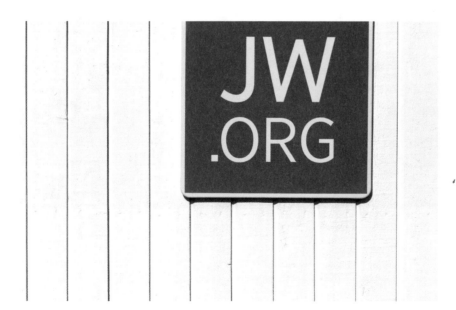

Fig. 6.4. Jehovah's Witnesses maintain an up-to-date and user-friendly website at JW.org.

39. Holden, *Jehovah's Witnesses*, 64.

Kingdom Halls

Let us start with the basics. Jehovah's Witnesses assemble in congregations called *kingdom halls* that are led by voluntary male leaders called *elders* as well as larger gatherings called *assembly halls* supervised by voluntary male leaders called *circuit overseers*. You are required to attend the kingdom hall closest to you. You do not get to choose.[40] Kingdom halls epitomize ecclesial austerity. They are devoid of crosses, bereft of artwork, and empty of ostentation. There are no collared priests, no stained-glass windows, and no burning candles. Every hall I have visited was made of either brick or aluminum, and their unadorned exterior reflects their unembellished interior. Inside, however, the members are generally warm and friendly, though they can be reserved if you arrive unannounced. They also tend to dress modestly and professionally. What is more, it becomes evident very soon that the halls are led by males only. Historically, only males publicly read scripture, teach, and pray.

Fig. 6.5. Places of worship of the Jehovah's Witnesses are called *kingdom halls*.

Although there are services throughout the week that members are expected to attend, the primary service is on Sunday morning and lasts a couple of hours. The Witnesses do not do things spontaneously, and every part of the service comes directly from the Jehovah's Witness

40. Chryssides, *Jehovah's Witnesses*, 206.

digital app that everyone uses, which is easy to navigate. Witnesses like to say that no matter where you are in the world, the same service is happening at the same time. Everything is on the app: the service, the Bible verse and translation, the suggested length, the teaching, and the questions. It is all thoroughly centralized. Services contain parts not too different from mainstream Christianity. For example, although using distinct terminology (for instance, "Treasures from God's Word" or "Apply Yourself to the Field Ministry"), the service consists of Bible readings and teachings, songs, a time for questions, an offering, short videos or presentations, and a charge to continue evangelizing. Although both water baptism and the Lord's Supper—called a *memorial*—are practiced, they are not regarded as sacraments or salvific. Instead, water baptism is understood to be a requirement to be a committed disciple of Jehovah (meaning that a public profession must be made), and it is usually done in larger assembly halls during certain times of the year. Similarly, the memorial is offered only once a year during Passover (Nisan 14). It consists of unleavened bread and wine, but it is reserved only for the 144,000 anointed class, meaning that "it is common for everyone in the congregation simply to pass the emblems along the row, and for no one at all to partake."[41]

Evangelism and Publishing or Pioneering

One of the most enduring practices of the Jehovah's Witnesses is door-to-door evangelism. Witnesses receive rigorous training to be able to perform this duty in a way that is consistent, calculated, and competent. Having been evangelized multiple times by those performing this house-to-house service, I know exactly what to expect when they come knocking at my door. In short, they never travel alone, they are well dressed and courteous, they distribute their organization's literature (through a *Watchtower* or *Awake!* pamphlet or magazine), and their ultimate goal is to persuade me to let them lead a Bible study with me with the hopes that I will eventually visit their local kingdom hall, get baptized, and become one of them.

Door-to-door evangelism is not the only way that Witnesses proselytize, however. As I have witnessed in cities across Europe, Asia, Latin America, Africa, and everywhere in between, Witnesses engage in what they call *street work*. This involves setting up a makeshift display containing the Society's literature in a prominent place within a city and hoping that someone will stop, select a pamphlet, and show interest.

41. Chryssides, 220.

When I see Witnesses doing street work, I usually stop and say hello, and I sometimes ask questions. They are always friendly, but their goal in this context is not to argue but to arrange a time when they can study with you in a more private setting.

Although their approach may come across as unplanned, sincere, and altruistic, members in the organization are required to do evangelism. Different terms are used internally to refer to how devoted one is. The most basic level is called a *publisher*. All baptized members of the Jehovah's Witnesses are expected to distribute ("publish") the Society's literature for the purpose of conversion. This has been an expectation since 1919. Those who want to advance beyond a publisher can become a *pioneer*. There are actually several sublevels of pioneer: (1) auxiliar, (2) regular, and (3) special. Historically, each level required a certain number of hours, or a quota, spent pioneering. But this is not always the case nowadays. Suffice it to say, though, that each level illustrates a deeper commitment or devotion. Naturally, the more committed one is, the less time there is for other full-time work, and the more time is dedicated to publishing. In fact, both publishers and pioneers are required to keep records of their evangelistic efforts and report them to the elders in their kingdom hall.[42] The Society takes this data very seriously. And those who do not put in sufficient hours of evangelism cannot advance to leadership positions.

Part 6: Point of Contact

I have known Jehovah's Witnesses my whole life. I can still remember wondering why certain kids in my elementary classes exited the room when we said the Pledge of Allegiance, why they considered all holidays "Pagan," and why they were never allowed to play sports with me after school. Being a curious person, I started asking them what they believed and why they were different. "We're Jehovah's Witnesses," they said, as if I knew what that meant. Over time, I came to befriend some of them—only at school, of course—and I came to understand that all their beliefs and practices were based on what they were taught from the Bible. The only problem, of course, was that I also read the Bible and attended church, yet I had never learned what they were taught. Over the years, we had endless conversations at the lunch table, where we would hurl Bible verses at each other as we ate our peanut-butter sandwiches. I would occasionally accept an invitation to attend one of their kingdom

---

42. Chryssides, *A to Z of Jehovah's Witnesses*, 109, 114.

hall meetings, but I found them forced and unattractive, and besides, these friends never accepted my invitations to attend my church.

Eventually, however, I moved away from an antagonistic approach in which I simply shouted my Bible verses louder than they shouted theirs. I realized that I was operating exclusively on their terms, and that the interpretation and presentation of isolated Bible verses that favored their religious system had been drilled into them for years. The Bible was all they knew. And yet, ironically, as I progressed into being a professor who taught biblical languages and world religions, none of the Jehovah's Witnesses I talked to—including their leaders— could ever engage any conversation about actual issues relating to the translation of the Bible, the history of the interpretation of the Bible, or the history of Christianity. I thought it sad that people who had given their lives to the Bible knew so little about it, and I felt compassion for them. I decided to stop trying to demolish their beliefs from the book they so admired.

For the last few years, for example, I have moved away from argumentation from the Bible and instead engaged them on topics that were closer to home: their own literature that has consistently yet erroneously predicted the end of the world. It is truly fascinating to read the revolving door of revisions made by the Jehovah's Witnesses about any number of theological matters. The revisionist history of the Jehovah's Witnesses is notorious, and comparing one edition of something to another illustrates just how frequently the Society changes its mind.[43] For instance, upon recently rereading Charles Taze Russell's six-volume *Studies in the Scriptures*, in which he rewrote all the prefaces in 1916 to conform to his ever-evolving teachings, I was dumbfounded at how often and unashamedly he admitted to making mistakes in his previous editions. For a man who so confidently declared that all creeds, churches, and theologians before him were wrong, you would think that he would not fall into the same error. And yet he readily admitted to doing so.

For example, below I have collected passages that Russell himself wrote in his revised prefaces to each of the six volumes of his magnum opus that show how wrong he was about the Bible. For instance, in volume 1, *The Divine Plan of the Ages*, he wrote, "After seeing the Truth, the errors [of this previous edition] are more and more seen to be absurd, worthless, injurious, and are gladly abandoned." Then, in volume 2, *The Time Is at Hand*: "Dealing with subjects so difficult that they are rarely touched by others, it is not to be considered strange if some of the suggestions made in this Volume have not been fulfilled with

---

43. Chryssides, *Jehovah's Witnesses*, 4.

absolute accuracy." Also, there is volume 3, *Thy Kingdom Come*: "The work of Harvest has progressed and is still progressing—even though at one time we supposed that the Harvest work would have been fully accomplished with the ending of the Times of the Gentiles. That was merely a supposition, which proved to be without warrant." Next, in volume 4, *The Battle of Armageddon*, he conceded, "None need be surprised to find that some of its statements, although startlingly strong, come short now of the full Truth." Then, in volume 5, *The Atonement between God and Man*: "The differences are not of a kind that will permit us to say that the expressions in the book are wrong—merely they are not as full and clear as they might have been if the writing were to be done now." Finally, in volume 6, *The New Creation*, Russell stated: "We call attention to the fact that since this Volume was written the light has grown still clearer. . . . If writing this Volume today, the author would make some slight variations."[44]

This sampling illustrates a serial weakness to the entire enterprise of the Jehovah's Witnesses. Why would people subject their eternity—and that of their family members—to an organization that so whimsically changes its mind, that does not apologize, and that does not even recognize how destructive this is? As Russell wrote in reference to his own errors of interpretation, "We are not able to see behind the veil; we are not able to know the things progressing under the direction of our glorious Lord."[45] This system of the Jehovah's Witnesses has made its members enslaved to whatever new doctrine it will promulgate in the future. This twisted logic makes God subject to the whims of human innovation, and the gospel becomes an ever-changing yet never-attainable illusion. The God of the Bible, however, is the same yesterday, today, and forever. We can rest assured that God's revelation to the world is not held captive by a few men in private meetings who change their minds as often as they change their socks.

Discussion Questions

1. How would you summarize the primary teachings and practices of the Jehovah's Witnesses? How are they different from mainstream Christianity?

2. How does the early history of the Jehovah's Witnesses compare to the history of other new religious movements at the time discussed in this book, for example, Mormonism and the Nation of Islam?

44. Russell, *Studies in the Scriptures*, 1:ii, 2:ii, 3:i, 4:3, 5:v, and 6:i, iii, respectively.
45. Russell, 2:iii.

3. What are the similarities and differences between the earliest leaders of this movement, for instance, Charles Taze Russell, Joseph Rutherford, and Nathan Knorr?

4. How would you respond to Jehovah's Witnesses who came to your house and told you that the Bible does not teach the Trinity? Would you reason with them from the Scriptures, refrain from engaging them, or go in a different direction?

5. What would you say is the greatest appeal of the Jehovah's Witnesses to those who convert? What do you think would attract a person to the Witnesses over, say, a more mainstream Christian church?

For Further Reading

Beckford, James A. *The Trumpet of Prophecy: A Sociological Study of Jehovah's Witnesses.* Oxford: Basil Blackwell, 1975.

Chryssides, George D. *Jehovah's Witnesses: Continuity and Change.* London: Routledge, 2016.

Holden, Andrew. *Jehovah's Witnesses: Portrait of a Contemporary Religious Movement.* London: Routledge, 2002.

Knox, Zoe. *Jehovah's Witnesses and the Secular World: From the 1870s to the Present.* London: Palgrave Macmillan, 2018.

Penton, M. James. *Apocalypse Delayed: The Story of Jehovah's Witnesses.* 3rd ed. Toronto: University of Toronto, 2015.

PART 4

Pagan New Religious Movements

In this section, we discuss the two most influential new religious movements emerging out of Paganism. This term—*Paganism*—means different things to different people, and a growing body of scholarship focuses on religions relating to it. In a word, *Paganism* is an elusive and catchall term for a variety of new religious movements that do not precisely correspond to classical religions such as Buddhism, Christianity, and Islam. Within this larger category of Paganism are many new religious movements such as Heathenism and Druidism. Arguably the two most influential, however, are Wicca and Scientology. As you read the two chapters discussing them below, it is important to keep in mind that they embody all the hallmarks of religion even though they may seem to function differently. And although both Wicca and Scientology emerged at the same time, they are very different from each other.

chapter 7

Wicca: The Story of Witches

I made the discovery that the witch cult, that people thought to have been persecuted out of existence, still lived. . . . I discovered the inner meaning of that saying in one of Fiona MacLeod's books: "the Old Gods are not dead. They think we are."

Gerald Gardner[1]

The past century has born[e] witness to a growing interest in the belief systems of ancient Europe, with an array of contemporary Pagan groups claiming to revive these old ways for the needs of the modern world. By far the largest and best known of these Paganisms has been Wicca, a new religious movement that can now count hundreds of thousands of adherents worldwide.

Ethan White[2]

There is not, and can never be, one "pure" or "true" or "genuine" form of Wicca. There are no central governing agencies, no physical leaders, no universally recognized prophets or messengers. Although specific, structured forms of Wicca certainly exist, they aren't in agreement regarding ritual, symbolism, and theology.

Scott Cunningham[3]

1. Gerald Gardner, *The Meaning of Witchcraft* (New York: Magickal Childe, 1959; repr., 2004), 11.
2. Ethan Doyle White, *Wicca: History, Belief, and Community in Modern Pagan Witchcraft* (Eastbourne, UK: Sussex Academic Press, 2015), i.
3. Scott Cunningham, *Wicca: A Guide for the Solitary Practitioner* (St. Paul, MN: Llewellyn, 1988), 12.

Part 1: The Beginning

World War II was just days underway, and he was already getting antsy. Restless by nature, this Englishman had recently returned from years of living overseas in the Far East. He was retired now, but certainly not sedentary. Although he did not miss his post as a civil servant working for the King of England, he did miss the excitement of exploring new lands, interviewing the fascinating people he met, and absorbing as many new ideas from them as possible. He was also interested in writing about some of the things he had learned and experienced in his travels. And over time, he would write about them. Eventually the man found his stride among a few intriguing souls who were part of an eccentric theater company with connections to a centuries-old secret society. This was right up his alley. Although many people were associated with the theater company, a group of women began focusing their attention on the Englishman, claiming that they knew him from a previous life. As they confidently asserted: "You belonged to us in the past. You are of the blood. Come back to where you belong." He found this titillating and eagerly accepted a private invitation to the mansion where one of the women lived.

Upon entering, they cast a circle of fire and ordered him to disrobe. Being a long-term nudist and ever-accommodating risk-taker, he removed his clothes, entered the circle, took a binding oath, and performed a secret ritual that he never divulged. "I realized," he later confessed, "that I had stumbled on something interesting; but I was [only] half-initiated before the word 'Wicca,' which they used, hit me like a thunderbolt." Things were getting clearer, and a second thunderbolt later, he began to understand the significance of the moment. At long last, the historic and presumed-dead religion of Witchcraft was alive and well. Witchcraft existed—and he was now an official Witch! It was September of 1939, and this experience would soon lead to the creation and growth of one of the fastest-growing religions in the world. The religion of Wicca, the historic craft of Witches, was being resurrected, and the Witchfather himself, Gerald Gardner, was the one resurrecting it.[4]

Road Map to Wicca Creation Story. Although witches have been around for thousands of years, the Wiccan religion is recent. It involves Gerald Gardner, a very curious British man who lived in the twentieth century. Importantly, law codes against the practice of witchcraft existed for millennia in Western countries such as England until the first half of the 1900s.

---

4. This account is based on the personal anecdotes of Gerald Gardner from his own works, for instance, *Meaning of Witchcraft*, 11. The term *Witchfather* stems from the most definitive biography of Gerald Gardner, which appears in two volumes under that name: Philip Heselton, *Witchfather: A Life of Gerald Gardner*, vol. 1, *Into the Witch Cult* (Loughborough, Leicestershire, UK: Thoth, 2012), and vol. 2, *From Witch to Cult to Wicca* (Loughborough, Leicestershire, UK: Thoth, 2012).

Part 2: Historical Origin

Combining magical rituals with prehistoric beliefs and fusing ancient traditions with modern sensibilities, Wicca is perhaps the world's most famous Pagan religion. It originated in the West in the first half of the twentieth century, where it spread globally through books, Hollywood, the internet, and countercultural movements ranging from disillusioned Christians to curious college students to social progressives. Although often portrayed by outsiders as dark, devilish, and demonic, insiders praise it for its inclusion, freedom, and equality. In fact, it has found success among those with whom the Christian church has been unsuccessful, namely, members of the LGBTQ+ community, women who have been burned by patriarchy, and those deeply concerned about the environment. Gaining momentum while historic religions subside, Wicca engages many matters important to contemporary people.

Wicca

Wicca is a modern religion based on ancient ritual. Although the religion attempts to re-create antique practices that existed before Christianity, scarce resources are available from which to make conjectures, accounts in the historical record conflict on how Pagans practiced their beliefs, and much of the available material was written by Christians who rejected the Craft and so had little incentive to cast it in the best light. Consequently, James Baker was not wide of the mark when he wrote that "Wicca is not the survival of an ancient tradition, but rather the modern syncretization of a number of old and new elements that never co-existed, much less were united, before."[5] In a word, Wicca is as old as the fortune cookie. Despite its air of antiquity and ubiquity in every Chinese restaurant from Albuquerque to Tokyo, it was invented in the second decade of the twentieth century. Pulled from a grab bag of rituals, practices, beliefs, and accoutrements that never really existed at the same time or in the same place, Wicca was reassembled to manufacture a religion.[6]

At the same time, plenty of authors, scholars, and especially practitioners claim that Wicca is centuries old. As Silver Starhawk, a prominent Witch, writes: "Witchcraft is a religion, perhaps the oldest religion extant

Understanding the Terms. A variety of overlapping terms are used in reference to Wicca. Although some authors and practitioners try to keep them distinguished, others use the following interchangeably: *Wicca, Witchcraft, Pagan Witchcraft, the Craft, Wiccan Religion,* and sometimes *Neopaganism.*

The Name Game of Religious Spaces. While Christians assemble in *churches,* Jews in *synagogues,* and Muslims in *mosques,* Wiccans gather in *covens,* Druids in *groves,* and Heathens in *hearths.* Within Wicca, when members of covens are actively planting a new community, they are called *hives.*

---

5. James W. Baker, "White Witches: Historic Fact and Romantic Fantasy," in *Magical Religion and Modern Witchcraft,* ed. James R. Lewis (Albany: State University of New York Press, 1996), 178.

6. Hugh B. Urban, *New Age, Pagan, and New Religious Movements: Alternative Spirituality in Contemporary America* (Berkeley: University of California Press, 2015), 165.

in the West. Its origins go back before Christianity, Judaism, Islam—before Buddhism and Hinduism."[7] In many ways, the source of disagreement about the antiquity of the religion hinges on whether you believe that Wicca was equivalent to Witchcraft or whether it was invented by Gerald Gardner. In short, lacking sufficient historical data, I think it better to frame Wicca as a modern religion that draws from ancient rituals. In the end, nothing stands or falls on antiquity. For instance, I am a committed Christian even though I know full well that most of the world's religions predate mine. In this way, I agree with Wiccan author Scott Cunningham that being ancient "isn't necessarily more powerful or effective" than being new.[8]

Gerald Gardner (1884–1964)

The religion of Wicca was built from either the shocking revelations or the inventive machinations of Gerald Gardner. Heralded as "the father of Wicca," Gardner was a British national who traveled widely both as a child and while stationed overseas as an adult. Throughout his life, he nurtured an abiding interest in the paranormal and also became a member of the Freemasons. Fascinated by the exotic cultures of the East where he lived for so long, he studied local customs, oversaw archaeological digs, and collected artifacts. This is also the setting in which he first began entertaining and adopting belief in reincarnation. Upon retirement in 1936, Gardner returned to England and settled close to the coast. There he hobnobbed with an eccentric theater company that claimed to be a successor to the Rosicrucians, an esoteric and secretive order with ancient roots that lurked in the shadows of Christianity. Although Gardner did not subscribe to all the tenets held, he did meet several people connected to the company who intrigued him. His friendship with these like-minded individuals was rewarded in 1939 with an invitation to a private ritual, during which time it was revealed that they were part of a coven, a clandestine community of Witches. Stripping naked as was required, he lay in the middle of a Witch circle and underwent a secret initiation through which he was ingrafted into the coven.

Though no one knew it at the time, Gardner's initiation into this coven of Witches in 1939 would be the defining moment of the movement. Gardner would go on to publicize his experience and propagate

What is Paganism? The word *pagan* is a catchall term ranging from someone who does not subscribe to someone else's religion to someone who actively worships the devil. Historically, however, in the Roman world, "a *pagus* was a country district, a *paganus* someone who lived there." Over time, *paganus* meant "civilian," a person in contrast to a Roman soldier.

James O'Donnell, *Pagans: The End of Traditional Religion and the Rise of Christianity* (New York: HarperCollins, 2015), 160.

---

7. Silver Starhawk, *The Spiral Dance: A Rebirth of the Ancient Religion of the Goddess: 20th Anniversary Edition* (New York: HarperCollins, 1999), 27.

8. Cunningham, *Wicca*, 12.

his faith in the form of several bestselling books, including *High Magic's Aid* (1949), *Witchcraft Today* (1954), and *The Meaning of Witchcraft* (1959). These books forever marked the religion, and the repealing of England's final laws against Witchcraft in 1951 allowed him to attract a revolving door of seekers who joined the coven he presided over as High Priest. Simply put, no Gardner, no Wicca. But how exactly should we understand this man's revelations? "Did Gerald Gardner discover, reconstruct, create, or merely popularize Witchcraft?"[9] That is the right question. But unfortunately, there is no objective answer. Gardner was as curious as a cat and had the spiritual appetite of a horse. In addition to serving as High Priest to his Wiccan coven, he joined other secret societies, was ordained a Christian priest, started a Witch museum, and actively participated in Druid ceremonies.[10] Opinions of Gerald Gardner have run the gamut, ranging from restorer of ancient truth to inventor of deception to sexual deviant to shameless promoter. Whatever his exact motivation, there is no denying that his writings have been incredibly influential in the development and practice of modern Witchcraft, especially Wicca.

Gardnerian Wicca

The most traditional denomination within Wicca is what is called *Gardnerian Wicca*. As its name implies, it is based on the teachings of Gerald Gardner. Surprisingly for a movement that is less than a century old, Gardnerian Wicca has come to dominate the religious landscape of Witchcraft. In fact, while Gardner was still alive and serving as High Priest in his coven, several coven-planting missions—called *hives*—were being founded in Australia, Canada, and the United States. As scholar Ethan White states, "Even in his lifetime, Gardnerianism had become a global phenomenon, with practitioners operating across the Anglophone West."[11] This growth and development, however, was not without conflict. Gardner had made many enemies and eventually moved to the Isle of Man to oversee his Witch museum. While on vacation in Tunisia in 1964, he died of a heart attack.

Almost every Wiccan tradition in existence owes its genesis to Gardnerian Wicca. In general, this tradition is based on the *Book of Shadows* that Gardner published. It is also quite distinct. First, Gardnerian Wicca is characterized by its emphasis on the Goddess over the God

Influences in the Development of Wicca. The modern religion of Wicca has drawn from many wells. To various amounts, this includes Paganism, folklore, the magical arts, the occult, Witchcraft, esotericism, naturalism, romanticism, secret societies, Eastern religions, and mystery cults.

---

9. Judy Harrow, foreword to *Witchcraft Today*, by Gerald Gardner, 50th anniversary ed. (New York: Citadel Press, 2004), 9.

10. See Philip Heselton, *Wiccan Roots: Gerald Gardner and the Modern Witchcraft Revival* (Milverton, UK: Capall Bann Publishing, 2001).

11. White, *Wicca*, 34.

and, consequently, on the High Priestess over the High Priest. Although it attracts a high percentage of female members, its rituals balance out male and female into pairs. Members of the community assemble in what are called *covens*. These covens are restricted to members only, in part because they are performed "skyclad," or completely nude.[12] Those interested in joining a Gardnerian community must go through extensive training in what is called the *outer court* (which I discuss below) for at least a "year and a day" before their initiation ceremony is considered. The initiatory ceremony is secret and not able to be disclosed to anyone outside the coven. But it involves being naked, joining a lighted circle, and taking vows to the Gods. There are advancement opportunities by degrees—just as in the Freemasons and many other secret organizations. These advancement opportunities also require "a year and a day" before rising to the next degree. Much of the Gardnerian tradition is focused on observing the seasons, performing spells, and joining a coven.

> **The New Age Movement?** Wicca and the New Age Movement are not the same. In general, Wiccans emphasize nature, rituals, and the past, whereas New Agers accentuate spirituality, the self, and the future. From an outside perspective, however, it is easy to highlight their shared beliefs in the afterlife, reincarnation, spiritual practices, and Pagan influences.

Alexandrian Wicca

Heated divisions among the Wiccan community erupted when Gerald Gardner was still alive, and several denominations formed in the decades that followed. Alexander Sanders (1926–88), another Brit intrinsically interested in the occult, founded the second-most-popular denomination within Wicca, referred to as *Alexandrian Wicca*. Similar to the reports of Gardner, there are conflicting accounts as to how and when Sanders became a Witch, but it appears that he was initiated into the Craft in 1962.[13] Before long he was a High Priest, nicknamed "the King of Witches," and overseeing an active coven that initiated hundreds of Witches. Alexandrian Wiccans share many similarities with Gardnerians. For instance, they follow similar protocols, use similar terms, and also practice the Craft skyclad.

Eclectic Wicca

Where there is religion, there is division. Wicca is no different. There are too many Wiccan denominations to list, but suffice it to say that what is called *Eclectic Wicca* is the largest. In a word, it is nondenominational Wicca in the sense that it freely and unashamedly draws from any source whatsoever. Others include—but are by no means limited to—American

12. Shelley TSivia Rabinovitch, "Spells of Transformation," in *Magical Religion and Modern Witchcraft*, ed. James R. Lewis (Albany: State University of New York Press, 1996), 79.
13. Jimahl diFiosa, *A Coin for the Ferryman: The Death and Life of Alex Sanders* (n.p.: Logios, 2010), 59.

Celtic, Church of the Crescent Moon, Circle, Coven of the Forest, Deboran Witchdom, Dianic, Far and Forever, Frost's, Georgian, Maidenhill, Northern Way, Nova-Wicca, Seax-Wicca, and Thessalonian.[14] As easily imagined, Eclectic Wicca enjoys fewer centralized beliefs and practices than those mentioned above. It can be practiced alone or with a group. If in a group, each community establishes its own beliefs and practices, but most assemble in robes (rather than in the nude).

Solitary Practice

Despite the importance of covens and community rituals, the majority of Wiccans practice Witchcraft alone.[15] In fact, even among those who are members of a coven, all of them are also involved in solitary practice. This makes a lot of sense. The most traditional Wiccans, after all, perform their rituals without clothes, over wine, at night, around fire, and with weapons (athames). This is hardly the place for the average person. What is more, Wicca is a hands-on religion. It is not a church that features one-sided Scripture readings, solitary sermons, and solo prayers. It is a community of practitioners in which everyone is expected to cast spells, conduct readings, and perform rites. Historically, and almost by necessity, all Wiccans embark on their spiritual journey as solitary practitioners. In my conversations with Wiccans over the years, virtually all of them have told me that they started with chat groups or specific sites on the internet. The conversations they had there eventually led them to a community of like-minded individuals, and from there, they were introduced to books, online Witch schools, private social media groups, and public festivals. In fact, because Wicca is such a new religion, most converts grew up in either another religious tradition (often Christianity) or none at all. They usually happened upon Wicca as a teenager or young adult, finding that it resonated with what they already believed. And even if they have children or are married, it is not assumed that either spouse or child will become Wiccan. Personal choice, completely free from coercion, is important to Wiccans. That said, the ritual of *wiccaning*, the equivalent of Christian christening, is practiced for Wiccans who present their children to the Craft.

---

14. Raymond Buckland, *Buckland's Complete Book of Witchcraft*, 2nd ed. (St. Paul, MN: Llewellyn, 2002), 309–14.

15. Helen A. Berger, *Solitary Pagans: Contemporary Witches, Wiccans, and Others Who Practice Alone* (Columbia: University of South Carolina Press, 2019), 36. Berger's meticulous research has unveiled that 60 percent of Wiccans identify as solo practitioners. Of this number, most are women.

Outer Court (or Outer Circle)

For those who start as solo practitioners and later join a coven, the process varies from denomination to denomination. In the most traditional denominations, such as Gardnerian Wicca, an interested person, called a *seeker*, must contact a coven and express interest. If approved for consideration, the seeker must undergo extensive training with the High Priest and/or High Priestess in a vetting experience called an *outer court*. This training involves reading books, practicing spells, meditating, and learning from their leader(s). This initiatory stage lasts "a year and a day"—whether literal or symbolical—before the seeker can be considered for initiation into the coven. The initiation ritual, conducted in the nude in the Gardnerian and Alexandrian denominations, is the equivalent of baptism in the Christian tradition (which, by the way, was also performed in the nude in the early church).[16] Once initiated into the coven, the seeker becomes a Priest or Priestess, and there are different degrees (traditionally, three) that can be attained. The person can also be promoted to High Priest or High Priestess. These positions, however, are not understood as hierarchical, and they are not paid positions as in the church.

Fig. 7.1. The High Priestess (HPS) is traditionally the most powerful leader in Wicca.

Wicca Today

The practice of Wicca today both parallels the wider culture and stands proudly against it. Although Wicca involves the widely

---

16. Derek Cooper, *Sinners and Saints: The Real Story of Early Christianity* (Grand Rapids: Kregel Publications, 2018), 68–69.

countercultural practice of communal nudity, it nevertheless fits snugly into the rugged individualism of Western society. Although it contrasts with traditional religions in that it does not seek converts but instead remains content to practice its rituals in small, clandestine communities, it nonetheless nurtures a vibrant and public presence both online and in bookstores. And although it goes against the grain of most religious movements by focusing on the Goddess and the feminine rather than a God and the masculine, it still resonates with a growing number of people who care deeply about the environment and consider it our responsibility to steward creation.

Part 3: Religious Writings

The religion of Wicca is unusual in the sense that no sacred book prescribes its beliefs or dictates its practices. Rather than drawing from a Bible, for instance, which contains special revelation from the divine, Wicca pulls from creation itself, which, it is believed, contains all the energies needed to perform magic.

Instead of discussing a specific sacred book, I will instead briefly list some influential authors within Wicca. First, the British archaeologist and anthropologist Margaret Murray (1863–1963) played a significant role in the development of Wicca. Sometimes referred to as the "Grandmother of Wicca," she wrote one of the classic texts on ancient Witchcraft that Wiccans have drawn from for decades. Published in 1921, *The Witch-Cult in Western Europe* resurrected ancient names, symbols, seasons, and rituals from history that Wiccans now utilize to reconstruct some of their most distinct beliefs and practices.[17] What is more, because Murray authored the "Witchcraft" article in the *Encyclopedia Britannica*, her legacy went on to influence ordinary readers interested in the Craft.

Next, I have already described the founder of modern Wicca, Gerald Gardner. Referred to as the "Father of Wicca," he was the genesis behind the resurrection of the Craft. In addition to the books of his that I already mentioned, one of his most enduring is *Book of Shadows* (often abbreviated as *BoS*). Originally a how-to-be-a-Witch book that was secretly passed down from initiator to initiate, it inevitably became public and now circulates in different versions across the Wiccan world. The equivalent of a liturgical book used by Christian priests for the performance of ceremonies, the *Book of Shadows* is the standard book

17. Margaret Alice Murray, *The Witch-Cult in Western Europe: A Study in Anthropology* (Oxford: Clarendon Press, 1921).

of spells and rituals that Witches use privately and publicly. In fact, all Witches are encouraged to write their own version, traditionally in a black journal, which contains their own spells, rituals, and practices. Gardner's *Book of Shadows*, of course, is the most famous, popularizing the most prominent features of Wicca (which I will discuss below), such as casting a circle, drawing down the moon, initiating new members, advancing members to new degrees, observing the sabbats, chanting, and casting spells.[18]

Fig. 7.2. Wiccans are encouraged to write out their own **Book of Shadows**, that is, a magic book of spells.

Finally, many popular writers of Wicca have played an important role in the growth of the movement, particularly among solitary practitioners who are not part of a physical coven. Examples are Doreen Valiente, Patricia Crowther, Dion Fortune, Alexander Sanders, Zsuzsanna Budapest, Robert Buckland, Silver Starhawk, Ed Fitch, Stewart Farrar, Leo Martello, Silver RavenWolf, Donald Kraig, Raven Grimassi, Heather Botting, Rachel Pollack, and Scott Cunningham—among many others. These men and women have written highly influential books, both fiction and nonfiction, attracting seekers, training practitioners, and raising up the next generation of Witches. Many of them have published their books with Llewellyn Worldwide, the leading publisher of books on Wicca, New Age, and Pagan practices.

18. To read the standard version, see "The Gardnerian Book of Shadows," https://www.sacred -texts.com/pag/gbos/index.htm.

Part 4: Beliefs

The religion of Wicca defies simple and shared beliefs. As Lil Abdo explains, "it has no single authority, no single canon of scripture, and an amazingly varied set of beliefs and practices. In fact, it seems hard to find any consensus."[19] Yet despite this constant claim, there is much more standardization than often admitted. Below, for example, is a summary of what is called the "Principles of Wiccan Belief," which was adopted by the Council of American Witches in 1974. It is based on thirteen principles, which is Wicca's equivalent to the number seven or twelve within Christianity.

Principles of Wiccan Belief (1974)

1. We practice rites to attune ourselves with the natural rhythm of life forces marked by the phases of the Moon and the seasonal and cross quarters.
2. We seek to live in harmony with nature.
3. We acknowledge a depth of power . . . sometimes called supernatural, but we see it as lying within that which is natural.
4. We conceive of the Creative Power in the universe as manifesting through polarity—as masculine and feminine. . . . We value neither above the other.
5. We recognize both outer worlds and inner, or psychological, worlds.
6. We do not recognize any authoritarian hierarchy.
7. We see religion, magick, and wisdom in living as being united . . . within . . . a worldview and philosophy of life that we identify as Witchcraft—the Wiccan way.
8. Calling oneself *Witch* does not make a Witch.
9. We believe in the affirmation and fulfillment of life in a continuation of evolution and development.
10. Our only animosity toward Christianity, or toward any other religion or philosophy of life, is to the extent that its institutions have claimed to be the only way.
11. As American Witches, we are not threatened by debates on the history of the Craft [or] the origins of various terms.
12. We do not accept the concept of absolute evil, nor do we worship any entity known as Satan or the Devil, as defined by the Christian tradition. We do not seek power through the suffering of others.

Aleister Crowley. Gerald Gardner was influenced by another Brit living at the time named Aleister Crowley (1875–1947). Crowley and Gardner were cut from the same cloth, sharing interests in the occult, travel, sexual experimentation, religious curiosity, secret societies, writing, publicity, and ritual. One of Crowley's most famous works, *The Book of the Law*, influenced Gardner's *Book of Shadows*.

19. Lil Abdo, "The Baha'i Faith and Wicca: A Comparison of Relevance in Two Emerging Religions," *Pomegranate* 11, no. 1 (2009): 124–48.

13. We believe that we should seek within nature that which is contributory to our health and well-being.[20]

Most of these principles are self-explanatory, especially when understood within the Christian and American context in which they were written. But some need a little more explanation, which I will provide below.

The Wheel of the Year, Sabbats, and Esbats

Wiccans believe that nature is sacred. And they frame their year based on the changing of the seasons, the phases of the moon, and the rotation of the sun. We can start with what is referred to as "the wheel of the year." This includes the four "greater sabbats" of Samhain, Imbolc, Beltane, and Lugnasad (Lammas), as well as the four "lesser sabbats" of Yule, Litha, Eostar, and Mabon. While the lesser sabbats are solar events marked by the two solstices and two equinoxes, the greater sabbats celebrate the four midpoints between them. The sabbats are based on annual seasons and solar phases, but they also carry religious significance. This is exactly how the different festivals in the Bible proceeded—first arising from agricultural seasons and then accruing religious meanings. Ideally, the festivals are celebrated on the exact days and in the outdoors. Yet Wiccans are not legalistic about this. Practical reasons, such as inclement weather, legal and safety issues, work responsibilities, property rights, and family obligations, impede them from performing their rituals on the exact days or outdoors. In addition to the sabbats, Wiccans also assemble on what are called *esbats*. Technically, an esbat is any nonsabbat Wiccan gathering, but esbats are often associated with the lunar calendar. Wiccan covens generally convene once a month during the full (or new) moon under the belief that this is the most prosperous time to cast spells and perform magic because of the additional energy being emitted by the moon.

Magic (Also Spelled "Magick")[21]

If popular culture gets one thing right about Wiccans, it is that they believe in magic. But from a Wiccan perspective, this is hardly unique to them. They see magic where every other religion sees sacrament, prayer, or ritual. For them, a Christian priest's conversion of bread and wine

---

20. Buckland, *Buckland's Complete Book of Witchcraft*, 12–13.
21. Within Wicca, the term *magic* is often spelled as "magick." The *k* is meant to distinguish Wiccan magic from the parlor-trick magic that is usually associated with stage performers.

into Christ's body is magic. A Muslim's interpretation of the Qur'an to discern Allah's will is magic. And a Buddhist's meditation under a sacred tree is magic. Definitions for *magic* within Wicca tend to be short and to the point. But one of the classic definitions comes from Aleister Crowley, who played a profound role in the development of Wicca. He classically defined *magic* (or, as he preferred, *magick*) as "the art or science of causing change in conformity with will."[22]

Fig. 7.3. Wiccans gather around fires during group rituals.

This definition grounds magic in the mundane. Rather than being supernatural, as in traditional Christianity, it is natural. It is about learning how to harness all the varied energies present in our body, in our planet, and in our deities. This gives a great deal of power to the individual will. But magic is never meant to be used for ill. Despite a lack of centralization, Wiccan ethics has traditionally followed a guideline called the eight-worded "Rede," also indebted to Crowley: "and you harm none, do what you will."[23] This effectively means that any ritual, spell, or practice can be performed as long as it does no harm to anyone. For it violates Wiccan ethics to cast spells that harm people—including oneself—much as it breaches Christian ethics to utter prayers that harm people. At the same time, just as hardly a day goes by that Christians do not violate Christian ethics by committing harm to someone in word,

22. As quoted in Ronald Hutton, *The Triumph of the Moon: A History of Modern Pagan Witchcraft* (Oxford: Oxford University Press, 1999), 174.

23. D. J. Conway, *Wicca: The Complete Craft* (Freedom, CA: The Crossing Press, 2001), 42.

deed, or thought, so, too, there are Wiccans who are involved in so-called gray or black magic rather than strictly white magic. Every religion has its excesses.

The Goddess and God

Wicca has variously been described as monotheistic, bitheistic, polytheistic, and atheistic. These are quite distinct worldviews. Which one is it? Traditionally, Wiccan religion is personified in equal and complementary entities: the Goddess and the God. In this way, it is bitheistic, duotheistic, or binitarian rather than Trinitarian as in Christianity. The Goddess, however, has the slight upper hand. And within Dianic Wicca, the Goddess is the exclusive deity invoked. But of course, not all Wiccans believe in physical deities; some, for instance, consider God a symbol or archetype. Either way, the Goddess and the God are symbolically invoked during rituals (whether they "really" exist or not), and they feature heavily in the religion. Rather than being all light, all purity, and all goodness, they are viewed by Wiccans more realistically as possessing a little of everything. While the Goddess symbolizes fertility and oversees the moon, the God is often depicted as a hunter and rules the sun. And classically, at least as defined by Margaret Murray, the God was a Horned God that Christians mistakenly identified with the devil, while the female deity was a Mother Goddess.[24] But Wiccans often invoke other Gods of the past whose names vary according to time, geography, and religion. As Wiccan High Priest Raymond Buckland writes, "The God and the Goddess are known by a wide variety of names; some classical, some local, some even made up."[25] Most covens, like most Roman Catholic and Orthodox churches, have patron deities that they are especially connected to.

According to Starhawk, one of the most prominent voices of Wiccan thought, there are three principles constituting the Goddess and God religion: (1) immanence, (2) interconnection, and (3) community. First, "Immanence means that the Goddess, the Gods, are embodied, that we are each a manifestation of the living being of the earth, that nature, culture, and life in all their diversity are sacred." This means that we are expected to preserve all life. For by caring for the earth, we are caring for the Gods. Second, "Interconnection is the understanding that all being is interrelated, that we are linked with all of the cosmos

Wiccan Terms. The Wiccan Goddess is identified as Maiden, Mother, and Crone, corresponding to the phases of the moon. The Maiden is connected to the new moon, the Mother to the full moon, and the Crone to the waning moon. When the High Priest invokes the Mother Goddess to enter the High Priestess, it is called "drawing down the moon."

---

24. Murray, *Witch-Cult in Western Europe*, 28–70.
25. Raymond Buckland, *Wicca for One: The Path of Solitary Witchcraft* (New York: Citadel Press, 2018), 28.

as parts of one living organism." This is why we cannot separate the pain that a human being feels when losing a loved one from the pain that a forest feels when destroyed for commercial enterprise, why we cannot divide stewardship of the environment from cultivation of the spirit, and why harm done to anyone is harm done to everyone. Third, because the religion is communal, "its primary focus is not individual salvation or enlightenment or enrichment but the growth and transformation that comes through intimate interactions and common struggles."[26]

Coven Autonomy

The authority structure of Wicca operates similarly to Christian denominations such as the Southern Baptist Convention. Other than assent to a small core of beliefs, individual congregations are free to join or leave the convention as they so choose. The same is true for Wicca. Although there are specific denominations within the Craft—such as Gardnerian or Alexandrian Wicca—no coven is able to dictate what another does. Instead, each coven is led by a High Priest (abbreviated as HP) and a High Priestess (HPS). It is these leaders, who personify the twin deities, who govern each coven. To be sure, most conform to the principles and traditions listed above, but they technically have oversight of autonomous communities.

Part 5: Worship Practices

"Wicca is not merely a religion of belief," writes author Ethan White; "it is fundamentally a religion of ritual."[27] In fact, it is the performance of rituals that distinguishes Wiccans from others within Paganism, Heathenism, and the New Age Movement. In short, Wiccans perform a variety of rituals in their ceremonies, several of which I will discuss in this section.

Initiation into a Coven

All religions have initiation ceremonies. For Christians it is baptism in water, for Muslims it is reciting the Shahada, and for Wiccans it is committing oneself to a coven. The exact process varies, but historically the initiation ceremony was modeled after Gardnerian Wicca. As I have

26. Starhawk, *Spiral Dance*, 22.
27. White, *Wicca*, 116.

already discussed, by the time a seeker is to be initiated into a coven, he or she has already fulfilled the preliminary training in the outer court lasting a year and a day. (And if you are a solo practitioner, you perform self-initiation by following instructions from any number of how-to Wicca books.) Although the actual initiation ceremony is private, enough Witches have shared the ceremony publicly that we can easily describe what happens. In more traditional covens, such as those that follow Gardner, the initiate is brought blindfolded and naked with the hands tied behind the back with a cord.

From there the initiate is brought into a circle by a High Priest or High Priestess and required to respond to specific questions in the presence of the coven. The High Priest or High Priestess anoints the initiate, bows, performs the fivefold kiss (on the feet, knees, genitals, breasts, and lips) before then making the initiate bow and make unbreakable promises. Afterward, the initiate is unbound, the blindfold is taken off, and he or she is presented with tools of the Craft. This is an initiation for the first degree, entitling one to be called a Priest or Priestess. The second and third degrees share similarities, but also follow additional ceremonies. Most infamously, the third-degree initiation ceremony involves the so-called Great Rite, in which the initiate has sex with the initiator (usually symbolically, that is, "in token"). Upon completion, the initiate is able to start his or her own coven.

Fig. 7.4.
Dozens of divining tools are used in Wicca. Here are just a few.

Tools of the Trade

The religion of Wicca is a Craft that consists of many tools or utensils. These can range from athames to crystals to pendulums to tarot cards to wands. At the same, time, as Starhawk states, "we have all [that] we need to make magic: our bodies, our breath, our voices, each other."[28] Still, much as a carpenter works with wood, a philosopher with ideas, and a drummer with drums, Wiccans employ any number of materials to perform magic. Below is a list of some of the more prominent tools. Depending on whom you ask, they have different significance, and many hold multiple meanings.

- **Athame:** Ritual knife, traditionally with a black handle, used to command or channel energy, especially for casting a circle, calling the quarters, and dipping in the chalice of wine (Great Rite).
- **Besom (Broom):** Ritually sweeps an area for the purpose of a ceremony.
- **Bolline:** Knife, usually with a white handle, used for cutting herbs.
- **Candles:** Used for a variety of purposes, especially in circles and on altars.
- **Cauldron:** Typically made of cast iron and used for holding candles or burning request papers.
- **Herbs:** Used to perform a variety of magical spells.
- **Incense:** Fragrances burned during the performance of rituals.
- **Pentagram:** Disc with five-pointed star symbolizing the grounding point for spiritual energy into the physical world.
- **Runes:** Carved stones from Nordic language usually based on twenty-four characters.
- **Tarot Cards:** Deck of seventy-eight cards used for divination.
- **Wand:** Like the athame, but used for directing energy rather than commanding it.

Circle Rituals

One of the most distinct features of Wiccan ritual is the casting of a circle. This is often accompanied by lighting (candles), dancing, and drumming. There are specific rituals performed to cast a circle that vary based on solitary practice or coven practice, but the circle is

28. Starhawk, *Spiral Dance*, 26.

usually purified by the four elements: fire, water, earth, and air. If a circle is cast in a coven, the High Priest and High Priestess cast the circle by following a specific liturgy. Inside the circle is an altar that faces north or east. And in the other cardinal directions there is placed a marking, for instance, a candle or a stone. Salt water is then distributed across the circle. Specific rituals are involved in casting, entering, and exiting the circle. In most instances, the athame is used to open and close the circle. Depending on the specific tradition, you will enter the circle in the nude or enrobed in pairs of opposite genders, be welcomed by a kiss, and proceed *deosil*, that is, sunwise or clockwise, possibly with a specific tool in hand. Once the circle is closed, it is sacred space, and various rituals are performed. It is recommended to not leave the circle until it is officially closed; but if necessary, you exit a circle by cutting it with your athame, which you will also use when returning.

What do Wiccans do inside a circle? The rituals performed inside the circle include saluting the cardinal directions ("charging the circle" or "calling the quarters"), invoking deities to enter or possess the High Priestess ("drawing down the moon"), evoking spirits to manifest outside the circle (in a designated triangle), blessing the food offerings ("wine and cakes") by the High Priest's striking his athame into a chalice of wine held by the High Priestess, sharing the wine and cakes with those assembled, performing chanting and breathing exercises with hands together in the shape of a Witch's hat ("raising a cone of power"), performing ritual dramas, and completing other spells as needed.

Fig. 7.5. An athame is a ritual knife used to command, cut, or channel energy in Wicca.

The Eightfold Way and the Five Essentials

Not unlike Pentecostal Christianity, Gardnerian Wicca seeks to create a highly experiential and heightened communal experience within the circle. Traditionally, Gerald Gardner emphasized eight ways in which coven members could be induced into an altered state of consciousness: (1) meditation, (2) trance, (3) chants, spells, and charms, (4) incense, drugs, and wine, (5) dance, (6) bleeding and breath control, (7) scourging (Gardner's favorite), and (8) the Great Rite. These are followed by the so-called Five Essentials: (1) intention, (2) preparation, (3) a correctly formed circle, (4) purification, and (5) proper tools. To create the most stimulating environment possible for the community, Gardnerian Wicca encourages the combination of these different actions, rather than observing them in isolation.[29]

The Devil, the Dark Arts, and Divination

In the popular imagination, Wiccans worship the devil at night during a full moon by channeling evil spirits. This is partly true. To begin with, Wiccans do not worship the devil. In fact, among all the Wiccans I have ever known, they are about as interested in engaging the devil as Christians are. That said, Wiccans perform rituals at night, and they both invoke and evoke various Gods and spirits, some of which are malevolent, malicious, or mischievous. It would be foolish, therefore, to not associate some of what they do with the dark arts. In this way, Wiccans certainly practice divination. *Divination* is a loaded term, but Wiccans generally use it to refer to methods used to hear from God. As Wiccan High Priest Raymond Buckland explains, divination is "the attempt to elicit from some higher power or supernatural being the answers to questions beyond the range of ordinary human understanding."[30] In fact, Wiccans are intensely interested in this. They practice divination in multiple ways: interpreting tarot cards, fortune-telling, reading tea leaves, following the zodiac, interpreting dreams, nurturing psychic abilities, communicating with the dead (necromancing), reading crystal balls, studying astral planes and planetary movement, channeling spirits, practicing alchemy, swinging a pendulum, casting runes, looking into reflections (called *scrying*), and reading palms. Though a world away from Christian customs, Wiccans are quick to point out that Christians also practice divination in an attempt to receive divine guidance,

Invoking, Evoking, and Banishing. Experienced Wiccans *invoke* a Deity into the circle but *evoke* a spirit outside the circle. It is assumed that the Deity is benevolent, which is why it is safe to welcome it into the circle. However, a spirit can be unpredictable in which case it is safer to keep outside the circle. At the end of a service, Wiccans banish the God or spirit by thanking them and releasing them from the circle, triangle, or possessed person.

---

29. White, *Wicca*, 124–27.
30. Buckland, *Wicca for One*, 188.

whether by discerning God's will by reading the Bible, praying to a saint, or fasting from food.

Part 6: Point of Contact

I have always respected how seriously and lovingly Wiccans view the divine as close to us rather than far away. After all, life can sometimes be horribly inhumane, heartbreakingly lonely, and downright unfair. When in the midst of these struggles, I want to worship a God who hears my prayers, feels my pain, and comforts my soul. Within the religion of Wicca, the Gods are described as "immanent." This means that they are here, that they are there, and that they are everywhere. I resonate with this belief. And I think I would prefer it over the opposite: that God is way up there, that God is in another realm, and that God is occupied with more important matters. In fact, most (but certainly not all) Wiccans take their belief in divine immanence to a whole other level. God is not simply among us. God is inside us. God is us.

This is where my attraction to this Wiccan doctrine dissipates. I am eager to declare that God is among us, I am delighted to say that God's Holy Spirit is inside us, but I am disappointed to think that God is us. I will be honest—I do enjoy my own company. And I do believe that I am quite capable of good and beautiful things. But I am not God—not even a minor saint, not even on my best day, not even when leading a church service. Instead, I am loved by God the Father, I am redeemed by God the Son, and I am filled by God the Spirit. But I am most decidedly not God. And on this point, I think Christianity has the upper hand, since it allows us to have our cake and eat it, too. We can simultaneously be surrounded by God, be protected by God, and yet be vetoed by God. I do not want the responsibility to be God because I am not smart enough, compassionate enough, or powerful enough. And to imagine otherwise will eventually and inescapably lead to pain, embarrassment, and sorrow.

Discussion Questions

1. Did anything surprise you in this chapter? What?
2. What are the most distinct beliefs and practices in Wicca? How are they different from mainstream Christianity?
3. If you were to share your faith with a Wiccan, what direction would you go and not go? Why?

4. Do you think Wicca is best understood as monotheistic (one God), duotheistic (God and Goddess), polytheistic (many Gods), or atheistic (no God)? Why?

5. How would you respond to a Wiccan who said that Christians also invoke God to possess a person (by asking the Holy Spirit to indwell them), attempt magic (by praying for healing), and practice divination (by discerning God's will by reading Scripture)?

For Further Reading

Berger, Helen A. *Solitary Pagans: Contemporary Witches, Wiccans, and Others Who Practice Alone.* Columbia: University of South Carolina Press, 2019.

Buckland, Raymond. *Buckland's Complete Book of Witchcraft.* 2nd ed. St. Paul, MN: Llewellyn, 2002.

Clifton, Chas S. *Her Hidden Children: The Rise of Wicca and Paganism in America.* Lanham, MD: Altamira, 2006.

Cunningham, Scott. *Living Wicca: A Further Guide for the Solitary Practitioner.* St. Paul, MN: Llewellyn, 1993.

———. *Wicca: A Guide for the Solitary Practitioner.* St. Paul, MN: Llewellyn, 1988.

Gardner, Gerald. *Witchcraft Today.* 50th anniversary ed. New York: Citadel Press, 2004.

Heselton, Philip. *Witchfather: A Life of Gerald Gardner.* Vol. 1, *Into the Witch Cult.* Loughborough, Leicestershire, UK: Thoth, 2012.

———. *Witchfather: A Life of Gerald Gardner.* Vol. 2, *From Witch to Cult to Wicca.* Loughborough, Leicestershire, UK: Thoth, 2012.

Hutton, Ronald. *The Triumph of the Moon: A History of Modern Pagan Witchcraft.* Oxford: Oxford University Press, 1999.

RavenWolf, Silver. *To Ride a Silver Broomstick: New Generation Witchcraft.* St. Paul, MN: Llewellyn, 1993.

White, Ethan Doyle. *Wicca: History, Belief, and Community in Modern Pagan Witchcraft.* Eastbourne, UK: Sussex Academic Press, 2015.

York, Michael. *Pagan Ethics: Paganism as a World Religion.* Cham, Switzerland: Springer, 2016.

chapter 8

Scientology: The Story of Clarity

I have high hopes of smashing my name into history so violently that it will take a legendary form even if all the books are destroyed.

L. Ron Hubbard[1]

Though other non-traditional religious groups that have been involved in dramatic incidents have attracted more public attention for short periods of time, the Church of Scientology is arguably the most persistently controversial of all contemporary New Religious Movements.

James Lewis[2]

Scientologists have long argued that [it] is a legitimate religious movement that has been misrepresented, maligned, and persecuted by media witch-hunters and McCarthy-style government attacks.

Hugh Urban[3]

Part 1: The Beginning

Ninety-five million years ago, the head of the Galactic Confederation faced a problem. Of the existing seventy-six planets, roughly

---

1. As quoted in Stephen A. Kent and Susan Raine, eds., *Scientology in Popular Culture: Influences and Struggles for Legitimacy* (Santa Barbara, CA: Praeger, 2017), xvii.
2. James R. Lewis and Kjersti Hellesøy, eds., *Handbook of Scientology* (Boston: Brill, 2016), 1.
3. Hugh B. Urban, *The Church of Scientology: A History of a New Religion* (Princeton, NJ: Princeton University Press, 2011), 2.

200 billion people were alive per planet—much more than each planet could sustain. Something had to be done as a matter of planetary survival. For the good of the universe, the head of the Galactic Confederation, a politician named Xenu, concocted an idea. Though it was controversial, he was willing to implement it. Xenu decided that the best way to solve the problem of overpopulation was to take billions of his planet's inhabitants to a rock three planets from the sun called *Teegeeack*—what we today call *earth*. Xenu froze his inhabitants and then transported them on spaceships—much as truckers today ship frozen vegetables from manufacturing plants to grocery stores.

Fig. 8.1. Because so many teachings of Scientology are secret, many Scientologists can find insider information about their religion only on the internet.

While on earth, Xenu methodically, if not morbidly, placed his inhabitants at the base of volcanoes. He then ignited a hydrogen bomb. As the inhabitants erupted out of the volcano and into the air, their souls—what we might call *thetans*—were separated from their melting bodies. Xenu captured these thetans and imprisoned them on earth. As if things could not get any worse, Xenu then forced the thetans to watch horrible images from huge screens for thirty-six consecutive days, tattooing them with eons of horror and trauma. Destined to wander the earth as spiritual nomads and jolted from what they had experienced, these thetans clamor to enter human bodies in droves—in fact, almost every person alive today consists of dozens, if not thousands, of them.

Fortunately, Xenu was eventually caught and found guilty of committing these crimes against humanity, and he remains in prison to this day. But nothing could be done about the billions of body thetans roaming the world and searching for humans to inhabit until one man of unparalleled intellect and unrivaled bravery risked his life to figure out how to liberate them. His name was L. Ron Hubbard. And he developed the first step-by-step system whereby human beings could free body thetans and regain control of their own destiny.[4]

Part 2: Historical Origin

The Church of Scientology is one of the most controversial and contested religions in the world. Whether condemned by critics or idolized by insiders, everyone seems to have an opinion about it. Yet few are familiar with what it teaches, how it worships, and why it flourishes. Instead, they tend to associate the movement with famous celebrities, media exposés, and legal battles. Is it a dangerous cult, a scientific breakthrough, a new philosophy, or something completely different? In this chapter, I will highlight the most important features of Scientology.

L. Ron Hubbard (1911–86)

Lafayette Ronald Hubbard, abbreviated to *LRH* within Scientology, is perhaps the most interesting religious founder in modern memory. "Virtually every detail of Hubbard's life narrative . . . has been the subject of debate,"[5] making it difficult to present his biography in a neutral way that does not antagonize someone. Moving frequently as a child because his father was in the navy, Hubbard spent his early years living in Oklahoma, Montana, and Washington, DC. At a young age, he developed a keen interest in psychology and became fascinated with human thought and human potential. He also traveled overseas, where he was exposed to exotic cultures and spiritual traditions. In 1930, he enrolled in George Washington University, but did not perform well in his studies and dropped out. Disinterested in the doldrum of classes, he lived for

Road Map to Scientology Creation Story. Most Scientologists do not believe in a god, so Xenu is merely a bad man. In fact, if this story sounds like science fiction, you should know that the founder of Scientology was a science fiction author. Interestingly, this story is kept secret even among most Scientologists. Those who learn are sworn to secrecy.

---

4. The myth of Xenu within Scientology is unveiled only to those who have advanced to the third level within the designation of Operating Thetan, what is called OT III. There are multiple sources corroborating this story. For more, see Mikael Rothstein, "'His Name Was Xenu. He Used Renegades': Aspects of Scientology's Founding Myth," in *Scientology*, ed. James R. Lewis (Oxford: Oxford University Press, 2009), 365–87; and Susan Raine, "Colonizing *Terra Incognita*: L. Ron Hubbard, Scientology, and the Quest for Empire," in *Scientology in Popular Culture: Influences and Struggles for Legitimacy*, ed. Stephen A. Kent and Susan Raine (Santa Barbara, CA: Praeger, 2017), 11.

5. Urban, *Church of Scientology*, 31.

adventure—writing imaginative works of fiction, leading international boat excursions for college students, and honing his skills as a pilot. He initially took a job as a pulp-fiction author and specialized in Westerns, fantasies, and science fiction, pumping out hundreds of writings over the course of a few years.

Always yearning for adventure, Hubbard enlisted in the navy during World War II and assumed command of various ships. But he was plagued by a series of medically unverifiable mental and physical illnesses, which led to months of convalescence at a California naval hospital. "While recovering," one author writes, "he had time to give consideration to the larger questions of the nature of the human mind and to help some of his fellow patients who had not survived the war in the best of mental health."[6] Hubbard also claimed to rehabilitate himself, since doctors could never identify what, if anything, actually ailed him. This experience laid the groundwork for many concepts that Hubbard would develop in Scientology. Hubbard also became associated with the esoteric society called the Ordo Templi Orientis (OTO). This is the same secret and magical group spearheaded by Aleister Crowley (1875–1947) that Gerald Gardner (1884–1964), the father of Wicca, whom I discussed in the previous chapter, had joined around the same time in England. Inside the group, Hubbard learned magical practices, hypnosis techniques, and secret rituals that he may have incorporated into Scientology, but the church disputes any influence whatsoever.

After the war, but while still under commission of the navy, Hubbard had apparently conducted sufficient research to publicize his findings about the problem of the human mind. His first major publication was *Dianetics: The Modern Science of Mental Health* (1950). This was the book that put Hubbard on the map. Hubbard soon established Dianetics research centers across the country. In them he introduced the world to *auditing*, a sort of one-on-one counseling session in which participants were presented with a variety of questions elicited to "clear" the mass of bad experiences that the mind had accumulated over a lifetime. Though an overnight success, Hubbard's movement overextended itself and went bankrupt by 1952. Yet "out of the ashes of Dianetics," writes scholar Hugh Urban, "Hubbard created a new and even more ambitious movement—indeed, a 'church' and self-identified religion—called Scientology in December 1953."[7] Throughout the 1950s,

Suppressive Persons and Fair Game.
A Suppressive Person (SP) is someone whom Scientology declares to be an opponent of the religion. All members must disassociate with any SP. Fair Game is the doctrine that allows members to attack or discredit an SP's reputation or public image by any means necessary.

6. J. Gordon Melton, "Birth of a Religion," in *Scientology*, ed. James R. Lewis (Oxford: Oxford University Press, 2009), 20.

7. Hugh B. Urban, "Typewriter in the Sky: L. Ron Hubbard's Fiction and the Birth of the Thetan," in *Scientology in Popular Culture: Influences and Struggles for Legitimacy*, ed. Stephen A. Kent and Susan Raine (Santa Barbara, CA: Praeger, 2017), 39.

Hubbard's new religion made huge strides, flooding the market with international training centers, books, media campaigns, a journal, a publishing house, and a global faith.

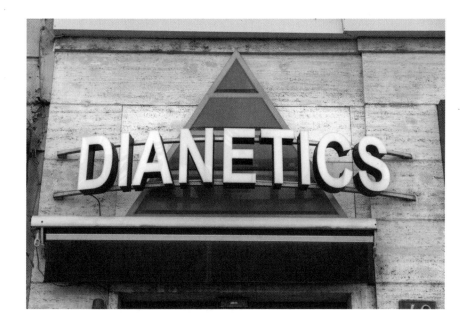

Fig. 8.2. Dianetics was a philosophy before turning into a religion.

Hubbard's decision to convert Dianetics from a scientific philosophy to a bona fide religion has generated intense controversy. And to this day, the Church of Scientology contests many sayings attributed to Hubbard in which he reportedly stated on various occasions: "I'd like to start a religion. That's where the money is."[8] As journalist Lawrence Wright explains, turning Dianetics into a religion offered Hubbard many advantages. For example, religions enjoy financial benefits as tax-exempt entities, they do not have to scientifically prove that they actually work, they transform occasional customers into lifetime members, and they protect the religion's founder from repercussions of what could otherwise be regarded as mental instability and erratic behavior.[9] Whatever his exact intentions, Hubbard legally incorporated three different churches for his new religion in 1953: the Church of American Science, the Church of Spiritual Engineering, and the Church of Scientology. It was the third that won the naming contest.[10]

8. Lloyd Eshbach, *Over My Shoulder: Reflections on a Science Fiction Era* (Hampton Falls, NH: Donald Grant Publishers, 1982), 125.

9. Lawrence Wright, *Going Clear: Scientology, Hollywood, and the Prison of Belief* (New York: Vintage Books, 2013), 97–103.

10. Wright, 101.

The first Church of Scientology opened in Los Angeles in 1954, setting up bases overseas in only a few years. Hubbard served as executive director from the Washington, DC, congregation before moving the central hub of the church to Sussex, England (in an estate called Saint Hill), where he lived for many years as he continued to refine the religion. He also traveled frequently, delivering lectures to enthralled audiences around the world from Australia to India. Still, the unorthodox methods of the movement caused ongoing controversy. Not only did the American Internal Revenue Service revoke Scientology's tax-exempt status as a religious nonprofit, but multiple countries followed suit by disputing the movement's religious claims and investigating its associations with global espionage. These actions no doubt reinforced Scientology's triggerlike tendencies toward litigation. The movement is notorious for the number of lawsuits it has filed worldwide, leading scholar James Richardson to conclude that Scientology is probably "the most litigious religious group in modern history."[11]

Hubbard responded to these attacks in stride, creating a culture within the movement that reflected the tactics he had learned in the military as well as tattooing it with the imperialist mindset he had cultivated as a Western explorer.[12] In fact, he even formed a naval order within Scientology called the *Sea Organization* (abbreviated to *Sea Org*). Drawing from the most dedicated members of the movement and notoriously requiring them to sign billion-year contracts of service, the Sea Org still constitutes the crème de la crème within Scientology and boasts the motto "We Come Back," indicating their reincarnation as enlightened thetans (see below).[13] Though initially confined to ships piloted by Hubbard that traveled the world in search of lands to conquer, evade, or escape (for legal, tax, or political purposes), the order eventually moved on land to Clearwater, Florida, where it remains to this day as the primary hub for Scientologists who want to advance in their training across the different levels of Operating Thetan (described below). After a period of significant growth yet ongoing criticism, Hubbard reorganized the church in the early 1980s into two entities: the Church of Scientology International, which oversees churches; and the Religious Technology Center, which oversees doctrine and licensing. Meanwhile, Hubbard receded into the background, eking out his remaining years in hiding in a motor home in the California desert.[14]

11. James Richardson, "Scientology in Court: A Look at Some Major Cases from Various Nations," in *Scientology*, ed. James R. Lewis (Oxford: Oxford University Press, 2009), 283.

12. Raine, "Colonizing *Terra Incognita*," 8–9.

13. Raine, 15.

14. Urban, *Church of Scientology*, 10.

Fig. 8.3. Though originating in the United States, Scientology quickly built an international following.

David Miscavige (b. 1960)

When L. Ron Hubbard died in 1986, he left behind not only a massive empire of churches, publications, training centers, and properties but also an organization with a bruised international reputation. For many years leading up to his death, Hubbard had grown increasingly paranoid, isolated from others in the organization, and the subject of countless lawsuits. His void was filled by David Miscavige, an American who dropped out of high school to join the Sea Org at the age of sixteen. Though characteristic of Scientology culture to recruit members at such a young age, Miscavige rapidly climbed the ranks within the organization to become the sole leader while still in his twenties. Miscavige's leadership of the organization is the source of ongoing investigation, and a flurry of accusations and lawsuits have been leveled against him among family members, former religious members, and even his own father.[15] In fact, "Miscavige has clearly generated as much as if not more scandal and media attack than L. Ron himself."[16] Still, he has managed to maintain control of the organization. And in his leadership, Miscavige has expanded the movement, rallied its members, beautified its buildings, celebrated its

15. See Ron Miscavige, *Ruthless: Scientology, My Son David Miscavige, and Me* (New York: St. Martin's Press, 2016).

16. Urban, *Church of Scientology*, 19, 205.

celebrities, battled its disputes, and done more to make Scientology a religious mainstay in our modern world than perhaps any other.

Scientology Today

Today, Scientology is known for its impressive buildings around the world, especially in and around Los Angeles (where the largest number of Scientologists live), its never-ending library of books by founder L. Ron Hubbard, an ever-expanding series of courses, notoriety surrounding its high-profile members, aggressive tactics it uses to maintain members, and its litigious tendencies toward outsiders—whether individuals, organizations, or governments. But none of these things get to the core of Scientology, which is centered on enrolling religious seekers into an ever-deepening labyrinth of books, courses, and truths that promise clarity of mind, soundness of body, and the removal of body thetans (see below).[17]

Fig. 8.4. Located in Los Angeles, this is probably the most recognizable building in Scientology.

In general, there are three levels of Scientologists today. The first are public members. These are ordinary men and women who pay money to take courses on any number of topics—whether relationships, work, happiness, communication, or the like. They are also encouraged to

17. Ironically, however, those who take courses or enroll in auditing sessions with Scientology are required to sign multiple legal forms indemnifying Scientology and legally protecting it against guaranteeing any results whatsoever.

read books by the religion's founder and pay for auditing sessions. The costs of courses and auditing sessions vary, but you can easily pay thousands of dollars for these within a relatively short amount of time. The next level are staff members. These are men and women who work for Scientology in some capacity, whether part time or full time. They are also required to enroll in as many courses and auditing sessions as possible and must complete a certain level before becoming staff. Finally, the most elite members in the organizations work in the Sea Org. The equivalent of clergy in other religions, Sea Org members sign a contract lasting a billion years and give their heart and soul to the organization. They are the most committed Scientologists, receiving room and board but little actual pay despite working grueling hours each week. They may be stationed anywhere in the world, and they are the recruiting ground for advancement within the organization. Sea Org members are easily recognizable by their militarylike uniforms. And if you visit any Scientology organization or church, you will eventually meet one.

Part 3: Religious Writings

Since Scientology is a religion created by the man who literally possesses the Guinness Book of World Records title for the most books ever published by a single author, it should come as no surprise that Scientology is not a religion of the book but a religion of the books. The sacred canon of writings within Scientology fills an entire bookshelf, and it all comes from one man: L. Ron Hubbard. As one scholar explains, Hubbard "remains the [sole] source of the spiritual practices and doctrines of the religion."[18]

Writings on Scientology

Of the countless books that Hubbard wrote about Scientology, I will discuss only some of the most foundational and influential ones. The three earliest are *Dianetics: The Original Thesis* (1948), *Dianetics: The Modern Science of Mental Health* (1950), and *Dianetics: The Evolution of a Science* (1950). These represent the building blocks of Dianetics (based on the Greek terms *dia* and *nous*, meaning "through the mind"). In them Hubbard argues that auditing clears the reactive mind of bad experiences and leads a person to discover his or her real identity. Initially, Hubbard believed that Dianetics was a scientific breakthrough that

18. Melton, "Birth of a Religion," 26.

would be enthusiastically embraced by the medical, pharmaceutical, and psychiatric establishment.[19] But when exactly the opposite occurred and Dianetics was panned by professionals, Hubbard began nurturing a deep antagonism toward psychiatry, pharmaceutical companies, and traditional medicine, pivoting the movement away from being portrayed as a medical breakthrough and closer toward being regarded as a religious system. As Urban explains, "Scientology began to adopt ever more elements drawn from Eastern religions, alternative spiritualities, and science fiction, such as the notion of an eternal spirit, reincarnation, past-life memories, supernatural powers, and a vast 'space opera' history of the universe."[20]

Life Is a Game. Axiom 48 in Scientology states, "Life is a game wherein theta as the static solves the problems of theta as MEST." This highlights the contrast between spirit (the original nature of theta) and matter (the false nature of theta). Scientology believes that life is a game in which our original natures have to solve the problems of materiality.

This period coincides with Hubbard's publication of *Science of Survival* (1951), *Self Analysis* (1951), and *Scientology: A History of Man* (1952), which introduced essential Scientology beliefs about thetans; past lives; the triangle of affinity, reality, and communication (ARC); how thetans interact with the material universe—which is made up of matter, energy, space, and time (MEST)—as well as the source of all human problems. Hubbard next wrote books focused on thetans and the origin of life in *Scientology 8–80* and *Scientology 8–8008*, both published in 1952. These two books discussed how thetans create energy and how thetans can reduce their matter, energy, space, and time to nothing (hence the zeros in the title) while also being able to expand the creation of their own universe to infinity (hence the eights in the title). Finally, Hubbard wrote a few other books in the mid-1950s titled *The Creation of Human Ability* (1954), *Dianetics 55!* (1954), and *Scientology: The Fundamentals of Thought* (1956). These books make comparisons between Scientology and other world religions, discuss exteriorization of the thetan outside the body, and describe life as a game.

Recordings, Lectures, and Films

Although Scientology probably has more sacred books than do other faiths, its history as the world's youngest religion has the advantage of possessing more than merely written words. It also features the recorded words of Hubbard in the form of lectures, films, and interviews. Altogether, this constitutes thousands of recordings delivered across the world to various audiences. Of these, perhaps the most noteworthy are the approximately 450 lectures that Hubbard recorded from 1961 to 1966 at Saint Hill in England, which at the time was the central hub

19. Kent and Raine, *Scientology in Popular Culture*, xvi–xvii.
20. Urban, *Church of Scientology*, 3.

of Scientology and where Hubbard lived as the movement was gaining momentum. These recordings are called the *Saint Hill Special Briefing Course Lectures*. Hubbard also wrote dozens of scripts that were filmed for training purposes for Scientologists. These coincide with Scientology's filming department that regularly writes scripts and records short videos and tutorials used for coursework.

Part 4: Beliefs

Scientology is a gnostic religion promising salvation in the form of mental clarity upon completion of a rigorous—and expensive—process of study, questioning, reflection, and reprogramming. Constructed by a founder with an unusually fertile imagination and penchant for coining words and phrases, the Church of Scientology is full of terms that require further explanation. Of the fifty-eight axioms that undergird the belief system within Scientology as outlined by L. Ron Hubbard in 1954, I will isolate the most significant terms and concepts below.

God, Theta, and Thetans

It might surprise you that an organization calling itself a religion does not advocate or endorse any particular concept of God. But that is the case with Scientology. While not averse to using the term *God*, "the exact nature of God is not defined by Scientology."[21] Instead, Scientology has always been more interested in human creation than a divine creator. Although a Scientologist—particularly if belonging to another religion such as Christianity—may believe in God, most are atheists. This illustrates the influence of Asian religions on Hubbard, who reasoned that terms such as *soul* and *spirit* contained too much baggage, so he coined the words *theta* to mean "life force" and *thetan* to refer to an individual life force—such as a human being.

This concept of theta stands in contrast to the physical world, which consists of matter, energy, space, and time—what Scientologists abbreviate to *MEST*.[22] In Scientology, theta surpasses MEST, and in fact, it was theta that created MEST. The combination of these two generated thetans, who are composed of mind, theta, and body. Stated differently,

21. Dell deChant and Danny L. Jorgensen, "The Church of Scientology: A Very New American Religion," in *World Religions in America: An Introduction*, ed. Jacob Neusner, 3rd ed. (Louisville: Westminster John Knox Press, 2003), 226.

22. Church of Scientology International, *Scientology: Theology and Practice of a Contemporary Religion* (Los Angeles: Bridge Publications, 1998), 18.

human beings like you and me are inhabited by countless thetans. Specifically, we are a mixture of thetans and MEST, which is why we can accurately describe Scientology as a gnostic religion in the sense that thetans (the spiritual) are good while matter, energy, space, and time (the material) are bad. Although thetans were originally good, immortal, and immaterial, they eventually became obsessed with the physical and forgot their true nature. This is the most pressing problem that human beings face. It is only through auditing and putting into practice the principles of Scientology that we may realize our true thetan selves and learn that we can fully and perfectly function without a body—thereby becoming Operating Thetans, or OTs (discussed below).

Analytical and Reactive Mind

Scientology teaches that the mind is made up of two parts: (1) the analytical or conscious mind and (2) the reactive or unconscious mind. Everything that happens in life is recorded on a "time track" that is divided into one of these two minds. The analytical mind is the center of awareness and the storehouse of all experiences from a person's life. It is the rational part. It is the good part. The reactive mind, by contrast, is the receptacle of all our fears, failures, and insecurities. It is what holds us back from attaining greatness, and it perfectly records everything our mind encounters when unconscious—including smells, feelings, and all accompanying sensations. According to Scientology, the reactive mind stores bad experiences as *engrams*, which have to be sought, retrieved, processed, and "cleared" in order to achieve one's full potential. Much of auditing, in fact, involves removing these deep-lodged engrams that have been stored in the unconscious or reactive mind from current or previous lifetimes.

Eight Dynamics

Scientologists follow the Eastern religious worldview of reincarnation rather than the Abrahamic belief that we have one lifetime in which to live. This gets to the core of Scientology's conviction that life is about survival—and this survival involves the so-called Eight Dynamics. In short, thetans strive to survive, and they do so by means of an interlocking web that illustrates our natural inclination toward preservation of (1) the self, (2) the family unit, (3) groups or community, (4) all human beings, (5) all life forms, (6) the physical universe, (7) the spiritual realm, and (8) the concept of infinity, or what we might call the *divine*. It takes

Engrams and the Mind.
L. Ron Hubbard wrote: "The reactive mind consists of a collection of experiences received during an unanalytical moment which contain pain and actual or conceived antagonism to the survival of the individual. An engram is a perceptive entity which can be precisely defined. The aggregate of engrams composes the reactive mind."

L. Ron Hubbard, *Dianetics: The Original Thesis* (Los Angeles: Bridge Publications, 2007), 39.

time and training to unlock and understand these dynamics, but they are like a sequential series of breakthroughs in which a person comes to have a greater understanding of oneself and his or her relationship to the other dynamics, culminating in the desire to survive forever at the highest level of infinity. These Eight Dynamics also contain Scientology's understanding of ethics in which all of life is related, and it is the responsibility of human beings to ensure that each dynamic is conserved and cared for. As one progresses through the Operating Thetan levels, a person is supposed to gain a better understanding of his or her role to "clear the planet" by restoring everyone to the original thetan nature.[23]

ARC Triangle

Scientology teaches that the Eight Dynamics are foundational to our survival and success and that they are closely connected to three other elements: affinity, reality, and communication. These three terms are often referred to as the *ARC Triangle*. The bottom left portion of the triangle refers to affinity. This includes our emotional state, and it involves the degree to which we like or dislike something. The bottom right portion contains reality. This describes what we agree or ascribe to be real. At the top of the triangle is the most important: communication. This is the interchange of ideas. Scientology teaches that "when a thetan has total affinity, reality and communication across all eight dynamics, complete understanding of the entirety of life and full spiritual awareness follow."[24]

Part 5: Worship Practices

The Church of Scientology is a hands-on religion that emphasizes doing rather than worshiping. In this way, it is "primarily a religion of action."[25] And perhaps the primary action is the series of steps a person takes in order to go clear and then become a fully functioning Operating Thetan (OT), which means that a person becomes completely capable of handling oneself independent of a body.

Going Clear and Becoming an Operating Thetan

Scientologists seek two primary experiences: going clear and advancing along the Operating Thetan levels. The first is the state

---

23. DeChant and Jorgensen, "Church of Scientology," 229.
24. Church of Scientology International, *Scientology*, 29.
25. Rothstein, "His Name Was Xenu," 366.

of being completely "cleared" of all engrams—or bad experiences and thoughts that inhibit a thetan from understanding its true identity. You "go clear" by undergoing extensive auditing at a Scientology church (discussed below). For those who become clear and therefore who remove all engrams, the next milestone is becoming an Operating Thetan. This process involves eight levels, advancing from Operating Thetan Level I to Level VIII. Each of these steps was designed by L. Ron Hubbard, and they progress sequentially. These are very expensive courses to take, and you must be invited to take them. They supposedly reveal the most secretive and mysterious elements of the cosmos, and those who take these courses sign nondisclosure agreements, are filmed, and are closely monitored. You are not allowed to publicize any of the information learned during the Operating Thetan levels.

Fig. 8.5. *Freewinds* is a ship that performs the highest levels of Scientology training.

Hubbard believed that Scientologists who progressed through his training would eventually be able to move not only several feet away from their bodies but even eons and light-years away, exploring the cosmos unhindered by the physical MEST. He taught that Operating Thetans were superhuman and godlike.[26] In fact, it is quite common for those undergoing this training to eventually experience what is called *exteriorization*. This refers to the ability of a thetan to travel outside the physical body, illustrating the true nature of thetans. It is also quite common for those at these levels to report on past lives, since it is believed that

26. Urban, "Typewriter in the Sky," 42.

thetans are immortal. While you can train to go clear at virtually any Scientology church, you can receive training as an Operating Thetan only at an Advanced Organization (*AO* for short). There are only a few AOs in the world, and it is these that provide training from Level I to Level V. The Scientology organization in Clearwater, Florida—commonly referred to as *Flag*—is the training center for Levels VI and VII, while the course for Level VIII can be taken only aboard a ship named *Freewinds*.[27] The secretive nature of these levels—as well as the layers of security that one must go through to attain them and the amount of money that one must spend—is legendary. And many ex-members have discussed it.

The Bridge to Total Freedom: Processing and Training

One of the most common metaphors that Scientologists use to describe how a person advances spiritually in the pursuit of "going clear" is that of a bridge. And if you ever visit a Scientology organization, you may see a large chart called *The Bridge to Total Freedom*, abbreviated to *The Bridge*. If you want to think about how a person is "saved" in Scientology—to use a Christian term—it is through the Bridge. There are two ways to reach the Bridge, that is, two ways to experience salvation: training and processing. While *training* refers to studying Scientology scriptures, *processing* refers to auditing. You can enter the Bridge through either one. Let's start with the right side of the Bridge: processing.

Processing: Auditing, Engrams, and E-Meters

Auditing is the bread and butter of Scientology. We could describe it as Scientology's core "religious" practice. It was designed by L. Ron Hubbard when *Dianetics* was first published, and in fact, Hubbard audited himself until the day he died. Auditing is a mixture of counseling, confession, meditation, processing, and therapy. The purpose of auditing is to restore a human being to full capacity by clearing negative thoughts called *engrams*. This has the effect of transitioning a person from the status of being a *preclear* (an uninitiated person, often abbreviated to *PC*) to a *clear* (an insider who achieves total recall and perfect knowledge), who is then eligible for the Operating Thetan levels. (By definition, no preclear can become an Operating Thetan.)

I have received auditing before, and it follows a step-by-step process that auditors are expected to follow. It can begin almost anywhere

Operating Thetan Level III. The most infamous level within the Operating Thetan training occurs at Level III when a person is introduced to the story of Xenu. The "clear" signs a nondisclosure agreement and is taught that the thetans that were blown up in the Xenu story are "body thetans," as opposed to ordinary "thetans." These "body thetans" attach to human bodies, and part of what Scientologists learn how to do is to remind these body thetans of their true selves, namely, that they do not need human bodies.

27. Kjersti Hellesøy, "Scientology: The Making of a Religion," in *Controversial New Religions*, ed. James R. Lewis and Jesper Petersen, 2nd ed. (Oxford: Oxford University Press, 2014), 263.

and usually proceeds according to topics, but eventually the preclear is asked to recall one's earliest engram. You will then retell the incident in as much detail as possible with eyes closed and with prompting from the auditor, who is seated directly facing you. While you are responding to questions, the auditor closely watches fluctuations in the E-meter. Because Scientology teaches that engrams located in the reactive mind contain electrical charges that can be measured by the device, the E-meter is an important tool that accompanies auditing. Until the electrical charge from the engram has sufficiently dissipated on the E-meter, you may be asked to reprocess the same engram a dozen or more times. And because Scientologists believe that you live forever, you may have to go back to many previous lives to retrieve this. Auditing sessions can last a few hours at a time, so they are usually divided into multiple sessions. Detailed records of each session are meticulously kept by auditors and will be consulted as you progress through your training. Preclears are also expected to write about successes they encounter as a result of the auditing session. These records are kept in private storage by the church.

Training: Studying Scientology Scriptures and Training Routines

The other way to enter the Bridge to salvation within Scientology is through training. This involves detailed study of books and lectures by L. Ron Hubbard, taking courses that expand on his teachings, doing advanced training as an auditor, and looking up words that one does not understand. In fact, one of the distinct features within Scientology is its insistence that you cannot pass by any word or idea that you do not understand. And in the preface to any book published by Scientology, you will see some variable of the following note: "In studying Dianetics and Scientology be very, very certain you never go past a word you do not fully understand. The only reason a person gives up a study or becomes confused or unable to learn is that he or she has gone past a word or phrase that was not understood."[28]

The importance of this note becomes apparent almost immediately in any Scientology book, for not only is Hubbard's language technical and mechanical, but he uses words and phrases in unique ways. This focus on reading books authored by Scientology's founder and looking up words while doing so has led to the formation of reading rooms inside many Scientology churches (called *orgs*). It is not uncommon to see Scientologists at tables, reading through Hubbard's extensive corpus of

What Is Auditing? During auditing, the auditor (listener) asks questions to the preclear that seek to identify and remove engrams. Although Scientologists portray auditing as a religious practice, it is simply a person's walking another person through a series of scripted questions. Scientologists undergo auditing their entire lives.

28. Hubbard, *Dianetics*, i.

writings. This practice is accompanied by taking courses, which involve reading Hubbard's works, watching premade videos, and completing assignments related to the specific course. Those who train to become auditors also undergo Training Routines (TR). These represent a series of training techniques that attempt to simulate awkward and uncomfortable situations that may arise during auditing, such as staring at another person for long periods, asking repetitive questions, and making exact requests. There are also related training programs for preclears that involve rehabilitation from addiction and incarceration under the names Narconon, Criminon, and WISE.

Part 6: Point of Contact

There are many things to admire about Scientology. For instance, I think auditing can be a therapeutic process that helps people process traumatic events that could be holding them back. I also appreciate Scientology's emphasis on study, its encouragement for members to look up unknown words in the dictionary, and its warm embrace of lifetime learning. These are all positive elements that have the potential of furthering one's spiritual maturity and deepening one's intellectual development. After all, it is all too easy to become complacent about your faith, and I have encountered countless Christians who have made little, if any, progress in their walk with Christ since joining a church. So if there were an expectation among Christians that they had to process their thoughts and emotions with others, that they had to journal and reflect on what they discovered, and that they had to read theological books and take spiritual courses to strengthen their faith, I think it would more accurately reflect the kind of commitment, discipline, and discipleship that Christ seemed to expect from his followers.

One of my frustrations with Scientology is the fact that you can advance to the highest levels of spirituality only if you pay hundreds of thousands of dollars. In all my conversations with Scientologists over the years, they eventually lead down the same path. And that path is paved in dollar signs. Everything in Scientology comes with a price tag. Books, courses, auditing, levels, memberships—it all costs dearly. As I was, you are usually introduced to Scientology by means of a "free" personality test, but by the time you are finished, you are surrounded by a squad of staff members that could put used-car salespeople to shame.

Believe me, I agree with the apostle Paul that "the laborer deserves his wages" (1 Tim. 5:18), but I also agree with Paul that the worker's religion should be "rich in good works" and "generous" to those in need (6:18).

Especially upon regaining its tax-exempt status as a religious organization in the 1990s, Scientology has gone on a public-relations campaign, marketing itself as a church replete with creeds, clerics, and a canon of scripture.[29] I actually believe that Scientology is better described as a religion than a philosophy, but I have never heard of a religion that demands payment for every single service it provides—and hundreds of thousands of dollars at that. If Scientology wants to be a religion, it needs to act like one. In real religions, members donate money to the organization out of the overflow of their faith and for the ultimate purpose of helping others; they do not pay money because they are contractually obligated to do so and for the sole purpose of what they alone get out of the experience. And in real religions, members minister to homeless people and others in need even though they know that they will never receive a dime for doing so; they do not establish celebrity centers, cater to movie stars, and focus their attention only on those who can afford to spend millions of dollars on secret spiritual lessons that regular people, let alone poor ones, will never get the chance to receive.

Discussion Questions

1. Why do you think so many people find Scientology appealing? Is there anything in the religion that you think is helpful?
2. How would you describe what auditing is? What would it be most similar to in Christianity?
3. What are the most essential beliefs within Scientology? Explain each one.
4. If you had to describe Scientology more as a philosophy or more as a religion, which one would you choose? Why?
5. If you had to boil Scientology down into one primary or distinct belief or practice, what would it be? How would you do the same for Christianity?

For Further Reading

Kent, Stephen A., and Susan Raine, eds. *Scientology in Popular Culture: Influences and Struggles for Legitimacy.* Santa Barbara, CA: Praeger, 2017.

Lewis, James R., ed. *Scientology.* Oxford: Oxford University Press, 2009.

29. See especially Church of Scientology International, *Scientology.* This book reframes all of Scientology in terms of a religion.

Lewis, James R., and Kjersti Hellesøy, eds. *Handbook of Scientology.* Boston: Brill, 2016.

Melton, J. Gordon. *The Church of Scientology.* Salt Lake City: Signature Books, 2000.

Rinder, Mike. *A Billion Years: My Escape from a Life in the Highest Ranks of Scientology.* New York: Gallery Books, 2022.

Urban, Hugh B. *The Church of Scientology: A History of a New Religion.* Princeton, NJ: Princeton University Press, 2011.

Wright, Lawrence. *Going Clear: Scientology, Hollywood, and the Prison of Belief.* New York: Vintage Books, 2013.

PART 5

Uncommitted New Religious Movements

In this section, we discuss the two most influential nonreligious movements: atheists and nones. A wide range of names are used to refer to these groups, none of which is perfect. But both are on the rise in terms of sheer numbers. Yet they are also quite different. In fact, you might think it strange to include them in a book on new religious movements, since neither officially lays claim to religious beliefs. When you peel things away, however, you can begin to see that there are actually many similarities among atheists and nones compared to practitioners of organized religions.

chapter 9

Atheism: The Story of Unbelief

Atheism simply possesses no single, objective definition: it can be used correctly in a number of related, sometimes overlapping, and often mutually exclusive ways. This is not necessarily a problem, so long as one is always clear how exactly each author is deploying the term.

Stephen Bullivant[1]

It does not follow from the fact that atheism is not itself a religion that there are no atheistic religions.

Michael Martin[2]

In most religions, debates about belief are unimportant. Belief was irrelevant in pagan religion and continues to be unimportant in the religions of India and China. When they declare themselves unbelievers, atheists are invoking an understanding of religion that has been unthinkingly inherited from monotheism.

John Gray[3]

Part 1: The Beginning

It was just yesterday, it seemed, that he was an amateur naturalist living in the English countryside whose overbearing father had once

---

1. Stephen Bullivant, "Defining 'Atheism,'" in *The Oxford Handbook of Atheism*, ed. Stephen Bullivant and Michael Ruse (Oxford: Oxford University Press, 2013), 13.
2. Michael Martin, "Atheism and Religion," in *The Cambridge Companion to Atheism*, ed. Michael Martin (Cambridge: Cambridge University Press, 2007), 221.
3. John Gray, *Seven Types of Atheism* (New York: Picador, 2018), 5.

scolded him for showing more interest in catching rats than taking classes. Little did his father know that his late-blooming son was simply in the early stages of research into what would culminate in one of the most influential books of all time. Reluctant to publish his findings—either out of fear of upsetting Victorian English society or else being proved wrong and confirming his dad's suspicions that he was a scientific crackpot—the man was buying time as he classified beetles and drank brandy. Whatever the case, he knew he had to act soon. Upon hearing that an acquaintance—in fact, a trenchant enemy—was about to publish scientific findings similar to his own, the country gentleman hastily wrote out what he had been casually mulling over for more than twenty years.

Upon hearing the controversial idea advanced in the five-hundred-page book that ensued, the wife of the bishop of Worcester reportedly exclaimed: "Descended from the apes! My dear, let us hope that it is not true, but if it is, let us pray that it will not become generally known."[4] That prayer must never have been uttered, for the book was wildly successful. In fact, it was a bestseller before that term even existed. Not one copy of Charles Darwin's *On the Origin of Species* remained on the shelf for more than a few hours after the first edition was released on November 24, 1859. In fact, a second edition immediately followed, which was eagerly read by the general public and the professional scientist alike. Less than two centuries later, the book still remains in print—even if the ideas in it have evolved.[5]

Part 2: Is God Dead?

The publication by Charles Darwin (1809–82) of the theory of evolution by natural selection was a scientific breakthrough. Thomas Huxley (1825–95), called "Darwin's Bulldog" on account of his aggressive defense of his friend's theory, later remarked, "It is doubtful if any single book, except [Isaac Newton's] 'Principia,' ever worked so great and so rapid a revolution in science, or made so deep an impression on the general mind."[6] Continuing, Huxley wrote that "whenever science and orthodoxy have been fairly opposed, the latter has been forced to retire

Road Map to Atheist Creation Story. Though atheism existed for centuries, its social acceptability grew across cultures and regions of the world, and its cohesiveness as a worldview expanded during Darwin's time. So, we begin with Darwin because his theories represent a turning point in which religion came to be questioned as never before.

---

4. Patricia Horan, Foreword to *The Origin of Species*, by Charles Darwin (New York: Random House, 1979), v.

5. This opening section is modeled after Derek Cooper, *Twenty Questions That Shaped World Christian History* (Minneapolis: Fortress Press, 2015), 299–300.

6. Thomas Huxley, *Selected Works of Thomas H. Huxley*, 2 vols. (New York: Appleton & Co., 1893), 2:286.

from the lists, bleeding and crushed if not annihilated."[7] In addition to deeply influencing the general public, Darwin's book also sent shock waves across the Christian world—as well as across the other religions of the world. As historian of Darwinism Peter Bowler describes, some "declared Darwin to be the most dangerous man in England. If evolutionism implied that humans were merely improved apes, . . . where was the divine source of moral values?"[8]

Although the seed of atheism was planted in *On the Origin of Species*, it is not exactly certain that Darwin himself ever sprouted into a full atheist. But even then, we should not assume that Darwin would have been the world's first atheist. Not to put too fine a point on it, but atheism has probably always existed. Though not prominent, we see glimpses of it in virtually every ancient culture. In fact, a whole genre about the death of God had materialized well before Darwin. At that time, scientists and philosophers were feverishly conjecturing what role, if any, the divine played in the creation of the cosmos, the preservation of the world, and human affairs. They had a hunch that God's character should have never made it into the script, and they were intent on proving it. With the meteoric rise and almost immediate acceptance of evolution as well as the mounting influence of the Enlightenment among the educated class, the question of God's existence and providence only intensified, leading many an academic to posit that God was a figment of our imaginations and that religion would vanish as swiftly and completely as the dinosaurs did during the Cretaceous Period.

In more recent times, the advent of cloning, sequencing, and the human genome project, as well as faster-than-light technological advances in science, artificial intelligence, and robotics, have only accelerated our culture's suspicions that God has died, with many politicians, scientists, philosophers, and trenchant atheists placing in their crosshairs the very enterprise of religion, asking whether it deserves any place in intellectual society at all. In fact, public figures such as Stephen Hawking (1942–2018), Richard Dawkins (b. 1941), and Christopher Hitchens (1949–2011) have become the darlings of enlightened society, being richly rewarded on earth for their faithfulness in spreading the gospel of atheism. In his *New York Times* bestselling book *The God Delusion*, Dawkins declared that "God almost certainly does not exist" and that "religion can be seen as a by-product of the misfiring of several . . . modules [in the brain]," tantamount to "mental 'viruses'" that infect our understanding

Was Darwin an Atheist? It is impossible to enter another's mind, but I tend to agree with Frank Brown that Darwin's belief in God "never entirely ceased to ebb and flow...At low tide, so to speak, he was essentially an undogmatic atheist; at high tide he was a tentative theist; the rest of the time he was basically agnostic."

Frank Burch Brown, *The Evolution of Darwin's Religious Views* (Macon, GA: Mercer University Press, 1986), 27.

---

7. Thomas Huxley, "The Origin of Species," in *Darwiniana: Collected Essays*, vol. 2 (New York: Appleton & Co., 1894), 52.

8. Peter J. Bowler, *Evolution: The History of an Idea* (Berkeley: University of California Press, 2009), 177.

of reality.[9] Dawkins reasoned that religion evolved insipidly, stupidly, and arbitrarily, generating a "bewildering—and sometimes dangerous—... diversity" of thought and practice.[10] Is it indeed the case, as many respectable intellectuals would have us believe, that atheism has won the day and relegated the exercise of religion into a fairyland that only those who believe in Bigfoot and flying saucers inhabit? In this chapter, I will discuss unbelief.

Fig. 9.1. Charles Darwin's theory of evolution accelerated the division between religion and science.

Part 3: Defining Terms

Prominent thinkers such as Darwin and Dawkins descend from a fairly long line of questioners and skeptics, but before we lump them all together as equal adversaries of God and opponents of organized religion, we need to pause and ponder a few terms. As atheist author Armin Navabi explains in his book *Why There Is No God*, "Atheism exists on a spectrum."[11] Not all atheists think or believe alike. In fact, as one atheist author explains, some atheists "are religious,"[12] and there are

---

9. Richard Dawkins, *The God Delusion* (Boston: Houghton Mifflin, 2006; repr., Boston: Mariner Books, 2008), 189, 209, 218.

10. Dawkins, 220.

11. Armin Navabi, *Why There Is No God: Simple Responses to 20 Common Arguments for the Existence of God* (n.p.: CreateSpace Publishing, 2014), 12.

12. Graham Oppy, *Atheism: The Basics* (London: Routledge, 2019), 19.

denominations or subtraditions within virtually every world religion that are atheistic. What is more, the very definition of *atheism* has evolved over time—and is still in evolution. To repeat the quote I provided at the beginning of this chapter: "*Atheism* simply possesses no single, objective definition: it can be used correctly in a number of related, sometimes overlapping, and often mutually exclusive ways."[13] That stated, what makes an atheist different from an agnostic or secular humanist? In a related way, is atheism equivalent to communism or socialism, or is one a byproduct of the other? In this section, I will define our terms and classify them in relation to each other.

Defining Atheism

Etymologically, and strictly speaking, the terms *atheist* and *atheism* derive from the Greek language. The so-called alpha privative—the letter *a* (or α in Greek)—means "not" or "without," and *theos* (θεός) signifies "god" or "God." Although the concept must have existed earlier, the first recorded evidence we have of the exact term comes from the most famous philosopher in the West: Socrates (c. 470–399 B.C.). In the trial that led to his death, Socrates' peers accused him, among other things, of atheism. Socrates responded: "I do not understand whether you are saying that I teach people to believe in the existence of certain gods [θεούς]—in which case I do believe in the existence of gods [θεούς], and I am certainly not an atheist [ἄθεος] or guilty of that charge."[14] The ancient Greeks used this kind of language for centuries to refer to the absence of belief in the gods, but it was very rare for someone to openly acknowledge it.[15] In Socrates' context, *atheist* meant something like "godless" or "godforsaken."[16] For instance, the Greek philosopher and priest Plutarch (c. 46–119), living a generation after the time of Christ, wrote of those who had been called "atheists" [ἄθεοι],[17] defining an "atheist" [ἀθεότης] as someone who "has no belief in God" [δοκεῖ τῇ ἀπιστίᾳ θείου]—which, in that context, was a very bad thing.[18] Interestingly, atheism was one of the charges leveled against early Christians—partly because they rejected Pagan rituals and

Atheism in Ancient Israel? According to Psalm 14:1, "The fool says in his heart, 'There is no God.'" Although virtually all the cultures in the Bible had their own gods, there is no reason to think that some individuals did not actually believe in these gods— even within Israel.

---

13. Bullivant, "Defining 'Atheism,'" 13.

14. Plato, *Apology* 26c. This is my translation of the original Greek: ἐγὼ γὰρ οὐ δύναμαι μαθεῖν πότερον λέγεις διδάσκειν με νομίζειν εἶναί τινας θεούς—καὶ αὐτὸς ἄρα νομίζω εἶναι θεοὺς καὶ οὐκ εἰμὶ τὸ παράπαν ἄθεος οὐδὲ ταύτῃ ἀδικῶ.

15. David Sedley, "From the Pre-Socratics to the Hellenistic Age," in *The Oxford Handbook of Atheism*, ed. Stephen Bullivant and Michael Ruse (Oxford: Oxford University Press, 2013), 151.

16. Jan N. Bremmer, "Atheism in Antiquity," in *The Cambridge Companion to Atheism*, ed. Michael Martin (Cambridge: Cambridge University Press, 2007), 19.

17. Plutarch, *Against the Stoics* 1075a.

18. Plutarch, *Moralia* 165c.

partly because they worshiped in private and had no public venues from which to demonstrate their beliefs to outsiders.

In English, the term *atheist* came of age in the sixteenth century, at which time countless dictionaries and translations of ancient writings were prominent. Based on the literal meaning of Greek, these early usages of *atheist* in English were understood to apply to someone who did not believe in God. And under the cultural aegis of Christianity, the epithet was also tantamount to being an "infidel" or an "ungodly" person, the rough equivalent of how the ancient Greeks and Romans used it. As history has unfolded, and the terms have been in use for more than four centuries in English, scholarship has never reached an exact consensus. Few topics among scholars have. Nevertheless, both for our purposes and for the greater public, *atheism* is generally defined as "an absence of belief in the existence of a God or gods."[19] Thus, an *atheist* is a person who does not believe in God, which does not necessarily have anything to do with believing in religion. An *atheist* contrasts with a *theist*, a person who does believe in God or gods, without, however, suggesting which particular God or gods he or she believes in, or whether the person is a member of any particular religion. In short, atheism does not necessitate that you are irreligious in exactly the same way that theism does not necessitate that you are religious. The related term *deism* is similar to *theism*, but the difference is that deism affirms the existence of God but not the involvement of God in human affairs (as theism does).

Fig. 9.2. Although the concept existed millennia earlier, the term *atheism* developed in English in the sixteenth century.

19. Bullivant, "Defining 'Atheism,'" 13.

Defining Agnosticism

Though also etymologically connected to Greek, the terms *agnostic* and *agnosticism* were coined only in the nineteenth century. They were not used in the ancient world per se, though the concept certainly existed. Based on the alpha privative (α)—once again, signifying "not" or "without"—and the Greek word *gnosis* (γνῶσις), meaning "belief" or "knowledge," the term *agnostic* was first used by Thomas Huxley. A tireless champion of evolution and a close personal friend of Charles Darwin, Huxley first employed the term publicly in 1869 at a meeting of the Metaphysical Society in London, a society dedicated to philosophical and religious questions that held meetings from 1869 to 1880. Huxley invented the term *agnostic* in an attempt to define his own philosophical position in contrast to the existing but insufficient terms of *atheist, freethinker, idealist, materialist, pantheist, theist,* and, of course, *Christian.* As a lengthy quote of his attests:

> When I reached intellectual maturity and began to ask myself whether I was an atheist, a theist, or a pantheist; a materialist or an idealist; a Christian or a freethinker, I found that the more I learned and reflected, the less ready was the answer; until at last I came to the conclusion that I had neither art nor part with any of these denominations, except the last. The one thing in which most of these good people were agreed was the one thing in which I differed from them. They were quite sure that they had attained a certain "gnosis" [that is, "knowledge"]—[that they] had, more or less, successfully solved the problem of existence; while I was quite sure I had not and had a pretty strong conviction that the problem was insoluble. And, with [David] Hume and [Immanuel] Kant on my side, I could not think myself presumptuous in holding fast by that opinion. . . . So I took thought and invented what I conceived to be the appropriate title of "agnostic." It came into my head as suggestively antithetic to the "gnostic" of Church history, who professed to know so much about the very things of which I was ignorant; and I took the earliest opportunity of parading it at our Society, to show that I, too, had a tail, like the other foxes. . . . That is the history of the origin of the terms "agnostic" and "agnosticism."[20]

As a firm believer in science, Huxley found no scientific grounds for the existence of God, and so he coined the term *agnostic* to characterize

---

20. Thomas Huxley, "Agnosticism," in *Collected Essays,* vol. 5, *Science and the Christian Tradition* (Cambridge: Cambridge University Press, 2011), 237.

his skepticism. Far from describing agnosticism as sinister in nature, however, Huxley elaborated in his essay "Agnosticism and Christianity":

> Agnosticism is not properly described as a "negative" creed, nor indeed as a creed of any kind, except in so far as it expresses absolute faith in the validity of a principle, which is as much ethical as intellectual. This principle may be stated in various ways, but they all amount to this: that it is wrong for a man to say that he is certain of the objective truth of any proposition unless he can produce evidence which logically justified that certainty.[21]

The meaning of the term *agnosticism* was soon expanded by another British thinker. Bertrand Russell (1872–1970), a prominent philosopher who inspired a generation of skeptics with his calm reason, quick wit, and powerful writing, penned an entire essay on the question of agnosticism appropriately titled "What Is an Agnostic?" In short, Russell argued that agnostics are those who think "it is impossible to know the truth in matters such as God and future life."[22] In response to the question whether agnostics are atheists, he decidedly answered "No." "An atheist," he explained, "holds that we *can* know whether or not there is a God. . . . [But the] agnostic suspends judgment, saying that there are not sufficient grounds either for affirmation or for denial [of God's existence]."[23]

As regards the existence of God, Russell argued that agnosticism represents an intellectual position that is undecided, uncommitted, and uncertain. To be sure, a spectrum of agnosticism does exist, with those on the right holding God's existence to be "so improbable that it is not worth considering in practice,"[24] while on the left are those who deem it possible, though not to the point of pronouncing it categorically to be so. As historian of agnosticism Bernard Lightman explains, "there were a number of types of agnosticism [in Russell's day], including theistic and atheistic varieties."[25] In the rest of Russell's essay, he entertained a series of common questions posed to agnostics, to which all his answers reinforced his prior commitment to agnosticism, meaning that he could not affirm any traditional religious beliefs or practices. On the

---

21. Thomas Huxley, "Agnosticism and Christianity," in *Collected Essays*, vol. 5, *Science and the Christian Tradition* (Cambridge: Cambridge University Press, 2011), 310.

22. Bertrand Russell, "What Is an Agnostic?," in *Russell on Religion*, ed. Louis I. Greenspan and Stefan Andersson (London: Routledge, 1999), 41.

23. Russell, 41.

24. Russell, 41.

25. Bernard V. Lightman, *The Origins of Agnosticism: Victorian Unbelief and the Limits of Knowledge* (Baltimore: Johns Hopkins University Press, 1987), 3.

contrary, Russell was avowedly opposed to religions such as Christianity and thought them devoid of logical sense. But once again, agnosticism per se need not imply rejection of religion.

What about the Other -Isms? Atheist and Agnostic Worldviews

When coining the term *agnosticism*, Thomas Huxley listed a long series of rival philosophies that also end in *-ism*. These included communism, humanism, socialism, evolutionism, secularism, materialism, and naturalism. We might describe these as worldviews under the umbrella of atheism and agnosticism. Stated differently, most of the *-isms* listed are social and political byproducts of an atheist or agnostic worldview. As Karl Marx (1818–83) and Friedrich Engels (1820–95) wrote in *Communist Manifesto*—a sort of bible of nontheistic political systems—"Communism abolishes eternal truths, it abolishes all religion."[26]

The same holds for some of the other *-isms*. Still, as I mentioned above, these byproducts exist on a spectrum, and there is a marked difference between a rigidly atheistic culture and a reluctantly agnostic one. Nevertheless, a prior atheistic and agnostic worldview gives birth to such systems of thought. Many regions of the world can sustain multiple worldviews, but there is a fine line between a theistic worldview and its atheistic or agnostic counterpart. Just as Christianity stems from a theistic worldview, so communism descends from an atheistic one. But to keep things complicated and confusing, today there are Christians who do not engage in organized religion, just as there are communists who are members of churches.

Part 4: Varieties of Atheism

In his book *Seven Types of Atheism*, atheist philosopher John Gray outlines seven varieties of atheism. Although I quibble with this random number and his precise terminology, he is certainly correct that atheism exists on a spectrum and that it has never been as monolithic as people assume. In this section, therefore, I will isolate some of the more notable varieties of atheism, including both anti-religious and pro-religious kinds. As you read, you might try to imagine what kind of atheism you most often encounter in your walk of life.

---

26. Karl Marx and Friedrich Engels, *The Communist Manifesto*, trans. Paul M. Sweezy (New York: Washington Square Press, 1970), 92.

Modern Atheism

As scholar Denis Robichaud explains, "It is largely during the Renaissance and Reformation that the semantic field of modern atheism began to be assembled and articulated."[27] Before that time, the term *atheism* was equivocal and used in various ways; but because atheism was effectively illegal for millennia (and therefore one could be found guilty of it and sentenced to death), there was everything to lose by professing it and hardly anything to gain. In this way, it was mostly an amorphous term hurled against one's opponents until the modern era. Consequently, I will use the term *Modern Atheism* to include atheists and agnostics who were active from approximately the 1500s to the 1800s. This period included some of the most famous atheistic and agnostic philosophers and scientists across the Western world, such as Giordano Bruno (1548–1600), Herbert of Cherbury (1583–1648), Voltaire (1694–1778), John Toland (1670–1722), David Hume (1711–78), Thomas Paine (1737–1809), Charles Darwin, Karl Marx, and Friedrich Nietzsche (1844–1900). Of these authors, some of the more influential books they wrote are Toland's *On Truth* (1624), *Christianity Not Mysterious* (1696), and *Letter to Serena* (1704); Hume's *Dialogues concerning Natural Religion* (1779); Paine's *The Age of Reason* (1794–95, 1807); Darwin's *On the Origin of Species* (1859) and *Descent of Man* (1871); Marx's *Communist Manifesto* (1848) and *Das Kapital* (1867–83); and Nietzsche's *The Antichrist* (1888) and *Thus Spoke Zarathustra* (1892). Combined, these books made it intellectually and even morally respectable to adopt atheism and abandon any vestiges of God.

New Atheism

The term *New Atheist* was coined in the first half of the twenty-first century to refer to a growing cohort of atheists who are much more dogged in their stances against religion and more dogmatic in their support of science. In short, these are the feisty atheists. By this time in history, atheism was no longer illegal—at least in the West—and society's attachment to the concept of the divine had been increasingly loosened after the 1800s. According to philosopher Graham Oppy, New Atheism generally argues that "religion is an enemy of both philosophy and reason, a relic of our shameful past that ought to be put down with extreme rancour."[28] The leaders of the movement have written bestsellers that

Seven Types of Atheism. Atheist philosopher John Gray delineates seven varieties of atheism: (1) new atheism, (2) secular humanism, (3) science as morality, (4) atheism, gnosticism, and modern political religion, (5) God-haters, (6) atheism without progress, and (7) mystical atheism.

Gray, *Seven Types of Atheism*.

---

27. Denis Robichaud, "Renaissance and Reformation," in *The Oxford Handbook of Atheism*, ed. Stephen Bullivant and Michael Ruse (Oxford: Oxford University Press, 2013), 180.

28. Oppy, *Atheism: The Basics*, 138.

have sold millions of copies, they have been featured on countless media outlets, and they have debated and lectured in classrooms and auditoriums around the world. There are too many New Atheists to mention, but most are educated white men in middle age or older. And if anything, they have as much faith in science as priests have in religion. Some of the notables are Stephen Hawking, Richard Dawkins, Christopher Hitchens, Daniel Dennett (b. 1942), and Sam Harris (b. 1967).

Fig. 9.3.
Richard Dawkins is a leading figure in what is called *New Atheism*.

    Stephen Hawking, a famous physicist who taught at Cambridge, wrote popular books such as *A Brief History of Time* (1988) and *The Grand Design* (2010), which narrated the creation of the cosmos completely independently of a creator, arguing, "It is not necessary to invoke God to . . . set the universe going."[29] Richard Dawkins, a former professor at Oxford and perhaps more famous for his campaign against religion than for his scientific research, wrote *The God Delusion* (2006), which took aim at the concept of a deity. Daniel Dennett, an American philosopher, is author of *Darwin's Dangerous Idea* (1995) and *Breaking the Spell: Religion as a Natural Phenomenon* (2006), in which he maintains

29. Stephen Hawking and Leonard Mlodinow, *The Grand Design* (New York: Bantam Books, 2010), 180.

that evolution accounts for morality and explains how religion developed naturalistically. Christopher Hitchens, a British journalist, penned *God Is Not Great: How Religion Poisons Everything* (2007) and *The Portable Atheist: Essential Readings for the Non-Believer* (2007), asserting that all religions are hateful and violent. Finally, Sam Harris, an American neuroscientist, is author of multiple atheist-oriented books, including *The End of Faith* (2004), *Letter to a Christian Nation* (2006), and *Waking Up: A Guide to Spirituality without Religion* (2014). In these books Harris argues that religion is the source of most of our human and political problems, and that the best solution is to reject everything that is not scientifically verifiable—namely, faith and the religions that faith creates and sustains. He is especially critical of Islam.

Religious Atheism

Despite the representatives of the New Atheism mentioned above, plenty of atheists are religious. Yes, this means that they do not believe in God, but that they do believe in religion. Unfortunately, this is a topic that scholars have only recently begun exploring, and immense challenges are involved in quantifying the exact percentage of religious atheists. This is compounded by the fact that practically all countries have historically made atheism either explicitly illegal or socially unacceptable. Even in the West, as I discussed above, the centuries-long queue of would-be publicly avowed atheists had to wait until fairly recently to form, and atheism is still not a viable option among those living in many countries in the East where it is safer to suffer theism in silence than risk censure by professing atheism. This is further convoluted by the Western assumption that atheism implies irreligion, and that religion entails theism. But neither is necessarily true. As we will see below, atheism and religion have a complicated relationship.

Let me get right to the point: Every world religion has atheists. This may sound shocking—and you might not believe me—but there are atheists in Hinduism, Buddhism, Jainism, Sikhism, Confucianism, Daoism, Judaism, Christianity, and even Islam. In fact, I could even argue that world religions requiring belief in a personal, knowable, and omniscient God are the exception rather than the rule. For neither the Chinese nor Indian traditions—which, when added, make up the majority of world religions—have ever mandated such credence.[30]

First Public Jewish Atheist. Although atheistic Judaism has accelerated since the Holocaust, it has been around for centuries. One of the earliest atheistic Jews was Benedict Spinoza (1632–77). He was eventually excommunicated from his Jewish community. His two most influential books were *Theologico-Political Treatise* (1670) and *Ethics* (1677).

---

30. See especially Jacques Berlinerblau, "Jewish Atheism"; Andrew Skilton, "Buddhism"; Anne Vallely, "Jainism"; and Jessica Frazier, "Hinduism," in *The Oxford Handbook of Atheism*, ed. Stephen Bullivant and Michael Ruse (Oxford: Oxford University Press, 2013), 320–82.

This leaves only the Abrahamic religions of Judaism, Christianity, and Islam. But of these, it is no secret that a high percentage of Jews are atheists. Being Jewish, after all, has long been more about deeds than creeds and about ethnicity over faith. In this way, "ritual practice is much more important to being a Jew than belief."[31] And when it comes to Christianity, entire denominations have been created for atheists, such as Unitarian Universalism, which is perfectly content to have church but skip God. This reality is heightened in many Western European nations where growing numbers of atheists are still members of churches—not to mention the untold millions of so-called Christians in the Middle Ages and modern era who feigned belief in God at church to avoid arrest, suspicion, or censure and, by contrast, feigned belief to gain respectability, community, and opportunity. Even in Islam, secularism has eroded belief in God in certain Muslim nations, and among Muslims in European countries, this is even more pronounced.[32] But as alluded to above, "in most Muslim-majority societies today, atheism and nonreligion are strongly scandalized, and often also criminalized."[33] This has the result of muffling the number of atheist Muslims when polled.

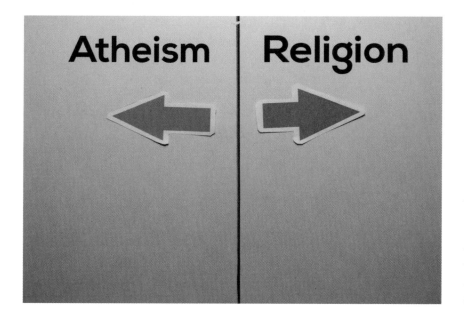

Fig. 9.4.
Atheism and religion are not always opposed. In fact, many religions are atheistic.

31. Aaron J. Hahn Tapper, *Judaisms: A Twenty-First Century Introduction to Jews and Jewish Identities* (Berkeley: University of California Press, 2016), 4.

32. See Paul Froese, "'I Am an Atheist and a Muslim': Islam, Communism, and Ideological Competition," *Journal of Church and State* 47, no. 3 (Summer 2005): 473–501.

33. Samuli Schielke, "The Islamic World," in *The Oxford Handbook of Atheism*, ed. Stephen Bullivant and Michael Ruse (Oxford: Oxford University Press, 2013), 647.

Is Atheism a Religion, Then?

In his book *The Atheist's Guide to Reality*, Alex Rosenberg contends that atheism is for those "who are comfortable with the truth about reality,"[34] meaning that it is not for those harboring incredible stories about gods, miracles, faith, and religion. In fact, he argues, atheism offers "a demanding, rigorous, breathtaking grip on reality, one that has been vindicated beyond reasonable doubt[,] . . . employing a real understanding of the natural world."[35] Instead of religion's providing the answers to life's basic questions, he believes that science does. This mindset characterizes the various *-isms* stemming from an atheistic or agnostic worldview that we explored above. Whether or not they explicitly set aside religion, these worldviews attempt to construct a personal, social, or political system purely out of the building blocks of what can be seen, heard, touched, and smelled. No room, or at least very little, is left for the miraculous, a *deus ex machina*, or a Messiah.

Fig. 9.5. Benedict Spinoza was a Jewish atheist who has been very influential. He was buried in his native country of the Netherlands.

This begs the question: Is atheism a religion? The answer depends on a whole host of matters. On the one hand, New Atheism believes in science just as much as religious practitioners do in God. After all, it does not take very long when reading Harris, Dawkins, and Hawking—all

---

34. Alex Rosenberg, *The Atheist's Guide to Reality: Enjoying Life without Illusions* (New York: Norton & Co., 2011), vii.

35. Rosenberg, viii.

of whom earned doctorates in the sciences, by the way—to learn that they have put all their eggs in one materialist basket. They leave no room for mystery, no room for spirituality, and no room for God. They are materialists who glorify the physical. On the other hand, atheism does not have the cluster of elements that constitute religions, namely, defined beliefs, worship practices, scriptures, hierarchies, bylaws, moral codes, and holy sites. In the absence of such elements, I personally do not consider atheism to be a religion. Nor do any of the actual figures listed above. It is more fitting to recognize that plenty of atheists are religious but not that atheism in and of itself is a religion.

Part 5: Point of Contact

Some of my closest friends are agnostics and atheists, and they each have their own reasons for why they cannot be certain that God exists. They know, of course, that I am a committed Christian, and that I have taken entire courses in apologetics in which I learned sophisticated arguments about why they must be wrong. Although we do occasionally talk about such things, I have never found the dozens of arguments for the existence of God that I have been taught to be very effective. It could, of course, just be my own limitations. Perhaps I simply do not understand the arguments. Or perhaps, like someone who tries to tell a joke but botches the punchline, I simply cannot articulate the arguments in the right order or the right way. Either way, I have mostly moved away from intellectual arguments for the existence of God and instead turned to a model I created called *Dodekagram*.

Coming from the Greek words for "twelve" and "written," "Dodekagram is a spiritual tool designed to uncover and understand the twelve ways people connect with God."[36] It is divided into six parts that correspond to the body: (1) head, (2) heart, (3) core, (4) limbs, (5) soul, and (6) spirit. As a Reformed Christian, I resonate with Abraham Kuyper's famous quote, "There is not a square inch in the whole domain of our human existence over which Christ, who is Sovereign over all, does not cry, Mine!" It is in this spirit that I believe that everything in creation gives evidence to God's existence, which, in the makeup of Dodekagram, contains the six parts mentioned above, each of which contains two sub-parts. The head consists of the Rationalist and Secularist, and I believe that both our thinking and our tendency to nurture communities point to God's existence. The heart consists of the Naturalist and Artist, and

---

36. www.Dodekagram.com.

I believe that both nature and our inclination toward creating attest to God's existence. The core consists of the Scripturalist and Traditionalist, and I believe that both the Bible and church history give voice to God's existence. The limbs consist of the Activist and Altruist, and I believe that our desire to both advocate for and serve others offers a reflection of God's existence. The soul consists of the Perfectionist and Ritualist, and I believe that our desire to both live morally upright lives and form religions that promote worship give witness to God's existence. Finally, the spirit consists of the Mysticist and Supernaturalist, and I believe that both our natural compulsion to pray and our inherent search for meaning testify to God's existence. As I engage atheists, I draw from Dodekagram, finding that I have at my disposal twelve completely different ways that illustrate God's existence. Perhaps you will find it a useful tool as well.

Discussion Questions

1. Discuss your reactions to the following quote: "*Atheism* simply possesses no single, objective definition: it can be used correctly in a number of related, sometimes overlapping, and often mutually exclusive ways. This is not necessarily a problem, so long as one is always clear how exactly each author is deploying the term."[37]
2. Look up online "arguments for the existence of God." Which arguments do you find most compelling? Why?
3. Have you ever had any exposure to any of the figures who make up what is called the *New Atheists*? What is your impression of their arguments, presentations, or images?
4. What is the difference between an atheist, agnostic, and deist? Of these three, which is most popular among people you may know? Would you respond to each of these three in the same way or a different way? How so?
5. What is Dodekagram? Check out the website at Dodekagram.com and explain how you think the twelve Dodekagram types could be used when interacting with atheists or agnostics. Which type do you resonate with most?

For Further Reading

Bullivant, Stephen, and Michael Ruse, eds. *The Oxford Handbook of Atheism*. Oxford: Oxford University Press, 2013.

37. Bullivant, "Defining 'Atheism,'" 13.

Gray, John. *Seven Types of Atheism*. New York: Picador, 2018.

Martin, Michael, ed. *The Cambridge Companion to Atheism*. Cambridge: Cambridge University Press, 2007.

Oppy, Graham. *Atheism: The Basics*. London: Routledge, 2019.

Walters, Kerry. *Atheism: A Guide for the Perplexed*. New York and London: Continuum, 2010.

chapter 10

Nones: The Story of Unaffiliation

The ranks of the Nones have ballooned in recent years, making "no religious affiliation" the fastest-growing category among religious affiliations.

Corinna Nicolaou[1]

Claiming no religion does not necessarily mean that people consider themselves anti- or nonreligious . . . , merely that they do not identify with any organized, public religion.

Joseph Baker and Buster Smith[2]

Rather than forming one homogenous secular group, individuals declaring having no religion are characterized by varying levels of religiosity.

Sarah Wilkins-Laflamme[3]

Part 1: The Beginning

Like so many others before him, he was moving to Los Angeles to make a name for himself. But unlike those aspiring to break into show business, he was breaking away from the religion that had made him a celebrity. Just weeks before, he had been preaching each Sunday

---

1. Corinna Nicolaou, *A None's Story: Searching for Meaning inside Christianity, Judaism, Buddhism, and Islam* (New York: Columbia University Press, 2016), xi.

2. Joseph O. Baker and Buster G. Smith, *American Secularism: Cultural Contours of Nonreligious Belief Systems* (New York: New York University Press, 2015), 1.

3. Sarah Wilkins-Laflamme, "How Unreligious Are the Religious 'Nones'? Religious Dynamics of the Unaffiliated in Canada," *Canadian Journal of Sociology* 40, no. 4 (2015): 478.

to ten thousand adoring Christians in a mall that had been converted into a megachurch. He was a rising star in the universe of American Christianity who had not only earned degrees from the flagship evangelical academic institutions of Wheaton College and Fuller Seminary but gone on to plant a megachurch, write bestselling books, and create out-of-the-box videos that connected with the coveted generational cohort of millennials who were otherwise deserting organized religion in droves. He could have been the next Billy Graham. But now he was spoiled goods. As a result of his latest book in which he questioned deeply rooted Christian beliefs, the gatekeepers of evangelicalism closed him off from the flock, decrying him as a wolf in sheep's clothing. To be avoided at all costs, he was labeled a heretic, an unbeliever, a universalist, and anything and everything in between.

Fig. 10.1. Rob Bell was a leading figure in evangelical Christianity before becoming a none.

Now living happily in Los Angeles where he hosts a popular podcast, continues to write spiritual books, and speaks to audiences across the globe, Rob Bell (b. 1970) is perhaps the founding member of a growing community of spiritual but not religious individuals who want little or nothing to do with organized faith. Although there has certainly always been a remnant of believers who did not feel as though they truly belonged to the religious communities with which they may have occasionally been affiliated, that number has been climbing year by year and decade by decade, currently capturing roughly a third of all adult Americans—and just as many, as I will discuss below, from other regions around the world. Like Bell, these individuals are called by many names, and also like Bell, they are a work in progress. They may differ in exactly what they believe, which religion they left, and why they did so, but they unite in their conviction that they are better off forging their own individual path without the supervision of an official and organized religious community overseeing them.

Part 2: Defining Terms

The West has been swept up in a revolution of religious apathy. And no matter where you seem to go, the trail is more evident than ever. As Jason Lantzer argues in his book *Mainline Christianity*, many individuals perceive religious spaces like Christian churches to be "vestiges of a different time."[4] It is not surprising, therefore, that 34 percent of Americans "either do not identify as religious or do not consider religion as important in their lives."[5] This percentage represents "a steady increase during the past two decades,"[6] with numbers only expected to rise in the years to come. In fact, "there are more individuals who consider themselves 'not religious' living in the United States than any other nation in the world except China."[7] Taken all together, this phenomenon "has been one of the most important trends on the American religious scene."[8]

A whole host of terms have emerged in the past few decades to describe this increasing number of individuals who retain their faith but ditch their religion. Some of the more common terms are *unaffiliated, nonaffiliated, disaffiliated, areligious, nonreligious, nonvert, postreligious,*

---

4. Jason S. Lantzer, *Mainline Christianity: The Past and Future of America's Majority Faith* (New York: New York University Press, 2012), 4.

5. Ryan Cragun et al., "North America," in *The Oxford Handbook of Atheism*, ed. Stephen Bullivant and Michael Ruse (Oxford: Oxford University Press, 2013), 602.

6. Frank Pasquale and Barry Kosmin, "Atheism and the Secularization Thesis," in *The Oxford Handbook of Atheism*, ed. Stephen Bullivant and Michael Ruse (Oxford: Oxford University Press, 2013), 458.

7. Baker and Smith, *American Secularism*, 15.

8. Barry A. Kosmin and Ariela Keysar, *ARIS 2008 Summary Report* (Hartford, CT: Institute for the Study of Secularism in Society and Culture, Trinity College), http://commons.trincoll.edu/aris/files/2011/08/ARIS_Report_2008.pdf.

liminal, none, done, and *spiritual but not religious.* Although scholars work hard to distinguish them—or at least to argue which are best—I will generally use these terms interchangeably to refer to those individuals who manage to maintain some semblance of faith without being affiliated with any religious organization. In case you are thinking that this phenomenon is safely confined to America and China, however, you will need to think again. The numbers of the unaffiliated are on the rise around the world. And although they do not perfectly correlate with all the new religious movements that we have discussed in this book, they are nonetheless a religious force that can no longer be denied, overlooked, or marginalized. In fact, within the horizon of history, we can easily make the case that the unaffiliated are new, they are spiritual, and they are a movement.

Part 3: Reasons for the Rises of Unaffiliation

Sociologist Callum Brown writes, "Losing religion has become a very important phenomenon of our times."[9] This is true. Losing religion, however, does not automatically mean abandoning spirituality. As Scott Adams explains, "The evidence seems to suggest that being unchurched does not necessarily equate to being unchristian, unspiritual, or unbelieving."[10] There are actually multiple reasons why nones have risen in the past several decades, few of which directly hinge on belief that God does not exist or that spirituality is bad. For instance, social scientist Ryan Burge, author of *The Nones*, argues that the unaffiliated do not participate in organized religion for myriad reasons, including loss of trust in institutions, experiences of abuse within religious contexts, frustration at widespread politicization among faith communities, changing family structures and values, no longer believing in the theologies propounded, forming better connections with people on the internet (rather than in person), increased lack of societal pressure to be part of a religious community, the continued growth of secularism, and, we might add, dissatisfaction at how religious organizations handled issues relating to the pandemic (masks, vaccines, attendance, and so on).[11]

Spiritual But Not Religious (SBNR). According to Linda Mercadante: "The most complex type of none is the 'spiritual but not religious' (SBNR). These people define spirituality as personal, heart-felt, and authentic, while claiming religion is external, structured, and non-essential...They are generally neither devoted atheists nor devout believers, instead occupying the middle space between these orientations.

Linda Mercadante, "Spiritual Struggles of Nones and 'Spiritual but Not Religious' (SBNRs)," *Religions* 11, no. 10 (2020): 513–14.

9. Callum G. Brown, *Becoming Atheist: Humanism and the Secular West* (London: Bloomsbury, 2017), 7.
10. Scott Lewis Adams, "The Spirituality of Jesus for the Unchurched and the Unaffiliated: A Pentecostal-Charismatic Perspective," *Religions* 13, no. 11 (November 2022): 1126.
11. Ryan P. Burge, *The Nones: Where They Came From, Who They Are, and Where They Are Going* (Minneapolis: Fortress Press, 2021), 35–68.

Fig. 10.2.
A growing number of individuals identify as spiritual but not religious (SBNR).

Christian-Based Nones

Let's start with nones who have a historical connection to the Christian religion. George Barna, the pioneering researcher of American religious statistics, writes, "The data show that the number of unchurched adults in the United States has increased by nearly 60 percent in the past decade."[12] And lest we assume that the unchurched consist only of the youth, Linda Mercadante, author of *Belief without Borders: Inside the Minds of the Spiritual but Not Religious*, reveals that nones can be found across the generational cohort of the Silent Generation, Baby Boomers, Gen Xers, Millennials, and Gen Zers.[13] On the one hand, many studies reveal that institutional Christianity's decline can be attributed to its escalating image problem. For instance, cultural commentators David Kinnaman and Gabe Lyons found that those between the ages of sixteen and twenty-nine who no longer affiliate institutionally with the Christian religion operate from the mindset that *Christianity* and *hypocrisy* are synonymous terms.[14] Even though Christians have historically served at the forefront of founding hospitals, funding health clinics, building schools, rescuing the abused, caring for the elderly, rehabilitating the imprisoned, sheltering the homeless, strengthening the family, offering

---

12. George Barna, *America at the Crossroads: Explosive Trends Shaping America's Future and What You Can Do about It* (Grand Rapids: Baker, 2016), 39.

13. Linda A. Mercadante, *Belief without Borders: Inside the Minds of the Spiritual but Not Religious* (New York: Oxford University Press, 2014).

14. David Kinnaman and Gabe Lyons, *unChristian: What a New Generation Really Thinks about Christianity . . . and Why It Matters* (Grand Rapids: Baker, 2012), 41.

mental health services, providing spiritual guidance, and generally seeking to improve society, many young nones think that Christianity is nothing more than a country club of judgmental, homophobic, racist, and excessively political hypocrites. In surveys conducted across the country, Kinnaman and Lyons discovered that 91 percent of younger nones think Christianity is homophobic, 87 percent believe Christians are judgmental, and 85 percent view Christians as hypocritical.[15]

Fig. 10.3.
Although the nones exist in every generational cohort, they are highest among Gen Z.

What Do Nones Have in Common?
"Regardless of where apostates have ended up—atheist, agnostic, unsure, spiritual, or something else—what all those I interviewed shared was a very clear and obvious distancing from their religion in terms of belief, adherence, identification, membership, and/or participation, and for the majority, an outright loss or rejection thereof."

Zuckerman, 151.

On the other hand, plenty of Christian nones have given up on church because they simply do not believe that it provides enough relevance to their lives. For instance, Barna has shared results from a study he encountered that roughly half of Americans do not affiliate with churches because churches are believed to offer "no value."[16] In a related way, Mercadante's research on this topic discovered that Christian nones prefer spiritual experiences over religious affiliation—with the implication being that religious affiliation is unable to muster enough meaningful personal experiences to keep the spiritual "in religion."[17] In fact, noted author Harvey Cox wrote an entire book on this topic, summarizing it by stating that "the experience *of* the divine is displacing theories *about* it."[18] Other scholars studying this subject have come to similar conclusions, maintaining that loss of belief in traditional doctrines leads a person to

15. Kinnaman and Lyons, 24.
16. Barna, *America at the Crossroads*, 42.
17. Linda Mercadante, "Do the 'Spiritual but not Religious' (SBNR) Want a Theology without Walls?," *Journal of Interreligious Studies* 34 (2022): 80.
18. Harvey Cox, *The Future of Faith* (New York: HarperOne, 2009), 20.

find little value in what churches or other religious institutions teach.[19] This is a clarion call to how many nones perceive Christianity, but it also puts into focus how wide a net secularism has cast.

The Effects of Secularization

According to secularization theory, the more developed a nation becomes, the more secular it becomes. To say it another way, organizational or institutional religion loses cultural and communal significance as modern societies become more individualistic, more specialized, more fragmented, and more differentiated.[20] What this effectively means is that a byproduct of a society's becoming more modern or developed is that it begins to display higher instances of individualism, pluralism, rationalism, consumerism, increase in lifespan, personal security, privatization, and technologization—all of which have the combined effect of eroding traditional religious organizations and practices. This mindset has been a dominant theory among scholars. And although it is not without its critics (and it does not work in every context), it does offer a shorthand explanation for why societies as far apart as Australia to France to Israel to Japan to Uruguay continue to witness consistent declines in religious attendance and affiliation at the exact time they become more modern, more economically robust, and more technologically advanced.

Historically, the topic of secularism and secularization has been discussed by philosophers, social scientists, and intellectuals for centuries. This especially includes figures such as August Comte (1798–1857), Karl Marx (1818–83), Sigmund Freud (1856–1939), Emile Durkheim (1858–1917), and Max Weber (1864–1920). Though arriving at different conclusions, they all witnessed the secularization of their societies and hypothesized why organized religion was disintegrating. Scholars today continue to interact with their theories in disciplines related to sociology, psychology, philosophy, religion, and other social sciences.

Building on the research of Durkheim, for example, who effectively argued that individualism was organized religion's nemesis, and that religion would decrease as individualism increased, sociologist Rob Warner organized Durkheim's cause-and-effect conclusions as follows:

1. Individualism diminishes the experience of social cohesion.
2. Individualism diminishes the practice of communal religion.

Secularization Theory. Secularization theory suggests that "there is evidence of a very broad tendency for religion(s) to weaken or religiosity to become more individualized as countries become more economically developed, as societies become more institutionally complex, and as individuals become more existentially— that is, economically, medically, psychologically — secure."

Phil Zuckerman, Luke W. Galen, and Frank L. Pasquale, *The Nonreligious: Understanding Secular People and Societies* (Oxford: Oxford University Press, 2016), 53.

---

19. Phil Zuckerman, *Faith No More: Why People Reject Religion* (New York: Oxford University Press, 2011).

20. Peter Ester and Loek Halman, "Empirical Trends in Religious and Moral Beliefs in Western Europe," *International Journal of Sociology* 24, no. 2/3 (Summer–Fall 1994): 81–110.

3. Protestantism elevates the individual and legitimates individualism.
4. Protestantism thereby diminishes social cohesion and the practice of religion.
5. The unintended consequences of Protestantism are the growth of individualism, the decay of social cohesion and the decline of religion.
6. Protestantism may therefore in the long-term become sociologically non-viable, subverting its own religious intentions by functioning as an accidental agent of secularization.[21]

Marx on Religion. "Religion is...the opium of the people. The abolition of religion as the illusory happiness of the people is the demand for their real happiness...The criticism of religion is therefore the germ of the criticism of the valley of tears whose halo is religion."

Karl Marx, *Critique of Hegel's "Philosophy of Right,"* trans. Joseph J. O'Malley (Cambridge: Cambridge University Press, 1970), 131.

Part 4: Unaffiliation around the Globe

The rise of the religiously unaffiliated and subsequent decrease in the affiliated is not confined to America. It is, in fact, rampant across the most developed regions in the world in Africa, Asia, Latin America, the Middle East, and Oceania.

Let us start in Africa and the Middle East. In the minority of countries on this continent that are modernized, they display the same kind of religious apathy that characterizes Western nations. For instance, although this region is historically Muslim, Christian, and Jewish, the more developed countries of Algeria, Azerbaijan, Botswana, Israel, South Africa, and Turkey are populated by high percentages of religious nones. In Algeria, this amounts to more than 40 percent who maintain no religious affiliation, while in Azerbaijan it is the majority of the country. In fact, in Azerbaijan only about 5 percent of the population are active Muslim practitioners. Religious nonaffiliation is also rampant in nearby Israel. For reasons that we discussed in the previous chapter, Israel has one of the highest religious none populations in the world. Only a little more than half the country participates in religious practices; and even then, most Israelis view these practices more as ethnically or culturally motivated than religiously so. Meanwhile, deep in sub-Saharan Africa, a region known for its religious devotion, the countries with the most stable economies and most advanced technological infrastructures—Botswana and South Africa—are growing in secularism. In Botswana, for example, 20 percent of the population are nones.[22] And in South Africa, the percentage is about the same.[23]

---

21. Rob Warner, *Secularization and Its Discontents* (London: Continuum, 2010), 23.
22. Zuckerman, Galen, and Pasquale, *Nonreligious*, 47–50.
23. Willem J. Schoeman, "South African Religious Demography: The 2013 General Household Survey," *HTS Teologiese Studies* 73, no. 2 (2017): 2.

Fig. 10.4. According to secularization theory, the more developed a nation becomes, the more secular it becomes.

The region of Asia illustrates similar characteristics. Although we tend to associate this part of the world with religions such as Buddhism, Confucianism, Daoism, and Hinduism, the most developed Asian countries display a population that is deeply nonreligious. This especially includes China, India, Singapore, South Korea, Japan, and Taiwan. In fact, in Japan, "religion has negative connotations." Although most Japanese believe in spirituality, the vast majority do not practice any religion. And "there is strong evidence of decline in 'traditional' religious practices" and "greater reported distrust of religious organizations and leaders."[24] In nearby China, the number of nones is staggering. According to surveys conducted over decades, "an average of 87 percent of Chinese mainland adults considered themselves not to be religious."[25] This is combined with an extremely loose, fragmented, and weak religious infrastructure, which is all the more fascinating given that China was formerly home to one of the most religiously fertile civilizations in the world.

Latin America is another region that presents interesting findings. Although Roman Catholicism—and in more recent decades, Pentecostalism—has played a significant role in historical religious affiliation, the countries in this region with the highest standards of living are experiencing widespread nonreligion. This is especially seen in places such as Argentina, Brazil, Chile, and Uruguay. Of these, Uruguay offers

24. Zuckerman, Galen, and Pasquale, *Nonreligious*, 39, 41.
25. Weixiang Luo and Feinian Chen, "The Salience of Religion under an Atheist State: Implications for Subjective Well-Being in Contemporary China," *Social Forces* 100, no. 2 (December 2021): 856.

compelling evidence for the secularization theory. Often compared to people of Western Europe, half the citizens in Uruguay do not place any importance on religious matters. They boast the highest "none" population in Latin America. Meanwhile, several nearby, modernizing countries are following in their footsteps. For instance, the nones are the fastest-growing segment in Argentina, where they have increased by more than 1,000 percent over the past half-century.[26] In a related way, Chile yields a population of more than 30 percent who do not have any religious affiliation. In fact, even less modernized Latin American countries such as El Salvador and Guatemala are experiencing widespread movement away from institutional Christianity. Nearly 30 percent of the population in those countries is composed of nones.[27]

Fig. 10.5. Nones are growing all around the world. In Azerbaijan, for example, they are the majority of the population.

In Europe, nones are not merely on the rise. They appear to be the majority. Scandinavia, for example, is perhaps the world's most politically stable yet religiously apathetic region. Although Christianity is the state religion, few Scandinavians feign any participation in the religious practices of the church. In Denmark, 93 percent do not attend church on a consistent basis.[28] Similarly, Norway is considered "the world's most secular [nation]," with about the same percentage of the population not being involved in services sponsored by the state church.[29] There are similar examples across Europe, with countries such as the Czech Republic, Estonia, France, and Russia containing extraordinarily high percentages of religious nones. In fact, being a none "is the norm" in these countries.[30] And when it comes to the British Isles, the United Kingdom is also deeply secular. In England, for example, "the scale and decline

26. Juan Cruz Esquivel, "Religiously Disaffiliated, Religiously Indifferent, or Believers without Religion: Morphology of the Unaffiliated in Argentina," *Religions* 12, no. 7 (June 2021): 472.

27. Zuckerman, Galen, and Pasquale, *Nonreligious*, 45–46.

28. Zuckerman, Galen, and Pasquale, 79.

29. Sivert Skålvoll Urstad, "The Religiously Unaffiliated in Norway," *Nordic Journal of Religion and Society* 30, no. 1 (May 15, 2017): 61–81.

30. Olaf Müller and Chiara Porada, "Towards a Society of Stable Nones: Lifelong Non-Denominationalism as the Prevailing Pattern in East Germany," *Religions* 13, no. 11 (2022): 1037.

[of church attendance] are staggering: English congregations have on average halved in size in the last quarter century."[31]

English Church Attendance Decline over 150 Years[32]

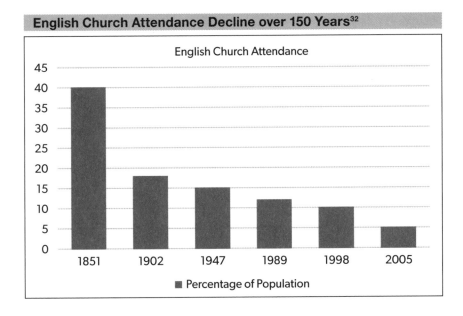

Finally, the two most developed countries in Oceania represent some of the most secular nations on the planet. I am, of course, referring to Australia and New Zealand. In Australia, "there has been a substantial and steady increase in the percentage of those declaring that they have 'no religion.'" Exact statistics vary, but that number hovers around 30 percent of the population.[33] This percentage is even higher in nearby New Zealand, with almost half the population claiming no religion.[34] As both these countries continue to modernize, it is projected that they will become even more secularized.

Part 5: Point of Contact

I completely resonate with nones in almost every way, and many of my closest friends would describe themselves as spiritual but not religious. All of them have their reasons for continuing to believe in God while

---

31. Warner, *Secularization and Its Discontents*, 6.

32. Warner, 11.

33. Gary Bouma and Anna Halafoff, "Australia's Changing Religious Profile—Rising Nones and Pentecostals, Declining British Protestants in Superdiversity: Views from the 2016 Census," *Journal for the Academic Study of Religion* 30, no. 2 (2017): 132.

34. Theis Oxholm et al., "Representing New Zealand Religious Diversity? The Removal of the Words 'True Religion' and 'Jesus Christ' from the Parliamentary Prayer," *Journal of Church and State* 64, no. 1 (Winter 2022): 87–109.

not going to church. Rather than berate them and convince them how wrong they are, which is an approach I once took, I now tread a different path. In short, I listen to their criticisms of the church as an invitation for me—as a representative of the church—to learn how those of us who are both spiritual and religious can do a better job. What do I mean?

When viewed through the prism of a humble desire to listen and learn, nones should encourage churchgoers to return to Scripture to reevaluate whether churchgoers' actions and behaviors are actually in step with the gospel. Taking my data from the research that books such as *Churchless*, *unChristian*, and *The Nones* have unearthed regarding why nones have abandoned the church, I agree with nones that rather than being spiritually shallow, churchgoers should embody spiritual maturity; rather than being overprotective, we should be so faith-oriented that we entrust all our loved ones and resources to the guidance of the Holy Spirit; rather than being antagonistic to science, we should unite the best of empirical research with the breadth of biblical wisdom, recognizing that there are no contradictions between natural revelation and supernatural revelation; rather than being judgmental, we should apply Jesus' commands to "judge not"; rather than being deemed haters of the LGBTQ community, we should universally exemplify what it means to be sexually whole and healthy; and rather than being hostile to those who express doubt, we should be the first to admit that faith meanders through peaks and valleys on the way to the celestial city.

Taken from a different angle, the data mentioned above from nones actually reveals values that are not at all antithetical to churchgoing: showing spiritual curiosity, illustrating intentional open-mindedness, taking mainstream science seriously, caring for the environment, acknowledging the gender gap, not shaming those who are different from us, accepting all people as image-bearers of God, and showing greater concern for social causes. To be sure, these "none" values will not perfectly coincide with churchgoing values (and I am not advocating that we let the tail wag the dog). Yet many of these overarching "none" values do coincide with churchgoing ones. For instance, according to research conducted by Barna and Kinnaman, the greatest "good" that the unaffiliated think churches can do for their communities is "addressing poverty."[35] This is one of the most recalcitrant social problems facing any developed nation, and it certainly qualifies as a value with which churchgoers should be concerned. The fact that those who are religiously unaffiliated believe that the church should be addressing poverty reveals many things, to be

---

35. George Barna and David Kinnaman, *Churchless: Understanding Today's Unchurched and How to Connect with Them* (Carol Stream, IL: Tyndale House, 2014), 25.

sure, but one stands out in particular. If nones think the church should be doing something that the church can and should be doing already as part of its biblical mandate, perhaps it is the church that is more at fault.

Discussion Questions

1. Do you know any nones? What would you say they think about religion?
2. Do you expect the number of nones to stay the same, decrease, or increase in the future? Why?
3. Why do you think there are so many nones around the world today compared to a century ago?
4. Explain what secularization theory is. Do you think it explains how religion and secularism function? How so? Is there a better theory?
5. If you had to share your faith with a none, what would you share? Do you think the person would find your testimony compelling? Why or why not?

For Further Reading

Baker, Joseph O., and Buster G. Smith. *American Secularism: Cultural Contours of Nonreligious Belief Systems.* New York: New York University Press, 2015.

Barna, George, and David Kinnaman. *Churchless: Understanding Today's Unchurched and How to Connect with Them.* Carol Stream, IL: Tyndale House, 2014.

Bullivant, Stephen. *Nonverts: The Making of Ex-Christian America.* Oxford: Oxford University Press, 2022.

Burge, Ryan P. *The Nones: Where They Came From, Who They Are, and Where They Are Going.* Minneapolis: Fortress Press, 2021.

Mercadante, Linda A. *Belief without Borders: Inside the Minds of the Spiritual but Not Religious.* New York: Oxford University Press, 2014.

Nicolaou, Corinna. *A None's Story: Searching for Meaning inside Christianity, Judaism, Buddhism, and Islam.* New York: Columbia University Press, 2016.

Zuckerman, Phil. *Faith No More: Why People Reject Religion.* New York: Oxford University Press, 2011.

Zuckerman, Phil, Luke W. Galen, and Frank L. Pasquale. *The Nonreligious: Understanding Secular People and Societies.* Oxford: Oxford University Press, 2016.

Conclusion

No matter how modern or post-modern or whatever else human societies become, religion will not wither and expire.... Anyone trying to comprehend our contemporary world [therefore] while neglecting religion is attempting the impossible.

Christian Smith[1]

Neither God nor Religion Is Dead

Gott ist tot! "God is dead!" This may be the most famous line that German philosopher and atheist social critic Friedrich Nietzsche (1844–1900) ever wrote. I distinctly remember the first time I encountered it. I was an undergraduate student at a secular university, studying political philosophy, and my professor inaugurated our class by shouting the phrase—first in its original German and then in its English translation—in front of a confused yet curious classroom. His act was partly theatrical and partly theological. As he continued his dramatic performance—with his left hand carefully holding a copy of some small book while his right hand gesticulated wildly—he read: "God is dead! God remains dead! And we have killed him!"[2] By now, my interest had been piqued, and I was excited to learn the rest of the story for myself—all theatrics aside. After class, I hastened to the library, snatched the last copy of Nietzsche's book (*Die Fröhlich Wissenschaft*), and consumed the content.

Although many people would have us believe that religion is on the verge of extinction, nothing could be further from the truth. Author Stephen Hunt confirms that "the attempt to measure religious decline by so-called hard empirical evidence is a notoriously hazardous enterprise."[3]

1. Christian Smith, *Religion: What It Is, How It Works, and Why It Matters* (Princeton, NJ: Princeton University Press, 2017), 250, 261.

2. Friedrich Nietzsche, *The Gay Science: With a Prelude in German Rhymes and an Appendix of Songs*, ed. Bernard Williams (Cambridge: Cambridge University Press, 2001; orig. published 1882), 120.

3. Stephen J. Hunt, *Religion in Western Society* (New York: Macmillan, 2017), 21.

Despite the rise and resilience of atheism, agnosticism, and secularism, religion is here to stay. As atheist A. C. Grayling concedes in his book *The God Argument: The Case against Religion and for Humanism*, "Religion is a pervasive fact of history,"[4] on top of which we may add that it will also be a pervasive fact of the future. Consequently, atheist author Alain de Botton is correct when he states that "religions merit our attention."[5]

Globally speaking, religion is on the rise. And this, of course, includes new religious movements. After all, as sociologist Christian Smith has demonstrated in his research, it is only logical to conclude that human societies "will continue to generate new religions" in the future just as much as they have in the past. To be sure, some of these new religious movements "will grow in size, strength, and significance, while others will decline."[6] But the expectation that humans will generate them is inescapable. It is, in a word, what we do. And with thousands of new religious movements in existence around the globe, it is clear that we have been hard at work.

Fig. C.1.
Friedrich Nietzsche was one of the West's most influential atheists. Although he famously wrote that "God is dead," religion is alive and well today.

Friedrich Nietzsche.

4. A. C. Grayling, *The God Argument: The Case against Religion and for Humanism* (London: Bloomsbury, 2013), 1.

5. Alain de Botton, *Religion for Atheists: A Non-Believer's Guide to the Uses of Religion* (New York: Random House, 2012), 18.

6. Smith, *Religion*, 5.

Go with the Great Commandment

In this book, I have isolated and discussed the most influential new religious movements in the world today. The purpose is twofold. And it is based directly on the two parts of Jesus' Great Commandment. First, as a committed Christian, I seek to follow and embody Jesus' command to love God. This is no small task. And every day I feel the weight of the command as I struggle to die to myself and live for God. As I strive to worship and devote myself to God in the most authentic and responsible way possible, the study of new religious movements reminds me how easy and seemingly natural it is to go astray, lose my bearings, and try to take shortcuts. This truth pushes me back to the well-trod and well-lit path, it cautions me to pay attention to warning signs, and it encourages me not to just follow my fancy.

Second, I am called to love others. This often assumes that others are different, which makes the task all the more challenging. As I reflect on how best to love others, it strikes me as only reasonable that it would entail really learning about what they most value. And for most people around the world and across the ages, what they most value is what we variously call *faith*, *spirituality*, or *religion*. For some, these manifest as world religions, which was the topic of my prequel, *Christianity and World Religions*.[7] For others, they go by the name *new religious movements*, which is, of course, the focus of this book. Either way, by learning about such things, and therefore being ready and able to engage them when I encounter the growing number of people who value them, I have had conversations that would blow your mind. What we as humans long for, after all, is connection, and the connection you can make with others by truly understanding and showing interest in what they most value will not just shock you. It will lead to interactions that you can scarcely imagine.

---

7. Derek Cooper, *Christianity and World Religions: An Introduction to the World's Major Faiths* (Phillipsburg, NJ: P&R Publishing, 2012).

Glossary

ablution. Ritual cleansing in water. Ablution is a common practice in many Asian religions and is similar to Christian baptism.

Adi Granth. Technically the first and foundational books of the holy scriptures within Sikhism. Even so, it is sometimes used to refer to all the holy scriptures (similar to how the word *Torah* can refer to the first five books of Judaism as well as all the Hebrew scriptures).

Adventism. A movement within Christianity developing in nineteenth-century America that put radical emphasis on the immediate return of Christ on earth. Many Christian denominations and new religious movements grew out of it.

agamas. Holy scriptures within Jainism written in the Prakrit language. The exact number of these scriptures is disputed within Jainism.

agnostic. A person who is undecided or uncommitted when it comes to the existence of a deity.

ahimsa. The core belief and practice of Jainism. It is variously translated as "nonharm" or "nonviolence."

ajiva. Often translated as "matter" in Jainism. It is the opposite of **jiva** ("soul," "spirit," or "life").

Al-Bab. Literally "the gateway," a common way to refer to the representatives of the Hidden Imam within Shia Islam. But it later came to be used as the name for the **Babi religion**'s founder, whose given name was Siyyid Ali Muhammad and who lived in the nineteenth century in Iran. He is also seen as the forerunner of the Baha'i Faith.

atheism. Absence of belief in any kind of deity. Atheism does not necessarily imply that one is irreligious.

auditing. A sort of one-on-one counseling session in which participants are presented with a variety of questions that they have to answer repeatedly and in great detail until sufficiently processed. Auditing is the primary ritual in Scientology.

Babi religion. Arising in the nineteenth century in Iran, the religion that immediately predated and led directly to the emergence of the Baha'i Faith. Though practiced today, it is quite small, and most followers eventually became practitioners of the Baha'i Faith.

Baha, Abdul. The son of **Baha'ullah**, the founder of the Baha'i Faith. Abdul Baha, whose name means "servant of Baha," became the official interpreter of Baha'i and served in that capacity until his death in 1921.

Baha'ullah. The founder of the Baha'i Faith, whose name means "Glory of God." He lived in the nineteenth century. Originally born in Iran, he died in prison in Israel.

bhakti. Devotional Hinduism, which is the most popular form of Hinduism today and which played a role in the development of Jainism and Sikhism.

caste system. A complex system of social privilege and restriction in classical Hinduism. It is traditionally grouped under four categories: priests (Brahmins), warriors (Kshatriyas), merchants (Vaishyas), and servants (Shudras). Under these categories is a noncategory of people referred to as *untouchables* (Dhalits). Classical Hinduism believed that people should act according to their station (caste) in life and perform their dharma (duty) according to where they resided within the caste system.

clear. A term in Scientology that essentially means the equivalent of *saved* in Christianity. The goal of Scientology is to "go clear," that is, to remove the bad thoughts (**engrams**) in one's mind.

coven. A group of believers within Wicca. Covens are usually small and private, following the seasons of the year and phases of the moon rather than holding weekly meetings.

Digambara. Of the two major denominations within Jainism, the more traditional one. The term translates as "sky-clothed" in reference to the historical custom of its practitioners (males only) to wear no clothes.

E-meter. In Scientology, an electric device that measures the electrical charge of an **engram**, or bad memory. It looks and operates like a lie-detector test, but can supposedly tell when an engram has been dissolved.

engram. In Scientology, a bad thought that must be cleared from one's mind in order to progress to spiritual and emotional health.

Fard, W. D. The founder of the Nation of Islam. His exact origin, name, ethnicity, and background is in dispute. He first appeared in Detroit, Michigan, in the year 1930 and disappeared mysteriously in 1934.

Farrakhan, Louis. The leader of the Nation of Islam beginning in 1977. He has played the most profound role within the movement since **Elijah Muhammad**.

Five K's. Distinctive clothing within Sikhism, comprising *kesh* ("uncut hair"), *kangha* ("comb"), *kirpan* ("sword"), *kachh* ("underwear"), and *kara* ("bangle").

Gardner, Gerald. The founder of Wicca. He was a British nationalist who died in 1964. Those who practice Wicca based on his tradition are called *Gardnerian Wiccans*.

Golden Temple. The central religious shrine in Sikhism, located in India and made of marble and gold.

gurdwara. A religious house of worship in Sikhism, similar to how a mosque is a Muslim house of worship.

guru. Sanskrit word meaning "teacher" in Indian religions (thus Hinduism, Buddhism, Jainism, Sikhism, and Baha'i). Gurus have important roles in thought and practice and seek to guide their pupils toward enlightenment.

High Priest/Priestess. Within the Wicca religion, leaders of **covens** (congregations). A coven has both a male High Priest and a female High Priestess. Historically, the High Priestess exercises more authority.

Hubbard, L. Ron. The founder of Scientology and the most prolific author ever. He died in 1986.

Jehovah. The preferred way to refer to God among Jehovah's Witnesses. Virtually all references to "God" in the Bible of the Jehovah's Witnesses (called the **New World Translation**) have been changed to "Jehovah."

jina. One of twenty-four figures in Jainism. The term is translated as "conqueror" or "victor." Those who follow the teaching of the jinas are called *Jains*, that is, practitioners of Jainism who have overcome earthly attachment.

jiva. Often translated as "soul," "spirit," or "life" in Jainism. It is the opposite of **ajiva** ("matter").

karma. An Indian (and thus Hindu, Buddhist, Jain, and Hindu) term, often translated as "action" or "deed," that refers to the universal notion of cause and effect. One's karma, which includes thoughts, deeds, and actions, remains with a living being (through the course of one's death and rebirth) until one reaches nirvana or extinction. Afterward, a being is no longer bound by cause and effect or karma.

Khalsa. Meaning "pure," the Sikh community known for being most committed to Sikhism, similar to the Pharisees in ancient Judaism. This community has undergone a special ceremony and is committed to the **Five K's**.

kingdom hall. The religious house of worship for Jehovah's Witnesses. A kingdom hall is open to all people and has meetings several times a week.

langar. Communal meal in Sikhism offered after a religious service, typically consisting of bread, lentils, potatoes, yogurt, and pudding. It is offered to all free of charge, irrespective of religion.

Mahavira. The last **jina** in our current eon and the primary figure of emulation in Jainism. He was a contemporary of Buddha and lived in the sixth century B.C.

Miller, William. A self-taught Bible interpreter in nineteenth-century America who predicted that the end of the world would occur in 1843–44.

Miscavige, David. In Scientology, the successor to the founder, **L. Ron Hubbard**. Miscavige joined the **Sea Org** at the age of sixteen and has been leading Scientology for decades with an iron fist.

moksha. Hindu term meaning "liberation." It refers to the release or liberation that living beings may attain from the shackles of **samsara**, the endless cycle of birth, death, and rebirth. It plays a role in Hinduism, Buddhism, Jainism, Sikhism, and Baha'i.

Muhammad, Elijah. The successor to **W. D. Fard** in the Nation of Islam. He led the movement from 1934 until his death in 1975.

Muhammad, W. D. The son of **Elijah Muhammad** who became leader of the Nation of Islam in 1975. He moved the religion much closer toward historic Islam, changing its name and becoming distant from the Nation of Islam when it was taken over by **Louis Farrakhan**. W. D. Muhammad died in 2008.

Nanak, Guru. Mostly living in the sixteenth century, the founder of Sikhism.

New World Translation. The official Bible translation of the Jehovah's Witnesses, completed in 1961.

none. Someone who does not have any particular religious affiliation. Such a person may be spiritual or unspiritual. The nones represent a growing number of individuals across the world.

Punjab. Region and language in North India where Sikhism arose.

Russell, Charles Taze. Founder of the Jehovah's Witnesses who died in 1916.

Rutherford, Joseph. The second leader of the Jehovah's Witnesses, who played a significant role in forming many beliefs and practices of Jehovah's Witnesses today. He died in 1942.

samsara. Literally meaning "continuous flow," an Indian (and thus Hindu, Buddhist, Jain, and Sikh) religious term referring to the repeated cycle of birth, life, death, and rebirth (or reincarnation). All living beings are trapped in samsara, and the goal of Indian religions is to escape samsara by achieving **moksha** or liberation.

sanatana dharma. A common way to refer to Hinduism, literally meaning something like "eternal religion," based on the common understanding that Hinduism is the world's oldest religion.

Sea Org. The crème de la crème within Scientology, drawn from its most dedicated members and notoriously requiring them to sign billion-year contracts of service. All leadership positions are drawn from Sea Org members.

secularization theory. A widespread hypothesis among sociologists of religion, maintaining that societies become more secular as they become more technically advanced.

Singh, Guru Gobind. The tenth and last human **Guru** within Sikhism. He was martyred in the year 1708.

Smith, Joseph. Founder of Mormonism. He grew up in upstate New York and authored the most foundational books of this new religious movement. He was killed in a gun shootout in 1844.

Standard Works. The four bodies of sacred writings in Mormonism: the Bible, the Book of Mormon, the Doctrine and Covenants, and the Pearl of Great Price.

Studies in the Scriptures. A six-volume publication by **Charles Taze Russell** that developed the basis for the beliefs of the Jehovah's Witnesses. Upon his death in 1916, a seventh volume was added.

Sufism. Devotional form of Islam that played a role in the development of Sikhism and the **Babi religion**.

Svetambara. Of the two major denominations within Jainism, the more recent one. The term translates as "white-clothed" in reference to its custom of its practitioners' wearing clothes, in contrast to the **Digambaras**.

theta. In Scientology, a "life force."

thetan. In Scientology, an individual life force such as a human being. In fact, human beings are made up of thousands of body thetans that live forever.

Twelfth Imam. An important doctrine within Shia Islam. The tradition developed in the ninth century that Muhammad's last physical male descendant (the twelfth imam since Muhammad) went into hiding (occultation) and would return on the day of judgment.

ward. Typically, a Mormon chapel where Mormon believers (and visitors) meet for worship and study. Wards are distinct from temples. For instance, temples can be entered only by Mormons in good standing who have a "temple recommend."

Wheel of the Year. In Wicca, the four "greater sabbats" of Samhain, Imbolc, Beltane, and Lugnasad (Lammas), as well as the four "lesser sabbats" of Yule, Litha, Eostar, and Mabon. While the lesser sabbats are solar events marked by the two solstices and two equinoxes, the greater sabbats celebrate the four midpoints between them.

Young, Brigham. The successor to **Joseph Smith** in early Mormonism. He led the fledgling community from Illinois to Utah during the latter half of the nineteenth century. He died in 1877, having established the entire infrastructure of Mormonism in Utah.

Bibliography

Abdo, Lil. "The Baha'i Faith and Wicca: A Comparison of Relevance in Two Emerging Religions." *Pomegranate* 11, no. 1 (2009): 124–48.

Adams, Scott Lewis. "The Spirituality of Jesus for the Unchurched and the Unaffiliated: A Pentecostal-Charismatic Perspective." *Religions* 13, no. 11 (November 2022): 1122–33.

Allah, Wakeel. *In the Name of God: A History of Clarence 13X and the Five Percenters*. Atlanta: A Team Publishing, 2007.

Babb, Lawrence A. *Understanding Jainism*. Edinburgh: Dunedin Academic Press, 2015.

Baha, Abdul. *Selections from the Writings of Abdul Baha*. https://www.bahai.org/library/authoritative-texts/abdul-baha/selections-writings-abdul-baha/1#324741256.

———. *The Will and Testament of Abdul Baha*. Wilmette, IL: Baha'i Publishing Trust, 1990.

Baha'ullah. *The Arabic Hidden Words*. https://www.bahai.org/library/authoritative-texts/bahaullah/hidden-words/2#439014978.

———. *Baha'i World Faith: Selected Writings of Baha'ullah and Abdul Baha*. Wilmette, IL: Baha'i Publishing Trust, 1976.

———. In *Consultation: A Compilation*. https://www.bahai.org/library/authoritative-texts/compilations/consultation/1#249611345.

———. *Gleanings from the Writings of Baha'ullah*. https://www.bahai.org/library/authoritative-texts/bahaullah/gleanings-writings-bahaullah/1#529444114.

———. *The Kitab-i-Aqdas*. https://www.bahai.org/library/authoritative-texts/bahaullah/kitab-i-aqdas/1#824700177.

———. *The Tablets of Baha'ullah*. Wilmette, IL: Baha'i Publishing Trust, 1988.

Baker, James W. "White Witches: Historic Fact and Romantic Fantasy." In *Magical Religion and Modern Witchcraft*, edited by James R. Lewis, 171–92. Albany: State University of New York Press, 1996.

Baker, Joseph O., and Buster G. Smith. *American Secularism: Cultural Contours of Nonreligious Belief Systems*. New York: New York University Press, 2015.

Barlow, Philip L. *Mormons and the Bible: The Place of the Latter-day Saints in American Religion*. New York: Oxford University Press, 2013.

Barna, George. *America at the Crossroads: Explosive Trends Shaping America's Future and What You Can Do about It.* Grand Rapids: Baker, 2016.

Barna, George, and David Kinnaman. *Churchless: Understanding Today's Unchurched and How to Connect with Them.* Carol Stream, IL: Tyndale House, 2014.

Beckford, James A. *The Trumpet of Prophecy: A Sociological Study of Jehovah's Witnesses.* Oxford: Basil Blackwell, 1975.

Berg, Herbert. *Elijah Muhammad and Islam.* New York: New York University Press, 2009.

Berger, Helen A. *Solitary Pagans: Contemporary Witches, Wiccans, and Others Who Practice Alone.* Columbia: University of South Carolina Press, 2019.

Bergman, Jerry. "The Adventist and Jehovah's Witness Branch of Protestantism." In *America's Alternative Religions*, edited by Timothy Miller, 33–46. Albany: State University of New York Press, 1995.

Berlinerblau, Jacques. "Jewish Atheism." In *The Oxford Handbook of Atheism*, edited by Stephen Bullivant and Michael Ruse, 320–36. Oxford: Oxford University Press, 2013.

Bidamon, Emma Smith. "Interview with Joseph Smith III, February 1879." In *Early Mormon Documents*, edited by Dan Vogel, 1:534–45. Salt Lake City: Signature Books, 1996.

Blythe, Christopher. "Was Jesus Married?" *BYU Studies Quarterly* 60, no. 3 (2021): 75–84.

Bouma, Gary, and Anna Halafoff. "Australia's Changing Religious Profile—Rising Nones and Pentecostals, Declining British Protestants in Superdiversity: Views from the 2016 Census." *Journal for the Academic Study of Religion* 30, no. 2 (2017): 129–43.

Bowen, Patrick D. *A History of Conversion to Islam in the United States.* Vol. 2, *The African American Islamic Renaissance, 1920–1975.* Leiden: Brill, 2017.

Bowler, Peter J. *Evolution: The History of an Idea.* Berkeley: University of California Press, 2009.

Bremmer, Jan N. "Atheism in Antiquity." In *The Cambridge Companion to Atheism*, edited by Michael Martin, 11–26. Cambridge: Cambridge University Press, 2007.

Brown, Callum G. *Becoming Atheist: Humanism and the Secular West.* London: Bloomsbury, 2017.

Brown, Frank Burch. *The Evolution of Darwin's Religious Views.* Macon, GA: Mercer University Press, 1986.

Buck, Christopher. *Baha'i Faith: The Basics.* London: Routledge, 2021.

———. "The Eschatology of Globalization: The Multiple-Messiahship of Baha'ullah Revisited." In *Studies in Modern Religions, Religious*

Movements, and the Babi-Baha'i Faiths, edited by Moshe Sharon, 143–78. Leiden: Brill, 2004.

Buckland, Raymond. *Buckland's Complete Book of Witchcraft*. 2nd ed. St. Paul, MN: Llewellyn, 2002.

———. *Wicca for One: The Path of Solitary Witchcraft*. New York: Citadel Press, 2018.

Bullivant, Stephen. "Defining 'Atheism.'" In *The Oxford Handbook of Atheism*, edited by Stephen Bullivant and Michael Ruse, 11–21. Oxford: Oxford University Press, 2013.

———. *Nonverts: The Making of Ex-Christian America*. Oxford: Oxford University Press, 2022.

Bullivant, Stephen, and Michael Ruse, eds. *The Oxford Handbook of Atheism*. Oxford: Oxford University Press, 2013.

Burge, Ryan P. *The Nones: Where They Came From, Who They Are, and Where They Are Going*. Minneapolis: Fortress Press, 2021.

Burton, Keith Augustus. *The Blessing of Africa*. Downers Grove, IL: IVP Academic, 2007.

Bushman, Claudia Lauper, and Richard Lyman Bushman. *Building the Kingdom: A History of Mormons in America*. New York: Oxford University Press, 2001.

Bushman, Richard L. *Mormonism: A Very Short Introduction*. Oxford: Oxford University Press, 2008.

———. *Rough Stone Rolling: A Cultural Biography of Mormonism's Founder*. New York: Vintage Books, 2007.

Butler, Jon. *Awash in a Sea of Faith: Christianizing the American People*. Cambridge, MA: Harvard University Press, 1990.

Chryssides, George D. *The A to Z of Jehovah's Witnesses*. Lanham, MD: Scarecrow, 2009.

———. *Jehovah's Witnesses: Continuity and Change*. London: Routledge, 2016.

Church of Scientology International. *Scientology: Theology and Practice of a Contemporary Religion*. Los Angeles: Bridge Publications, 1998.

Clifton, Chas S. *Her Hidden Children: The Rise of Wicca and Paganism in America*. Lanham, MD: Altamira, 2006.

Conway, D. J. *Wicca: The Complete Craft*. Freedom, CA: The Crossing Press, 2001.

Cooper, Derek. *Christianity and World Religions: An Introduction to the World's Major Faiths*. Phillipsburg, NJ: P&R Publishing, 2012.

———. *Introduction to World Christian History*. Downers Grove, IL: InterVarsity Press, 2016.

———. *Sinners and Saints: The Real Story of Early Christianity*. Grand Rapids: Kregel Publications, 2018.

———. *Twenty Questions That Shaped World Christian History.* Minneapolis: Fortress Press, 2015.

Cort, John E. *Jains in the World: Religious Values and Ideology in India.* New York: Oxford University Press, 2001.

———, ed. *Open Boundaries: Jain Communities and Cultures in Indian History.* Albany: State University of New York Press, 1998.

Cox, Harvey. *The Future of Faith.* New York: HarperOne, 2009.

Cragun, Ryan, et al. "North America." In *The Oxford Handbook of Atheism*, edited by Stephen Bullivant and Michael Ruse, 601–21. Oxford: Oxford University Press, 2013.

Cunningham, Scott. *Living Wicca: A Further Guide for the Solitary Practitioner.* St. Paul, MN: Llewellyn, 1993.

———. *Wicca: A Guide for the Solitary Practitioner.* St. Paul, MN: Llewellyn, 1988.

Curtis, Edward E., IV. *Black Muslim Religion in the Nation of Islam, 1960–1975.* Chapel Hill: University of North Carolina Press, 2006.

———. *Islam in Black America: Identity, Liberation, and Difference in African-American Islamic Thought.* Albany: State University of New York Press, 2002.

Dannin, Robert. *Black Pilgrimage to Islam.* Oxford: Oxford University Press, 2002.

Davies, Douglas J. *An Introduction to Mormonism.* Cambridge: Cambridge University Press, 2003.

Dawkins, Richard. *The God Delusion.* Boston: Houghton Mifflin, 2006. Reprint, Boston: Mariner Books, 2008.

de Botton, Alain. *Religion for Atheists: A Non-Believer's Guide to the Uses of Religion.* New York: Random House, 2012.

DeCaro, Louis A. *On the Side of the People: A Religious Life of Malcolm X.* New York: New York University Press, 1996.

deChant, Dell. "Apocalyptic Communities." In *World Religions in America: An Introduction*, edited by Jacob Neusner, 186–202. 3rd ed. Louisville: Westminster John Knox Press, 2003.

deChant, Dell, and Danny L. Jorgensen. "The Church of Scientology: A Very New American Religion." In *World Religions in America: An Introduction*, edited by Jacob Neusner, 220–28. 3rd ed. Louisville: Westminster John Knox Press, 2003.

diFiosa, Jimahl. *A Coin for the Ferryman: The Death and Life of Alex Sanders.* N.p.: Logios, 2010.

Dundas, Paul. *The Jains.* London: Routledge, 2002.

Effendi, Shoghi. In *Consultation: A Compilation.* https://www.bahai.org /library/authoritative-texts/compilations/consultation/3#668166237.

———. "Letter of March 12, 1923." In *Baha'i Administration*. https://www.bahai.org/library/authoritative-texts/shoghi-effendi/bahai-administration/3#904837722.

———. *Some Answered Questions*. https://www.bahai.org/library/authoritative-texts/abdul-baha/some-answered-questions/1#610118851.

———. *The World Order of Baha'ullah*. Wilmette, IL: Baha'i Publishing Trust, 1991.

Eshbach, Lloyd. *Over My Shoulder: Reflections on a Science Fiction Era*. Hampton Falls, NH: Donald Grant Publishers, 1982.

Esquivel, Juan Cruz. "Religiously Disaffiliated, Religiously Indifferent, or Believers without Religion: Morphology of the Unaffiliated in Argentina." *Religions* 12, no. 7 (June 2021): 472–92.

Ester, Peter, and Loek Halman. "Empirical Trends in Religious and Moral Beliefs in Western Europe." *International Journal of Sociology* 24, no. 2/3 (Summer–Fall 1994): 81–110.

Farrakhan, Louis. *A Torchlight for America*. Chicago: FCN Publishing, 1993.

Felber, Garrett. *Those Who Know Don't Say: The Nation of Islam, the Black Freedom Movement, and the Carceral State*. Chapel Hill: University of North Carolina Press, 2020.

Flügel, Peter. "Present Lord: Simandhara Svami and the Akram Vignan Movement." In *The Intimate Other: Love Divine in the Indic Religions*, edited by Anna King and John Brockington, 194–242. New Delhi: Orient Longman, 2005.

Franz, Raymond. *A Crisis of Conscience: The Struggle between Loyalty to God and Loyalty to One's Religion*. Atlanta: Commentary Press, 1983.

Frazier, Jessica. "Hinduism." In *The Oxford Handbook of Atheism*, edited by Stephen Bullivant and Michael Ruse, 367–82. Oxford: Oxford University Press, 2013.

Froese, Paul. "'I Am an Atheist and a Muslim': Islam, Communism, and Ideological Competition." *Journal of Church and State* 47, no. 3 (Summer 2005): 473–501.

Gallagher, Eugene. "The Branch Davidians." In *Controversial New Religions*, edited by James R. Lewis and Jesper Petersen, 67–80. 2nd ed. Oxford: Oxford University Press, 2014.

Gardell, Mattias. *In the Name of Elijah Muhammad: Louis Farrakhan and the Nation of Islam*. Durham, NC: Duke University Press, 1996.

Gardner, Gerald. "The Gardnerian Book of Shadows." https://www.sacred-texts.com/pag/gbos/index.htm.

———. *The Meaning of Witchcraft*. New York: Magickal Childe, 1959. Reprint, 2004.

———. *Witchcraft Today.* 50th anniversary ed. New York: Citadel Press, 2004.

GhaneaBassiri, Kambiz. *A History of Islam in America.* Cambridge: Cambridge University Press, 2010.

Givens, Terryl. *By the Hand of Mormon: The American Scripture That Launched a New World Religion.* New York: Oxford University Press, 2002.

———. *People of Paradox: A History of Mormon Culture.* New York: Oxford University Press, 2007.

Gospel Principles. Salt Lake City: Church of Jesus Christ of Latter-day Saints, 2009.

Gray, John. *Seven Types of Atheism.* New York: Picador, 2018.

Grayling, A. C. *The God Argument: The Case against Religion and for Humanism.* London: Bloomsbury, 2013.

Grewal, J. S. *The New Cambridge History of India.* Vol. 2, *The Sikhs of the Punjab.* Cambridge: Cambridge University Press, 1990.

Haddad, Yvonne Yazbeck, and Jane I. Smith, eds. *Muslim Communities in North America.* Albany: State University of New York Press, 1994.

Hardy, Grant. *Understanding the Book of Mormon: A Reader's Guide.* New York: Oxford University Press, 2010.

Harrow, Judy. Foreword to *Witchcraft Today,* by Gerald Gardner. 50th anniversary ed. New York: Citadel Press, 2004.

Hawking, Stephen, and Leonard Mlodinow. *The Grand Design.* New York: Bantam Books, 2010.

Hellesøy, Kjersti. "Scientology: The Making of a Religion." In *Controversial New Religions,* edited by James R. Lewis and Jesper Petersen, 257–69. 2nd ed. Oxford: Oxford University Press, 2014.

Heselton, Philip. *Wiccan Roots: Gerald Gardner and the Modern Witchcraft Revival.* Milverton, UK: Capall Bann Publishing, 2001.

———. *Witchfather: A Life of Gerald Gardner.* Vol. 1, *Into the Witch Cult.* Loughborough, Leicestershire, UK: Thoth, 2012.

———. *Witchfather: A Life of Gerald Gardner.* Vol. 2, *From Witch to Cult to Wicca.* Loughborough, Leicestershire, UK: Thoth, 2012.

Hess, Linda, and Shukdev Singh. *The Bijak of Kabir.* Oxford: Oxford University Press, 2002.

Holden, Andrew. *Jehovah's Witnesses: Portrait of a Contemporary Religious Movement.* London: Routledge, 2002.

Horan, Patricia. Foreword to *The Origin of Species,* by Charles Darwin. New York: Random House, 1979.

Hubbard, L. Ron. *Dianetics: The Original Thesis.* Los Angeles: Bridge Publications, 2007.

Hunt, Stephen J. *Religion in Western Society.* New York: Macmillan, 2017.

Hutton, Ronald. *The Triumph of the Moon: A History of Modern Pagan Witchcraft*. Oxford: Oxford University Press, 1999.

Huxley, Thomas. "Agnosticism." In *Collected Essays*, vol. 5, *Science and the Christian Tradition*, 209–62. Cambridge: Cambridge University Press, 2011.

———. "Agnosticism and Christianity." In *Collected Essays*, vol. 5, *Science and the Christian Tradition*, 309–65. Cambridge: Cambridge University Press, 2011.

———. "The Origin of Species." In *Darwiniana: Collected Essays*, 2:22–79. New York: Appleton & Co., 1894.

———. *Selected Works of Thomas H. Huxley*. 2 vols. New York: Appleton & Co., 1893.

Jaini, Padmanabh S. *Gender and Salvation: Jaina Debates on the Spiritual Liberation of Women*. Berkeley: University of California Press, 1992.

———. *The Jaina Path of Purification*. Berkeley: University of California Press, 1979.

Jenkins, Philip. *Mystics and Messiahs: Cults and New Religions in American History*. Oxford: Oxford University Press, 2001.

Jhutti-Johal, Jagbir. *Sikhism Today*. London: Continuum, 2011.

Johnson, David. "Archaeology." In *Encyclopedia of Mormonism*, vol. 1, *The History, Scripture, Doctrine, and Procedure of the Church of Latter-day Saints*, edited by Daniel Ludlow, 62–63. New York: Macmillan, 1992.

Jorgensen, Danny L. "The Latter-day Saint (Mormon) Religion in America." In *World Religions in America: An Introduction*, edited by Jacob Neusner, 272–90. 3rd ed. Louisville: Westminster John Knox Press, 2003.

Kent, Stephen A., and Susan Raine, eds. *Scientology in Popular Culture: Influences and Struggles for Legitimacy*. Santa Barbara, CA: Praeger, 2017.

Kinnaman, David, and Gabe Lyons. *unChristian: What a New Generation Really Thinks about Christianity . . . and Why It Matters*. Grand Rapids: Baker, 2012.

Knight, Michael. "Converts and Conversions." In *The Cambridge Companion to American Islam*, edited by Juliane Hammer and Omid Safi, 83–97. Cambridge: Cambridge University Press, 2013.

Knox, Zoe. *Jehovah's Witnesses and the Secular World: From the 1870s to the Present*. London: Palgrave Macmillan, 2018.

Kosmin, Barry A., and Ariela Keysar. *ARIS 2008 Summary Report*. Hartford, CT: Institute for the Study of Secularism in Society and Culture, Trinity College. http://commons.trincoll.edu/aris/files/2011/08/ARIS_Report_2008.pdf.

Land, Gary. *The A to Z of the Seventh-day Adventists*. Lanham, MD: Scarecrow Press, 2009.

Lantzer, Jason S. *Mainline Christianity: The Past and Future of America's Majority Faith*. New York: New York University Press, 2012.

Lee, Martha F. *The Nation of Islam: An American Millenarian Movement*. Lewiston, NY: Edwin Mellen, 1988.

Lefkowitz, Mary. *Not out of Africa: How Afrocentrism Became an Excuse to Teach Myth as History*. New York: Basic Books, 1997.

Lewis, James R., and Kjersti Hellesøy, eds. *Handbook of Scientology*. Boston: Brill, 2016.

Lightman, Bernard V. *The Origins of Agnosticism: Victorian Unbelief and the Limits of Knowledge*. Baltimore: Johns Hopkins University Press, 1987.

Lincoln, C. Eric. *The Black Muslims in America*. Boston: Beacon Press, 1961.

Long, Jeffrey D. *Jainism: An Introduction*. London: I. B. Tauris, 2009.

Luo, Weixiang, and Feinian Chen. "The Salience of Religion under an Atheist State: Implications for Subjective Well-Being in Contemporary China." *Social Forces* 100, no. 2 (December 2021): 852–78.

Mandair, Arvind-pal Singh. *Sikhism: A Guide for the Perplexed*. London: Bloomsbury Academic, 2013.

Mann, Gurinder Singh. "Canon Formation in the Sikh Tradition." In *Sikh Religion, Culture, and Ethnicity*, edited by Christopher Shackle, Gurharpal Singh, and Arvind-pal Singh Mandair, 10–24. London: Routledge, 2014.

———. *The Making of the Sikh Scripture*. New York: Oxford University Press, 2001.

Marsh, Clifton E. *The Lost-Found Nation of Islam in America*. Lanham, MD: Scarecrow Press, 2000.

Martin, Michael. "Atheism and Religion." In *The Cambridge Companion to Atheism*, edited by Michael Martin, 217–32. Cambridge: Cambridge University Press, 2007.

———, ed. *The Cambridge Companion to Atheism*. Cambridge: Cambridge University Press, 2007.

Marx, Karl. *Critique of Hegel's "Philosophy of Right."* Translated by Joseph J. O'Malley. Cambridge: Cambridge University Press, 1970.

Marx, Karl, and Friedrich Engels. *The Communist Manifesto*. Translated by Paul M. Sweezy. New York: Washington Square Press, 1970.

McConkie, Bruce R. *Mormon Doctrine*. Salt Lake City: Bookcraft, 1966.

McLeod, W. H. *Sikhs and Sikhism*. New Delhi: Oxford University Press, 1999.

McMullen, Mike. *The Baha'is of America: The Growth of a Religious Movement*. New York: New York University Press, 2015.

Melton, J. Gordon. "Birth of a Religion." In *Scientology*, edited by James R. Lewis, 17–34. Oxford: Oxford University Press, 2009.

———. *The Church of Scientology*. Salt Lake City: Signature Books, 2000.

———. "An Introduction to New Religions." In *The Oxford Handbook of New Religious Movements*, edited by James R. Lewis, 1:16–38. Oxford: Oxford University Press, 2008.

Mercadante, Linda A. *Belief without Borders: Inside the Minds of the Spiritual but Not Religious*. New York: Oxford University Press, 2014.

———. "Do the 'Spiritual but not Religious' (SBNR) Want a Theology without Walls?" *Journal of Interreligious Studies* 34 (2022): 77–82.

———. "Spiritual Struggles of Nones and 'Spiritual but Not Religious' (SBNRs)." *Religions* 11, no. 10 (2020): 513–29.

Metzger, Bruce M. "The Jehovah's Witnesses and Jesus Christ: A Biblical and Theological Appraisal." *Theology Today* 10, no. 1 (1953): 65–85.

Miller, William. *Evidences from Scripture and History of the Second Coming of Christ about the Year 1843 and of His Personal Reign of 1000 Years*. Brandon: Vermont Telegraph Office, 1833.

Millet, Robert L., and Shon D. Hopkin. *Mormonism: A Guide for the Perplexed*. London: Bloomsbury Academic, 2015.

Miscavige, Ron. *Ruthless: Scientology, My Son David Miscavige, and Me*. New York: St. Martin's Press, 2016.

Momen, Moojan. *An Introduction to Shi'i Islam: The History and Doctrines of Twelver Shi'ism*. Oxford: George Ronald, 1985.

Muhammad, Elijah. *Message to the Blackman in America*. Phoenix: Secretarius Memps Publications, 1973.

———. *Muhammad Speaks*. Special Issue. April 21, 1972.

———. *The Supreme Wisdom: Solution to the So-Called Negroes' Problem*. Chicago: University of Islam, 1957.

Müller, Olaf, and Chiara Porada. "Towards a Society of Stable Nones: Lifelong Non-Denominationalism as the Prevailing Pattern in East Germany." *Religions* 13, no. 11 (2022): 1024–52.

Murray, Margaret Alice. *The Witch-Cult in Western Europe: A Study in Anthropology*. Oxford: Clarendon Press, 1921.

Nabil-i-Azam. *Dawn Breakers: Nabil's Narrative of the Early Days of the Baha'i Revelation*. Wilmette, IL: Baha'i Publishing, 1932.

Nanak, Guru. Japji. In *A World Religions Reader*, edited by Ian S. Markham and Christy Lohr, 238–47. 3rd ed. Malden, MA: Blackwell Publishing, 2009.

———. Proem. In *A World Religions Reader*, edited by Ian S. Markham and Christy Lohr, 238. 3rd ed. Malden, MA: Blackwell Publishing, 2009.

Navabi, Armin. *Why There Is No God: Simple Responses to 20 Common Arguments for the Existence of God*. N.p.: CreateSpace Publishing, 2014.

Nesbitt, Eleanor. *Sikhism: A Very Short Introduction*. Oxford: Oxford University Press, 2005.

Newman, Andrew J. *Safavid Iran: Rebirth of a Persian Empire*. London: I. B. Tauris, 2009.

Nicolaou, Corinna. *A None's Story: Searching for Meaning inside Christianity, Judaism, Buddhism, and Islam*. New York: Columbia University Press, 2016.

Nietzsche, Friedrich. *The Gay Science: With a Prelude in German Rhymes and an Appendix of Songs*. Edited by Bernard Williams. Cambridge: Cambridge University Press, 2001. Originally published 1882.

O'Donnell, James J. *Pagans: The End of Traditional Religion and the Rise of Christianity*. New York: HarperCollins, 2015.

Oppy, Graham. *Atheism: The Basics*. London: Routledge, 2019.

Oxholm, Theis, et al. "Representing New Zealand Religious Diversity? The Removal of the Words 'True Religion' and 'Jesus Christ' from the Parliamentary Prayer." *Journal of Church and State* 64, no. 1 (Winter 2022): 87–109.

Pasquale, Frank, and Barry Kosmin. "Atheism and the Secularization Thesis." In *The Oxford Handbook of Atheism*, edited by Stephen Bullivant and Michael Ruse, 451–67. Oxford: Oxford University Press, 2013.

Penton, M. James. *Apocalypse Delayed: The Story of Jehovah's Witnesses*. 3rd ed. Toronto: University of Toronto, 2015.

Plato. *Apology*.

Plutarch, *Against the Stoics*.

———. *Moralia*.

The Promise of World Peace: A Letter by the Universal House of Justice to the Peoples of the World. College Park: University of Maryland Press, 2015.

Rabinovitch, Shelley TSivia. "Spells of Transformation." In *Magical Religion and Modern Witchcraft*, edited by James R. Lewis, 75–92. Albany: State University of New York Press, 1996.

Raine, Susan. "Colonizing *Terra Incognita*: L. Ron Hubbard, Scientology, and the Quest for Empire." In *Scientology in Popular Culture: Influences and Struggles for Legitimacy*, edited by Stephen A. Kent and Susan Raine, 1–32. Santa Barbara, CA: Praeger, 2017.

Raudvere, Catharina. *Islam: An Introduction*. London: I. B. Tauris, 2015.

RavenWolf, Silver. *To Ride a Silver Broomstick: New Generation Witchcraft*. St. Paul, MN: Llewellyn, 1993.

Regan, Michael. *Understanding Sikhism*. Minneapolis: Abdo Consulting Group, 2019.

Richardson, James. "Scientology in Court: A Look at Some Major Cases from Various Nations." In *Scientology*, edited by James R. Lewis, 283–94. Oxford: Oxford University Press, 2009.

Rinder, Mike. *A Billion Years: My Escape from a Life in the Highest Ranks of Scientology*. New York: Gallery Books, 2022.

Robichaud, Denis. "Renaissance and Reformation." In *The Oxford Handbook of Atheism*, edited by Stephen Bullivant and Michael Ruse, 179–94. Oxford: Oxford University Press, 2013.

Rosenberg, Alex. *The Atheist's Guide to Reality: Enjoying Life without Illusions*. New York: Norton & Co., 2011.

Rothstein, Mikael. "'His Name Was Xenu. He Used Renegades': Aspects of Scientology's Founding Myth." In *Scientology*, edited by James R. Lewis, 365–87. Oxford: Oxford University Press, 2009.

Russell, Bertrand. "What Is an Agnostic?" In *Russell on Religion*, edited by Louis I. Greenspan and Stefan Andersson, 41–50. London: Routledge, 1999.

Russell, Charles Taze. *Studies in the Scriptures*. 7 vols. 1886. Reprint, Brooklyn, NY: Watchtower Bible and Tract Society, 1916.

Rutherford, Joseph Franklin. *Jehovah*. Brooklyn, NY: Watchtower Bible and Tract Society, 1934.

———. *Millions Now Living Will Never Die*. Brooklyn, NY: International Bible Students Association, 1920.

Saiedi, Nader. *Gate of the Heart: Understanding the Writings of the Bab*. Waterloo, ON: Wilfrid Laurier Press, 2008.

———. *Logos and Civilization: Spirit, History, and Order in the Writings of Baha'ullah*. Bethesda: University Press of Maryland, 2000.

Schielke, Samuli. "The Islamic World." In *The Oxford Handbook of Atheism*, edited by Stephen Bullivant and Michael Ruse, 638–50. Oxford: Oxford University Press, 2013.

Schoeman, Willem J. "South African Religious Demography: The 2013 General Household Survey." *HTS Teologiese Studies* 73, no. 2 (2017): 1–7.

Scott, Latayne C. *The Mormon Mirage: A Former Member Looks at the Mormon Church Today*. 3rd ed. Grand Rapids: Zondervan, 2009.

Sedley, David. "From the Pre-Socratics to the Hellenistic Age." In *The Oxford Handbook of Atheism*, edited by Stephen Bullivant and Michael Ruse, 139–51. Oxford: Oxford University Press, 2013.

Shah, Ahmad. *The Bijak of Kabir*. Hamirpur: Indian Press, 1917.

Shipps, Jan. *Mormonism: The Story of a New Religious Tradition*. Urbana: University of Illinois Press, 1985.

———. "The Reality of the Restoration and the Restoration Ideal in the Mormon Tradition." In *The American Quest for the Primitive Church*, edited by Richard T. Hughes, 181–95. Urbana: University of Illinois Press, 1988.

Singh, Khushwant. *A History of the Sikhs*. Vol. 1, *1469–1839*. Princeton, NJ: Princeton University Press, 1963.

————. *A History of the Sikhs*. 2 vols. New Delhi: Oxford University Press, 1992–99.

————. "The Sikhs." In *The Religious Traditions of Asia: Religion, History, and Culture*, edited by Joseph M. Kitagawa, 111–18. London: Routledge, 2002.

Singh, Nikky-Guninder Kaur. *Sikhism: An Introduction*. London: I. B. Tauris, 2011.

Singh, Pashaura. *The Guru Granth: Canon, Meaning, and Authority*. New Delhi: Oxford University Press, 2000.

————. "An Overview of Sikh History." In *The Oxford Handbook of Sikh Studies*, edited by Pashaura Singh and Louis E. Fenech, 18–34. Oxford: Oxford University Press, 2014.

Singh, Patwant. *The Sikhs*. New York: Doubleday, 2001.

Skilton, Andrew. "Buddhism." In *The Oxford Handbook of Atheism*, edited by Stephen Bullivant and Michael Ruse, 337–50. Oxford: Oxford University Press, 2013.

Smith, Christian. *Religion: What It Is, How It Works, and Why It Matters*. Princeton, NJ: Princeton University Press, 2017.

Smith, Joseph. "How God Came to Be God." In *Joseph Smith: Selected Sermons and Writings*, edited by Robert L. Millet, 128–31. New York: Paulist Press, 1989.

Smith, Joseph Fielding. *Teachings of the Prophet Joseph Smith*. Salt Lake City: Deseret News Press, 1958.

Smith, Peter. *An Introduction to the Baha'i Faith*. Cambridge: Cambridge University Press, 2008.

Snow, Lorenzo. *Teachings of Lorenzo Snow*. Edited by Clyde J. Williams. Salt Lake City: Bookcraft, 1996.

Srutaprajna, Saman. *The Path of Purification*. Gujarat, India: Peace of Mind Training Center, 2005.

Starhawk, Silver. *The Spiral Dance: A Rebirth of the Ancient Religion of the Goddess: 20th Anniversary Edition*. New York: HarperCollins, 1999.

Stark, Rodney. "The Rise of a New World Faith." *Review of Religious Research* 26, no. 1 (September 1984): 18–27.

Stockman, Robert H. *The Baha'i Faith: A Guide for the Perplexed*. London: Bloomsbury Academic, 2013.

Talmage, James E. *The Articles of Faith: A Series of Lectures on the Principal Doctrines of the Church of Jesus Christ of Latter-day Saints*. 51st ed. Salt Lake City: Church of Jesus Christ of Latter-day Saints, 1974.

Tapper, Aaron J. Hahn. *Judaisms: A Twenty-First Century Introduction to Jews and Jewish Identities*. Berkeley: University of California Press, 2016.

Taylor, Ula Yvette. *The Promise of Patriarchy: Women and the Nation of Islam*. Chapel Hill: University of North Carolina Press, 2017.

Turner, John G. *Brigham Young: Pioneer Prophet*. Cambridge, MA: Belknap Press, 2012.

Urban, Hugh B. *The Church of Scientology: A History of a New Religion*. Princeton, NJ: Princeton University Press, 2011.

———. *New Age, Pagan, and New Religious Movements: Alternative Spirituality in Contemporary America*. Berkeley: University of California Press, 2015.

———. "Typewriter in the Sky: L. Ron Hubbard's Fiction and the Birth of the Thetan." In *Scientology in Popular Culture: Influences and Struggles for Legitimacy*, edited by Stephen A. Kent and Susan Raine, 33–52. Santa Barbara, CA: Praeger, 2017.

Urstad, Sivert Skålvoll. "The Religiously Unaffiliated in Norway." *Nordic Journal of Religion and Society* 30, no. 1 (May 15, 2017): 61–81.

Vallely, Anne. "Jainism." In *The Oxford Handbook of Atheism*, edited by Stephen Bullivant and Michael Ruse, 351–66. Oxford: Oxford University Press, 2013.

Vogel, Dan. "The Earliest Mormon Concept of God." In *Line upon Lion: Essays on Mormon Doctrine*, edited by Gary James Bergera, 17–34. Salt Lake City: Signature Books, 1989.

———, ed. *Early Mormon Documents*. 5 vols. Salt Lake City: Signature Books, 1996–2003.

———. *Joseph Smith: The Making of a Prophet*. Salt Lake City: Signature Books, 2004.

Walters, Kerry. *Atheism: A Guide for the Perplexed*. New York and London: Continuum, 2010.

Warner, Rob. *Secularization and Its Discontents*. London: Continuum, 2010.

Webb, Stephen H. *Mormon Christianity: What Other Christians Can Learn from the Latter-day Saints*. New York: Oxford University Press, 2013.

Weinberg, Robert. *The Ambassador to Humanity: A Selection of Testimonials and Tributes to Abdul Baha*. Oxford: George Ronald, 2020.

Weisenfeld, Judith. *New World A-Coming: Black Religion and Racial Identity during the Great Migration*. New York: New York University Press, 2016.

What Does the Bible Really Teach? Brooklyn, NY: Watchtower Bible and Tract Society, 2005.

White, Ethan Doyle. *Wicca: History, Belief, and Community in Modern Pagan Witchcraft*. Eastbourne, UK: Sussex Academic Press, 2015.

White, Vibert L., Jr. *Inside the Nation of Islam: A Historical and Personal Testimony by a Black Muslim*. Gainesville: University of Florida Press, 2001.

Wilkins-Laflamme, Sarah. "How Unreligious Are the Religious 'Nones'? Religious Dynamics of the Unaffiliated in Canada." *Canadian Journal of Sociology* 40, no. 4 (2015): 477–500.

Wright, Lawrence. *Going Clear: Scientology, Hollywood, and the Prison of Belief.* New York: Vintage Books, 2013.

X, Malcolm. *The Autobiography of Malcolm X: As Told to Alex Haley.* New York: Ballantine Publishing Group, 1973.

York, Michael. *Pagan Ethics: Paganism as a World Religion.* Cham, Switzerland: Springer, 2016.

Zuckerman, Phil. *Faith No More: Why People Reject Religion.* New York: Oxford University Press, 2011.

Zuckerman, Phil, Luke W. Galen, and Frank L. Pasquale. *The Nonreligious: Understanding Secular People and Societies.* Oxford: Oxford University Press, 2016.

Image Credits

Figure 4.5 © Kevin Duke via Dreamstime.com
Figure 4.6 © Jim Roberts via Dreamstime.com

CHAPTER 5

Figure 5.1 © via Dreamstime.com
Figure 5.2 © Walter Arce via Dreamstime.com
Figure 5.3 © Happykimmyj via Dreamstime.com
Figure 5.4 © Lizziemaher via Dreamstime.com
Figure 5.5 © Sean Pavone via Dreamstime.com
Figure 5.6 © Matthew Bamberg via Dreamstime.com

CHAPTER 6

Figure 6.1 © Photodynamx via Dreamstime.com
Figure 6.2 © Richard Van Der Spuy via Dreamstime.com
Figure 6.3 © Vchalup via Dreamstime.com
Figure 6.4 © Robert309 via Dreamstime.com
Figure 6.5 © Ricochet69 via Dreamstime.com
Figure 6.6 © Robynofexeter via Dreamstime.com

CHAPTER 7

Figure 7.1 © Creativefire via Dreamstime.com
Figure 7.2 © Rusticwitch via Dreamstime.com
Figure 7.3 © Dorothy Famiano via Dreamstime.com
Figure 7.4 © Tetiana Nazarenko via Dreamstime.com
Figure 7.5 © George Fairbairn via Dreamstime.com

CHAPTER 8

Figure 8.1 © Eric Robinson via Dreamstime.com
Figure 8.2 © Cineberg Ug via Dreamstime.com
Figure 8.3 © S Richardson via Dreamstime.com
Figure 8.4 © Michael Gordon via Dreamstime.com
Figure 8.5 © Helo80808 via Dreamstime.com

CHAPTER 9

Figure 9.1 © Georgios Kollidas via Dreamstime.com
Figure 9.2 © Juan Lopez via Dreamstime.com
Figure 9.3 © Wirestock via Dreamstime.com
Figure 9.4 © Bang Oland via Dreamstime.com
Figure 9.5 © Markovskiy via Dreamstime.com

CHAPTER 10

Figure 10.1 © Eugene Powers via Dreamstime.com
Figure 10.2 © Eldar Nurkovic via Dreamstime.com
Figure 10.3 © Alessandro Biascioli via Dreamstime.com
Figure 10.4 © Radzian via Dreamstime.com
Figure 10.5 © David Massie via Dreamstime.com

CONCLUSION

Figure C.1 © Nicku via Dreamstime.com

Index of Subjects and Names

Also by Derek Cooper

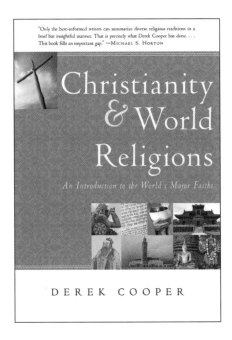

Derek Cooper takes us on a two-part tour of the world's most influential religions. The first discusses the essentials of each faith by looking at each faith's creation story, historical origin, beliefs, religious writings, and worship practices, and adds Christian reflections about it. The second surveys how biblical authors and important Christians in church history have responded to different religions. An appendix includes some helpful primary and secondary books relating to this theme.

Due to the increasingly global culture in which we live, it is important for Christians to know something about the major world religions so that we can speak confidently about our faith—there is no place in our interactions for fear. On the contrary, by learning about other religions we are able to learn more about God and Christianity, and how we can be more faithful to Christ.

"Peppering it with engaging personal anecdotes and supplementing it with helpful charts, tables, and sidebars throughout, Cooper has authored a truly helpful book."
—*Michael Lodahl*, Professor of Theology and World Religions, Point Loma Nazarene University